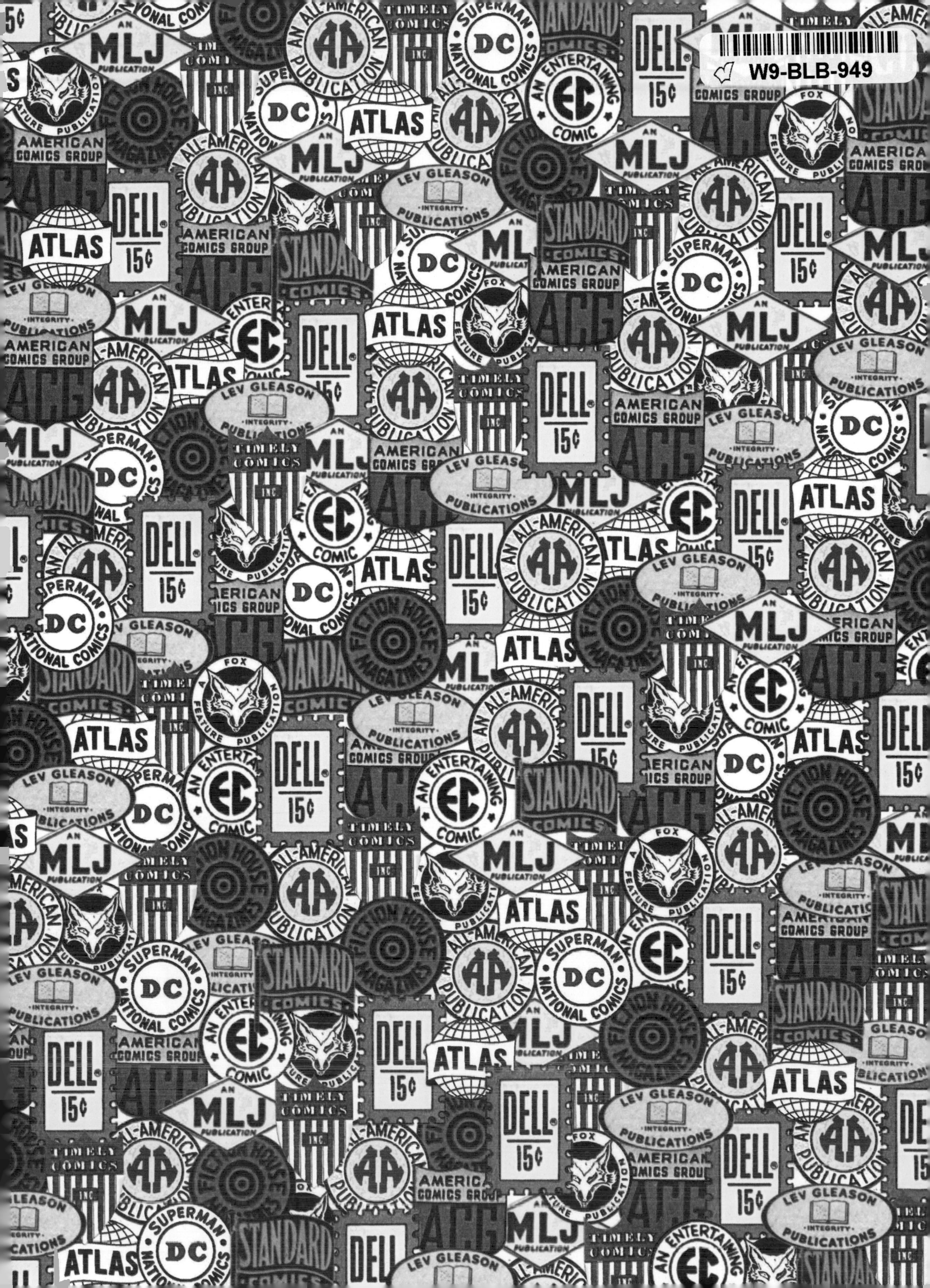
AN MLJ PUBLICATION
AN ALL-AMERICAN PUBLICATION
SUPERMAN DC NATIONAL COMICS
TIMELY COMICS INC.
AN ENTERTAINING EC COMIC
DELL 15¢
ATLAS
A FOX FEATURE PUBLICATION
AMERICAN COMICS GROUP ACG
FICTION HOUSE MAGAZINES
LEV GLEASON INTEGRITY PUBLICATIONS
STANDARD COMICS

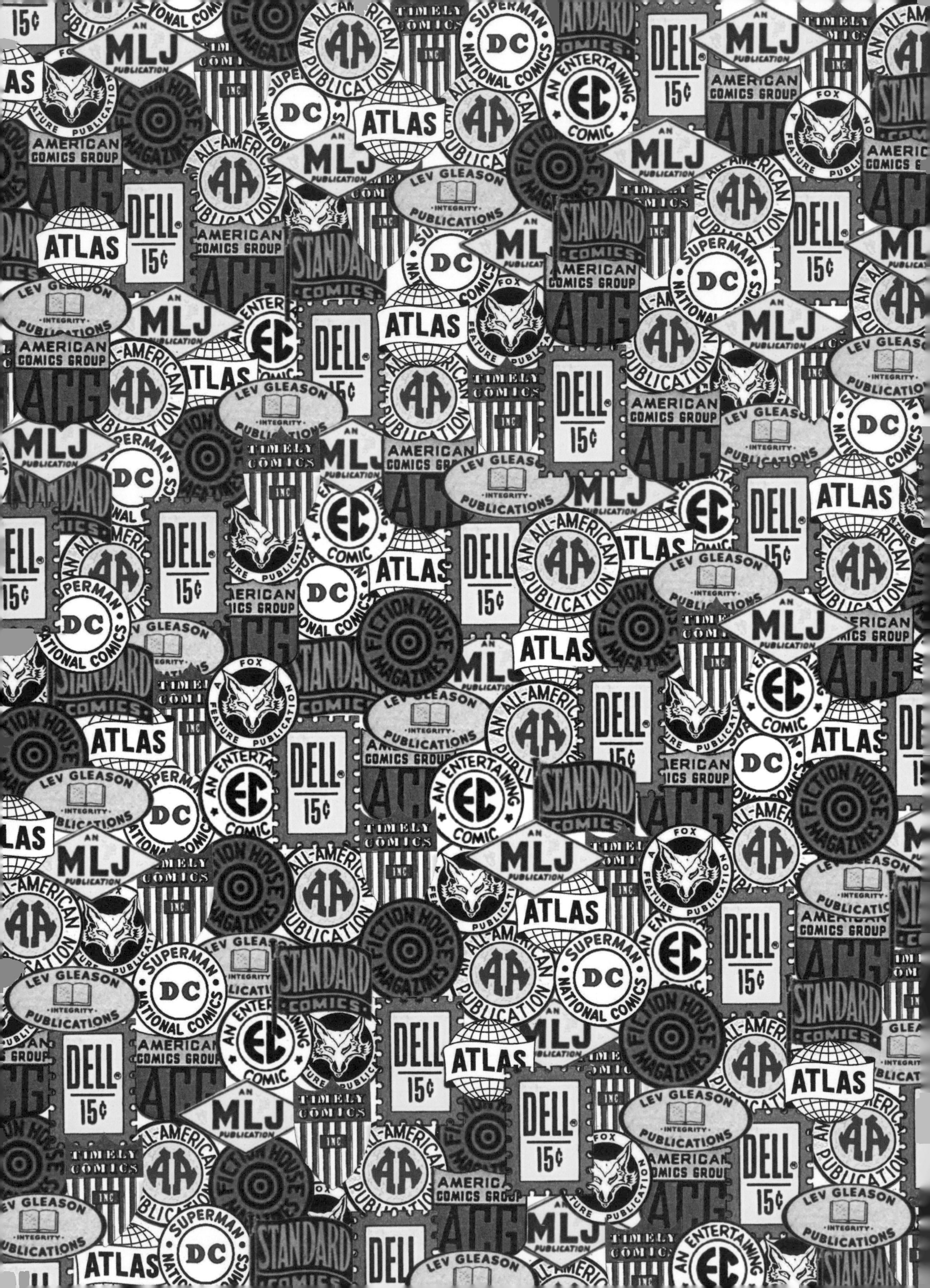
AN MLJ PUBLICATION
AN ALL-AMERICAN PUBLICATION
SUPERMAN DC NATIONAL COMICS
AN ENTERTAINING EC COMIC
DELL 15¢
ATLAS
AMERICAN COMICS GROUP ACG
LEV GLEASON INTEGRITY PUBLICATIONS
STANDARD COMICS
TIMELY COMICS INC
FICTION HOUSE MAGAZINES
A FOX FEATURE PUBLICATION

HEROES
of the COMICS

HEROES OF THE COMICS

Fantagraphics

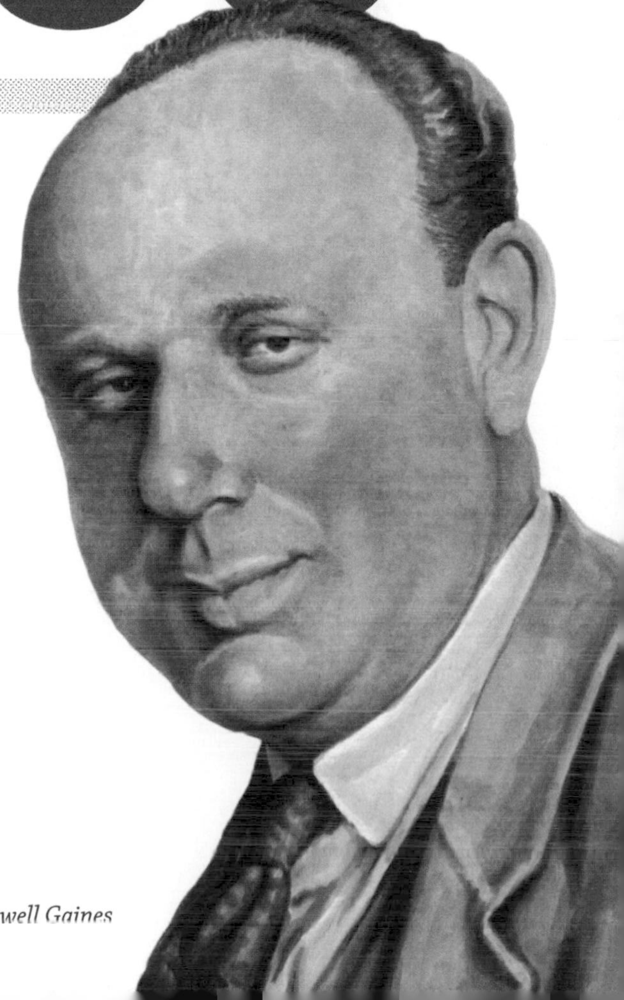

Maxwell Gaines

ACKNOWLEDGMENTS

I'd like to thank the following people for all of their generous help, suggestions, research, and encouragement during the creation of this book:

Thanks to my wonderful wife and collaborator (and copyeditor), Kathy, who continues to be patient with whatever my current obsessions may be.

Thanks to Kevin Dougherty, David Burd, Diane Wanek, Roger Hill, Iden Goodman, Wendy Gaines Bucci, and Richard Gelman for finding and sending me rare photo references of many of the heroes included in this book.

Thanks to Mark Newgarden, Glenn Bray, Roy Thomas, Mike Carlin, Nick Meglin, Grant Geissman, John Covello, Steven Brower, Ben Schwartz, Eddie Gorodetsky, Monte Beauchamp, Phil Felix, Gary VandenBergh, and the late Bhob Stewart for all their support and excellent suggestions.

Thanks to Jesse Marinoff Reyes for his astounding front and back cover designs, and Keeli McCarthy for her elegant interior design.

Thanks to Sean Howe, Paul Levitz, Arnold Roth, and Harlan Ellison for their kind and thoughtful blurbs.

Thanks to the one and only Al Jaffee for his wonderful foreword.

Thanks to Eric Reynolds and Gary Groth at Fantagraphics for instantly believing in this project and to all their terrific staff, including Michael Catron, who supplied several logos for the endpapers.

Special thanks to Mark G. Parker.

Heroes of the Comics is dedicated to two amazing heroes, Peter W. Kaplan and Kim Thompson.

Editor and Associate Publisher: Eric Reynolds
Book Design: Keeli McCarthy
Jacket Design: Jesse Reyes
Copy Editor: Janice Lee
Production: Paul Baresh
Publisher: Gary Groth

FANTAGRAPHICS BOOKS, INC.
Seattle, Washington, USA

ISBN 978-1-60699-731-4
First printing: August, 2014
Printed in China

THE HEROES of the COMICS

Foreword by Al Jaffee   ⁂   Introduction by Drew Friedman

Boyhood friends Al Jaffee and Will Elder in the cafeteria of the High School of Music & Art, c. 1937.

FOREWORD

by Al Jaffee

Drew Friedman has created an extraordinary gallery of writers, artists, editors and publishers who helped make comic books the worldwide phenomenon that it has become. During my seventy-plus years as an active cartoonist I have had the privilege of knowing and working with many of these legendary creative people. Some I knew from art school and others I met while working for various publications. This was in the early 1940s. They were difficult times. The Great Depression was still with us and joblessness was still high. Many of us had lived through this bleak period and were now, at last, finding work and paychecks in the exciting, creative field of comic books. The only fly in the ointment was the approach of World War II. But even this provided enormous amounts of inspiration for writers and artists who created fascist-battling superheroes. Until, of course, many of us were called upon to fight these bad guys for real.

I knew, on a personal level, about a third of the people represented in this superb collection. The rest I knew only from their amazing contributions to this uniquely American art form. My first job as a cartoonist was with Will Eisner, who was a packager of comic books at that time. He was not only brilliant in his own right but he also opened the door for many wannabe young writers and artists. Many of these talented people went on to become famous in fields other than comic books.

The inclusion of several comic book publishers in this collection is entirely necessary and appropriate. They gambled and brought new ideas and talent into a world of publishing that had no track record. Many artists and writers were unhappy with the distribution of financial rewards that eventually accrued but that's a subject for a different book. It's a sort of chicken-and-egg quandary. Without the egg would there be a chicken, and without the chicken, would there be an egg? Who's the egg and who's the chicken among writers, artists, and publishers?

In any case, the lowly ten-cent comic book has gone on to jumpstart many other entertainment industries. We now have blockbuster films based on comics as well as TV series, video games, etc.

We all owe a debt of gratitude to some of the creative geniuses depicted in these Drew Friedman portraits. Speaking of the people here whom I've known personally, I'm hugely impressed with how well Drew has captured not only their likenesses but their personalities as well. I am proud and honored to play my small part in this excellent collection.

Ten-year-old Drew Friedman with his comic book collection, 1969

INTRODUCTION ⟫ by Drew Friedman

From as early as I can remember, I've been drawn to comic books. The plots, the panels, the word balloons. The characters, the colors, the sound effects. The look of them, the feel of them, even the smell of them. Especially old comic books, worn, yellowed, crackling with age from multiple readings. I even loved that they were called "comic books," a perfect name for the cheaply produced, dispensable children's ephemera they were meant to be—*All in Color for a Dime*! I've also always been interested in learning as much as possible about the (mostly) unsung creators behind the comics.

I couldn't really avoid the inevitable onslaught of comic books in my life; it was my destiny. In 1954, my dad, fresh out of the air force and newly married, was hired to edit several men's adventure magazines (among them *Man's World* and *True Action*) for a company called Magazine Management (MM), run by a prematurely white-haired man named Martin Goodman (my dad, always referring to him as "Mr. Goodman," once told me that Martin Goodman's own brothers who worked for his company also called him "Mr. Goodman"). MM published a wide range of magazines and comic books, which were originally pub-

lished under the banner of Timely, then Atlas, and finally Marvel. In the late 1930s, Mr. Goodman's company helped usher in the first Golden Age of comic books, publishing the early adventures of Captain America, the Sub-Mariner, and the Human Torch. Martin Goodman's wife's young cousin, Stanley Lieber, a.k.a. Stan Lee, was hired by Timely in 1939, and when my dad joined MM, Stan was already a fifteen-year veteran of the company. My dad's desk was side by side with Stan's, separated by a thin partition, and they got along well. But soon my father began feeling sorry for Stan, as the once vast comics empire he controlled had been slowly downsized to one desk and one secretary, ravaged by the comic book witch hunts of the midfifties, which put an end to horror and crime comics and resulted in the enactment of the strict Comics Code. Mr. Goodman was seemingly attempting to phase out the comics division altogether. That all changed in the early sixties, when the miraculous rebirth of Marvel took hold and the Silver Age arrived.

I was born in 1958, and as early as I can remember, my dad would deposit a pile of Marvel comic books in my bedroom every Friday evening after returning from the city via the Long Island

William M. Gaines, early fifties

Rail Road. Before I was five, my brothers and I had already amassed a large collection of Marvels, among them early issues of *The Fantastic Four*, *The Amazing Spider-Man*, *The Incredible Hulk*, and *Millie the Model*. I loved the bright, vivid artwork, especially the covers, and took special notice of the artists' names, mainly the amazing Steve Ditko and Jack Kirby. I prided myself on figuring out who drew what, even if the particular artist wasn't credited, a practice prevalent in early comics.

Aside from art class, I never had much use for school. I received a far more enriching education from watching TV (*The Three Stooges*, *Adventures of Superman*, *Popeye*, *Soupy Sales*, etc.) and reading *Mad*, monster magazines, and comic books. When we got a little older, my brothers and I would sometimes pay visits to our dad up at his MM office on Madison Ave, and I inevitably made a beeline toward the comics department, which by the early sixties had returned to its former glory. I rarely caught a glimpse of the elusive Mr. Goodman, but Stan Lee was omnipresent and holding court, a tall, pudgy, balding man, as charming as could be, like a favorite smiling uncle who instead of dispensing candy dispensed brand-new comic books. When my dad mentioned to Stan that I liked to

draw, Stan proclaimed: "Someday, Drew is going to draw for MARVEL!"

In truth, I was already more focused on drawing funny stuff and dreamed of working for *Mad* magazine, joining the ranks of "the usual gang of idiots," which included my cartooning idols Mort Drucker, Don Martin, Al Jaffee, and Dave Berg. I was already aware that *Mad*'s publisher was one William M. Gaines, and thanks to my recent purchases of several Bantam horror and science fiction comics paperbacks, I connected the dots and realized Gaines had once also published a line of comic books under the banner of EC, which had originally published *Mad* as a comic book. I was instantly taken with the quality of the EC art drawn by comics greats like Johnny Craig, Jack Davis, George Evans, Wally Wood, and particularly "Ghastly" Graham Ingels. I was also trying to learn as much as I could about the early creators and the origins of comic books, especially after absorbing Jules Feiffer's essential book *The Great Comic Book Heroes*. Soon, like so many others, I would be startled, my mind blown, by *Zap* and early underground comics, mainly by the art of Robert Crumb, who forever changed my perception and outlook about comics, art, and life.

Martin Goodman, midfifties

While away at summer camp, I discovered DC's *Jimmy Olsen* comics. I was fascinated by how a young red-headed guy who was supposed to be making a living as a cub reporter at a metropolitan newspaper was instead being transformed monthly into a rock-and-roll star, a multimillionaire, a werewolf, a Nazi officer, a giant turtle man, or a slave on the "Planet of the Capes," yet always retaining his red hair and freckles. I thought those comics were out of control! I began collecting not only DC's *Jimmy Olsen*, but anything I could get my hands on that DC published: *Detective Comics* featuring Batman and Robin, *Action Comics* featuring Superman, and *Adventure Comics* featuring Supergirl, Superdog, Supermonkey, etc. I was slightly confused by *World's Finest Comics* though, which teamed up Batman and Superman. How could Superman, who had genuine superpowers, take on the mortal Batman as a partner in fighting crime? You would think that fact might slow him down a bit. From an early age I questioned comic book plausibility. No matter; at age nine I was an official obsessive DC comic book collector, and thanks to monthly pilgrimages (courtesy of my ever patient dad) to J. B.'s Back-Date Magazines on West Thirty-second Street (forever known to us as "the back-issue store"), I satisfied my craving. J. B.'s was a vast third-floor walk-up warehouse with countless aisles containing millions of aging magazines and comic books, and there I was able to feed my addiction. Soon, I possessed thousands of yellowing 1950s–1960s DC comics, stacked up so high in my Great Neck bedroom that there was little room to walk. I was a comic book junkie, craving a constant comic book fix, dreaming nightly of new comic book acquisitions, so much so that I'd settle for any comics, Archie, Gold Key, Harvey, even the lowly Charlton.

This all ended circa 1971, when I purchased an oversized hardcover called *Horror Comics of the 1950s*, which featured classic EC stories that, unlike the earlier black-and-white paperback collections, were published in full color! I was hooked.

I streamlined my comics buying to EC (and any Robert Crumb comics I could get my hands on). My family was now living in Manhattan, and monthly comic book conventions were being held at several low-rent hotels close to Penn Station, hosted by a former Brooklyn schoolteacher named Phil Seuling. I soon joined the faceless comic-collector rabble, seeking out original EC comics and attempting to negotiate the best possible prices from the Burger King–munching comics dealers. The Seuling cons sometimes featured special guests, and I found myself in the presence of comic book legends, among them Bill Everett, Bob Kane, William M. Gaines, Will Eisner, Wally Wood, Al Williamson, and the brilliant creator of *Mad*, Harvey Kurtzman. Out in the real world, these men were merely mortal, but at the comic cons they were treated like royalty, and I watched them from afar, not daring to invade their space aside from meekly asking for an occasional auto-

Jack Kirby, midsixties

graph. Watching "The King" Jack Kirby entering a comic book convention was like watching Jesus Christ entering the Vatican.

I still found the time to incessantly draw and attempt to improve as an artist (I was already obsessed with drawing faces) and held on to my dream of one day working for *Mad*. In late 1972, my high school, Baldwin, required ninth-grade students to seek out an interesting occupation for one week, then write a report about the experience. Since retiring from MM in 1966 to work as a full-time writer, my dad had kept in occasional touch with Stan Lee, so I asked if he could possibly call Stan and see if he could arrange for me to

Stan Lee, midsixties

work at Marvel for a week, fulfilling Stan's prophecy. Stan instantly agreed, but asked that my dad and I stop by the office the next day so he could introduce me to his secretary and set things up. We arrived at Marvel the next afternoon, which was headquartered in a large, sleek modern suite high above Madison Avenue. A trimmed-down Stan welcomed us, sporting a thick mustache and,

somehow, a full head of hair, and still smiling, still as charming as ever. We were seated in his expansive office, and he reminisced a little with my dad, then mentioned that he had just been shown a male model wearing a brand-new skin-tight Spider-Man costume: "Bruce, it's . . . AMAZING!" Then Stan looked over at me and said, "Yes sir, it's gonna be GREAT having Drew Friedman working here at Marvel next week!" He looked over at my dad and continued, "And, it's gonna be GREAT to have Bruce Jay Friedman write the *Spida-Man* film!" Stan was called out of his office briefly, and my dad looked over at me and murmured, "Son of a bitch. That's why he agreed to let you work here. Son of a bitch." Half a minute passed in silence, my dad mulling it over, and finally, pragmatically, he inquired, "So, how *did* he become *Spider-Man*?"

My career at Marvel began the following Monday, the always effusive Stan welcoming me and his secretary Carla Davis creating odd jobs for me to perform around the office: hanging new covers in the mail room, opening packages and mail (I was told to put the letters actually addressed to Iron Man into the "Iron Man bin"), running errands for staffers, and chatting with editors, including Roy Thomas and comics veteran Sol Brodsky. I was naturally drawn to the Marvel bullpen, where revolving Marvel artists could always be found sitting at their desks working. The particular week I spent at Marvel, the bullpen was inhabited by Marie Severin, the legendary EC comics colorist, who was drawing Marvel's current attempt at a *Mad*-like comic book, *Spoof*; *The Incredible Hulk* artist and Alan Alda look-alike Herb Trimpe; and John Romita, who was drawing *The Amazing Spider-Man*. Romita took a liking to me and spent time looking at some of my drawings and advising me to make sure to go to art college someday. He even set up a small desk next to his and asked me to help him out by tracing a particular *Fantastic Four* panel (most likely just to keep me busy). Overall, I was pleased with my time as a Marvel staffer and was paid fifty dollars for my ef-

Will Eisner, circa 1970

forts, but left with no particular desire to return, content with my one-week career. Drawing superheroes just wasn't in my game plan, as my sights were still set on working for *Mad*.

The following year I became friends with a younger kid at Baldwin named Chris Gaines, the son of *Mad* publisher William M. Gaines and the grandson of Max Gaines, one of the early pioneers of comics. I called Chris "Mr. Gaines" and he called me "Mr. Friedman." He pulled a few strings with his dad, and it was arranged that I would spend an afternoon up at *Mad* magazine. I somehow got the day off from school and was pretty nervous when I arrived at the *Mad* offices, but was welcomed by a friendly receptionist who ushered me right into Bill Gaines's office. Gaines, fifty-two at the time, was bearded with long, stringy, gray hippie-like hair. Legend has it that a newly divorced Gaines, who sported a crew cut up until the late sixties, woke up one morning and decided he just no longer wanted to shave or have his hair cut. The rest is history. He was hugely fat and wearing sloppy clothing—quite the sight and intimidating at first, but he instantly put me at ease by enthusiastically shaking my hand and inquiring about my artistic goals. I wanted to stay in his office and just

stare at all the EC, *Mad*, *King Kong*, and Zeppelin mementos covering the walls, but he encouraged me to make the rounds and talk to all the staffers. All were super friendly and encouraging, except *Mad*'s editor and former EC artist/writer Al Feldstein, who deigned to look up at me from his desk for one split second before returning to his paperwork, clearly having no interest in a fifteen-year-old. Slowly, I backed out of his office. Oh well. The most worthwhile part of my visit was courtesy of *Mad*'s art director, John Putnam, who after patiently sifting through my stack of drawings, sobered me up by strongly advising me that I needed to study anatomy and go to art school. I would dutifully follow his orders. Two years later, I enrolled at the School of Visual Arts (SVA).

I chose SVA mainly for one reason. The one and only Harvey Kurtzman was listed as a cartooning instructor in their catalog. At first I thought I was seeing things, but it was true. Harvey has been criticized by some for not being a great teacher, but never by me. Just being in his presence was enough; he was a guru. Harvey chose to teach "gag cartoons," preparing his students for a career as, say, a *New Yorker* or *Playboy* cartoonist. Rarely did he bring up the subject of comics, but if a student occasionally did, particularly referring to his early

Bill Gaines, 1971

Mad or war comics for EC, he clearly took great pride that anyone still cared and was interested in that work of his. Still, most of his students just thought of him as their amiable cartooning instructor, perhaps some aware that he had some vague connection to *Mad*, but mainly that he wrote that sexy comic strip in the back of *Playboy*. But to me and several other friends, including cartoonist classmates Mark Newgarden and Kaz, and future Marvel/DC editor Mike Carlin, Harvey was the methodical, turtle-faced living legend in our midst, and once a week for three hours his class was the main meeting place for like-minded young cartoonists.

Another comics legend, the creator of The Spirit, Will Eisner, also taught a comics course at SVA, and unlike the informal atmosphere of Kurtzman's class, Eisner presented a structured course in how to create comics the Will Eisner way. For example, one class would be dedicated to word balloons: "Always draw your word balloons FIRST!" he would admonish. Will was an entertaining raconteur and loved to reminisce about the golden days of running his comics shop: "Lou Fine had these big hands . . . Dave Berg worked for me before he met God . . . Jerry and Joe showed me Superman . . . I honestly didn't see the potential . . . I didn't think it would fly!" Although he admired my work ethic, Will couldn't quite fathom why I was spending my time drawing a comic strip featuring, say, William Frawley. To Will, comics were about heroes and villains, not Fred Mertz.

After four years at SVA, I felt I was prepared to begin my career as a cartoonist and illustrator. The satiric comics my brother Josh and I created were getting published and gaining some attention. Another SVA instructor, Art Spiegelman, included our comic strip about an innocent black man visiting Mayberry in his new graphics publication *Raw*, which would have a huge influence on the future of comics. My work was soon published in Robert Crumb's new comics magazine *Weirdo*, then regularly in *Heavy Metal*, *National Lampoon*, *Spy*, *Blab!*,

etc. I would eventually decrease the number of comics I was drawing to focus more on editorial illustration, caricature, and finally more realistic portraiture (old jewish comedians). I'd also fulfill my childhood goal of becoming a regular *Mad* contributor, one of the usual gang of idiots.

A couple of years ago my wife, Kathy, and I attended an outdoor party at my friend and former SVA classmate Phil Felix's home. Phil had lettered Harvey Kurtzman and Will Elder's *Little Annie Fanny* for *Playboy* for a decade, and the Elder family was in attendance. I was introduced to Will, "The Mad Playboy of Art," another longtime hero of mine, as well as his daughter Nancy and son-in-law Gary. Soon after Will died, Gary contacted me and asked if I would create a portrait of Will as a gift for Nancy. I agreed, but asked if there

Stan Lee, early seventies

were any photos of Will's art studio, as I've always been fascinated to observe cartoonists' working environments, and I wanted to place him in his if at all possible. Gary only had one photo of Will's studio, but his back was to the camera. The photo showed enough of his studio for me to incorporate it into my portrait, and Gary and Nancy seemed delighted with the final results. I was pleased with it too, and decided to create a companion piece, a portrait of Will's longtime collaborator, the late

Bill Everett, early seventies

Harvey Kurtzman, also placing him in his attic studio in Mount Vernon. Again, I was happy with the results and let the *Comics Journal* run it along with my Kurtzman reminiscence. The art also became a limited edition print and sold out quickly. I felt I was onto something and decided to expand the series to all of the original *Mad* comics artists,

adding Wally Wood, John Severin, and the twisted Basil Wolverton. I then took it a step further and decided to include all of the EC artists, and finally I began adding some Golden Age comics pioneers, among them Martin Goodman, Jack Kirby, Joe Simon, and Stan Lee. Soon, I envisioned the series as a book, presenting portraits of the early and in many cases ordinary-looking pioneers of comics, who began their careers within the first twenty years of the comic book's existence (1935–1955). I've created over eighty portraits of these talented and inventive men and women, presented mostly in middle age or older, not idealized or romanticized, but depicting the years of dedication etched into their faces. These were the pioneers who helped to shape a new medium, the American comic book. Some are still celebrated, some are more obscure, some died forgotten, and some are vilified. Several became rich and famous, several were exploited, and some were bamboozled, but all of them are legends: HEROES OF THE COMICS.

Harvey Kurtzman, midseventies

M.C. GAINES

1894–1947

plate

1

Maxwell Charles "M. C." Gaines (born Maxwell Ginsburg) was a pioneer of the early comic book industry. In 1933 he hatched the first four-color saddle-stitched newsprint pamphlets of comic strip reprints, known as "premiums" or "give-aways," first published as *Funnies on Parade*. Gaines (a Bert Lahr look-alike) was responsible for maneuvering two teenagers from Cleveland, Jerry Siegel and Joe Shuster, to newly installed publisher Harry Donenfeld at National Comics (DC) in 1938, urging Donenfeld to publish their character and playing a central role in the onset of Superman. He then formed a partnership with Donenfeld and his accountant Jack Liebowitz, creating a sister company to DC called All-American Comics and introducing Wonder Woman, the Green Lantern, and Hawkman. Relations between the partners eventually soured, and Gaines was bought out for half a million dollars and left to start his own company, Educational Comics (EC), at 225 Lafayette Street. At first he published reprints of Bible stories in comic book form, then expanded to a hodgepodge of undistinguished titles, some aimed at young children under the "Entertaining Comics" logo, among them *Tiny Tot*, *Dandy*, and *Animal Fables*. The bland company was limping along when, in 1947, Max Gaines was drowned in a freak boating accident in front of his home on Lake Placid, and the company fell into the hands of his reluctant twenty-five-year-old son Bill.

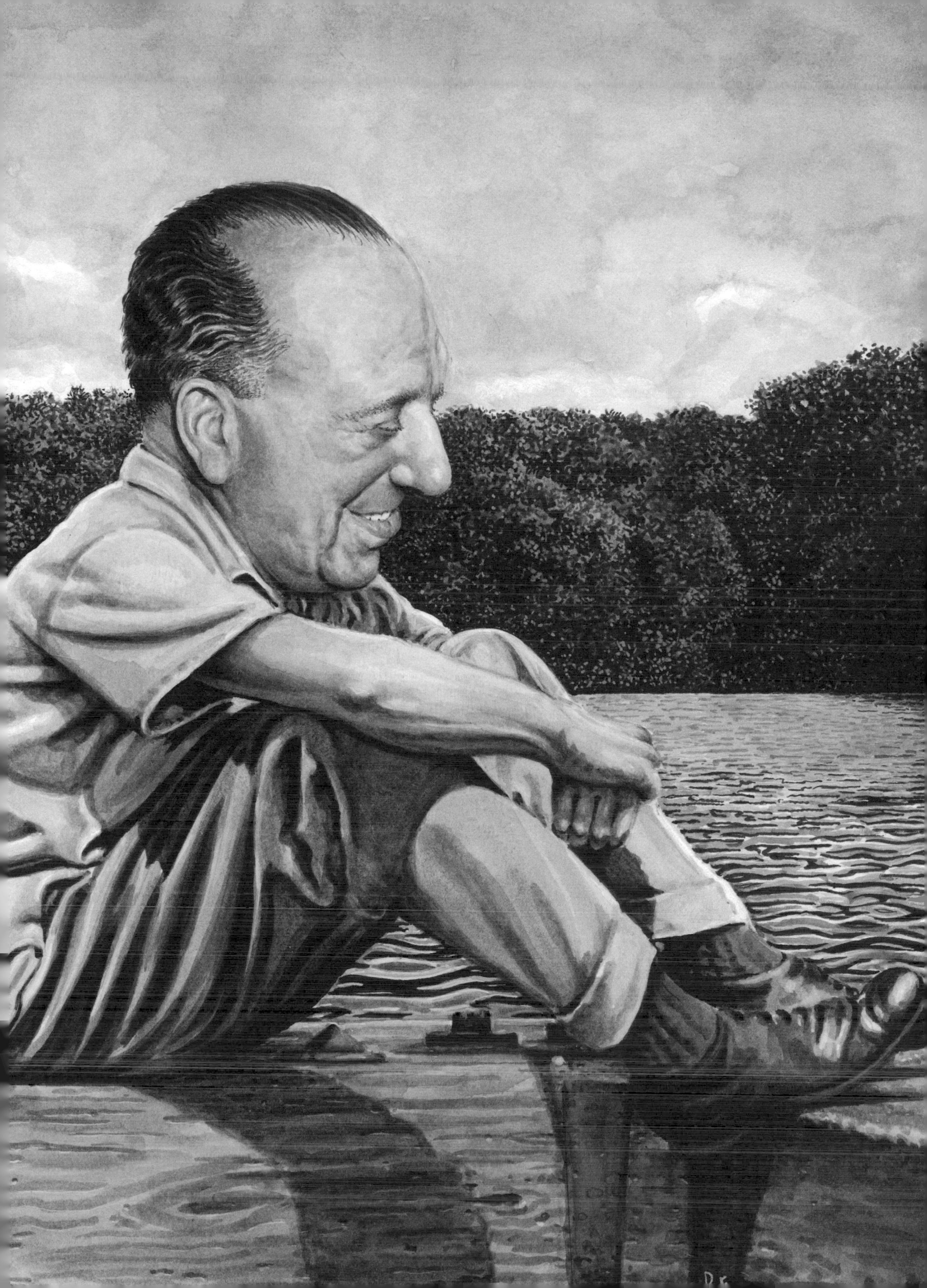

MALCOLM WHEELER-NICHOLSON

1890–1965

plate
2

Malcolm Wheeler-Nicholson joined the US Cavalry in 1917 and rose to become one of the youngest majors in the army. Subsequently he was forever addressed as "The Major." An entrepreneur, he is also credited with being the creator of the modern comic book. The Major returned from the war and became a vocal, outspoken critic of war. He was a vocal, outspoken critic of some of the practices of the US military. He also penned adventure and western short stories for pulp magazines. In 1935 he formed National Allied Publications, releasing a tabloid-sized comics publication called *New Fun*, which was soon converted to *More Fun* and printed in the standard comic book size. *More Fun* was a humor and adventure comic and the first comic book to publish original material, much of it written by The Major himself.

The Major was credited with discovering Jerry Siegel and Joe Shuster, the young and eager writer/artist partners from Cleveland. He ran their early comics adventures of Slam Bradley and others in his various National titles, including the first issues of *Detective Comics*. He also saw the potential in their newly created character Superman, but before he could act on it, he experienced cash-flow problems and was compelled to sell his publishing business to his partner at National, Harry Donenfeld, and Donenfeld's accountant, Jack Liebowitz, in 1937. National's new publishers soon introduced the characters Superman (quickly securing full ownership) and Batman. National became DC Comics, whose comics caused an instant sensation, launching the Golden Age. The Major retired from publishing and returned to writing his war stories and continuing his critiques of the American military.

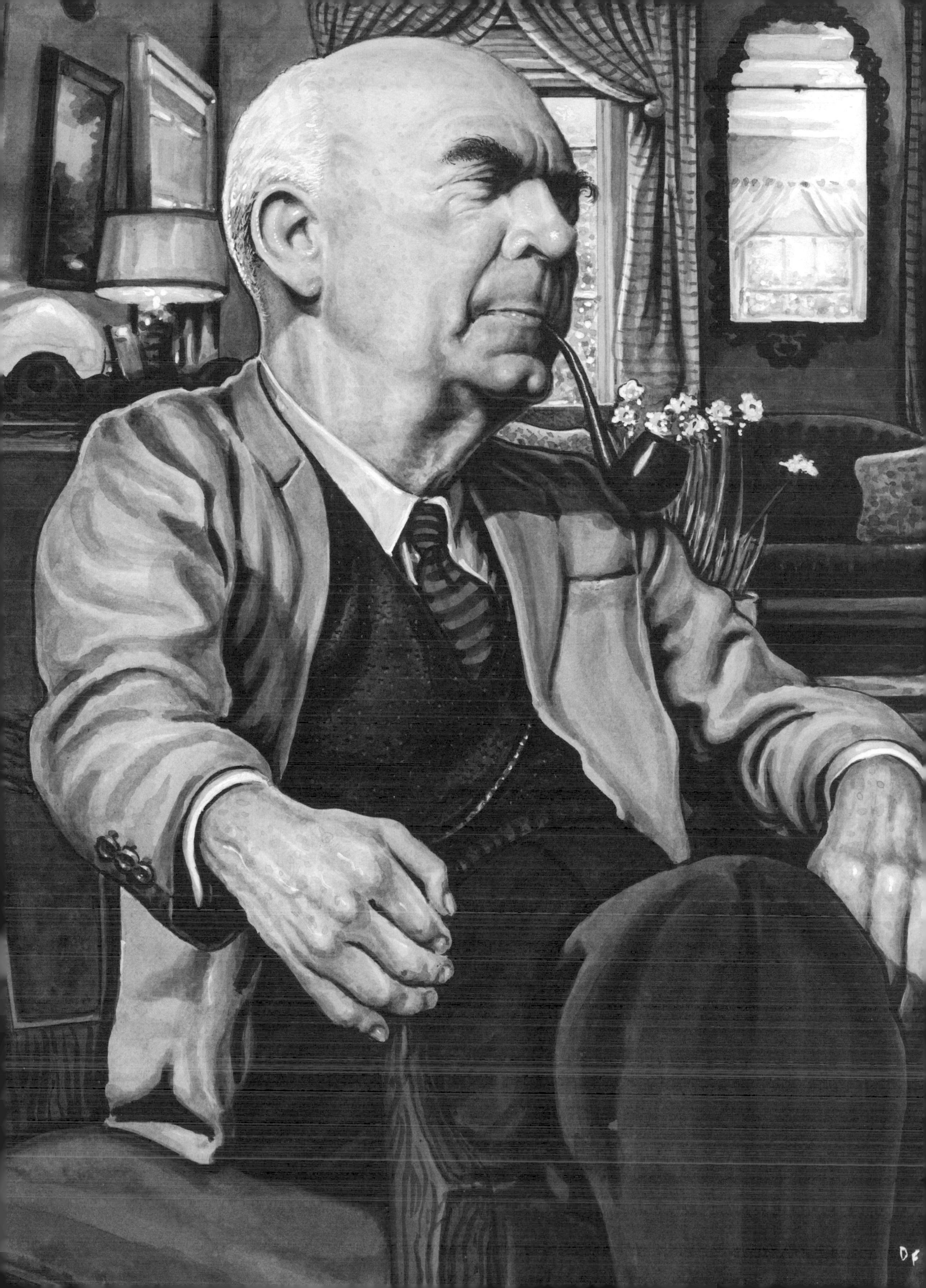
DF

HARRY "A" CHESLER

1898–1981

plate
3

Harry "A" Chesler was a cigar-chomping, fedora-wearing entrepreneur and a pioneer of packaging and outsourcing comic book material for new publishers in the emerging medium of comics. In the midthirties he opened the first of what would be referred to as comic book "shops," supplying completed comic book pages to the growing market of new comic book publishers by employing an assembly line of young comics artists to churn out hundreds of pages for little money but great experience. A strict taskmaster, Harry "A" Chesler, the "A" standing for "anything," opened his Dickensian New York "sweat" shop in 1936 and soon gobbled up dozens of young and eager artists looking to jump-start their careers and develop their craft in the new field of "funny books." Among them were Creig Flessel, Jack Cole, Carmine Infantino, Charles Biro, Mort Meskin, Mac Raboy, and even a twelve-year-old Joe Kubert. At one point Chesler had forty artists working in his crammed studio on West Twenty-third Street.

The Chesler shop (some referred to him as "Chizzler") always followed the current comics trends: first, funny books featuring humor, adventure, and western stories; then, following in the success of Superman and Batman, superheroes; and finally horror. Chesler also published comics under his own imprint beginning in 1941, following the booming superhero market, and labeled each cover "Harry 'A' Chesler, World's Greatest Comics." Chesler was less successful as a publisher though, and his comics—basically a hodgepodge of unmemorable titles and characters—were sadly not the "World's Greatest" and didn't meet with much success. He would later rehash many of his comic titles, such as *Dynamic*, using newly created macabre covers in an attempt to cash in on the emerging horror trend. His comics shop remained active on and off until 1953. He would eventually donate over four thousand pages of original art, much of it created in his studio, to Fairleigh Dickinson University's library.

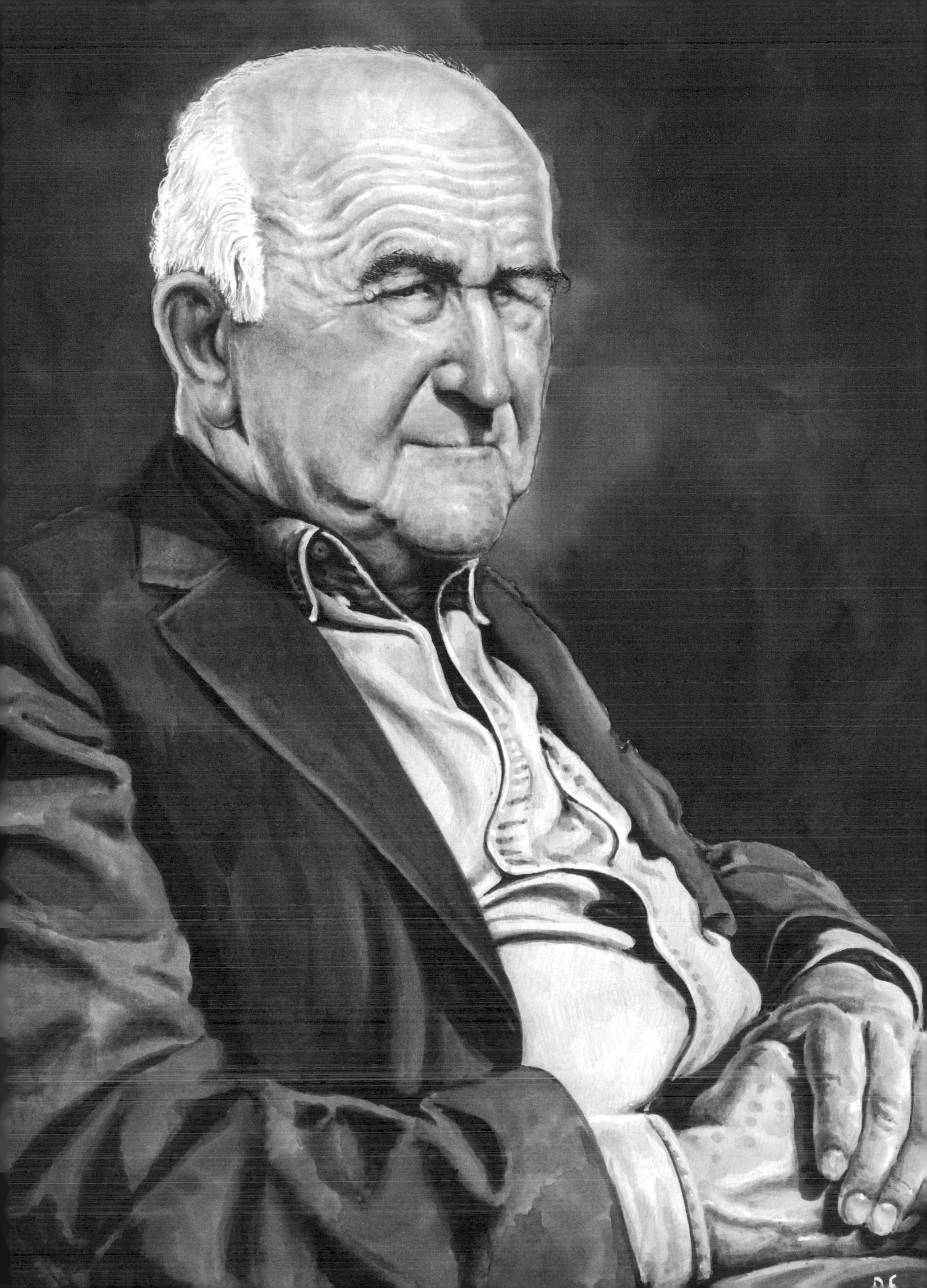

SHELDON MAYER

1917–1991

plate
4

Sheldon Mayer was one of the earliest artist/writers to work in comic books, doing odd jobs in 1934 at age twelve at National Allied Publications (later DC) under Major Malcolm Wheeler-Nicholson. While working at the McClure Newspaper Syndicate in the late thirties, he came across an unsold comic strip proposal by two Cleveland teenagers named Jerry Siegel and Joe Shuster in the rejection pile. Mayer fell in love with their character Superman and saw its potential for becoming something special. He instantly showed it to his boss, M. C. Gaines, who also worked at McClure at the time. Gaines agreed with Mayer and contacted Harry Donenfeld at National (who had taken over the company from the Major), urging him to publish it, which led to Superman's debut in the safely titled *Action Comics* #1 in 1938. The next year Gaines cofounded a sister company (but separate entity) to National/DC, All American Publications, and hired Mayer to join him as the company's first editor. Mayer edited and helped create *The Flash*, *Green Lantern*, *Wonder Woman*, and *All-Star Comics*. He also kept busy with his own quirky, appealing cartoon work, creating covers for comic book reprints of *Mutt and Jeff* and working on his semiautobiographical comic *Squiggly*, which chronicled the haphazard daily existence of a novice cartoonist. In the late forties Mayer would dedicate himself to cartooning full-time for DC, writing and drawing *Leave It to Binky* and his most endearing creation, *Sugar and Spike*—featuring two adorable toddlers who communicated with each other in baby talk but weren't understood by adults—which he'd continue for decades.

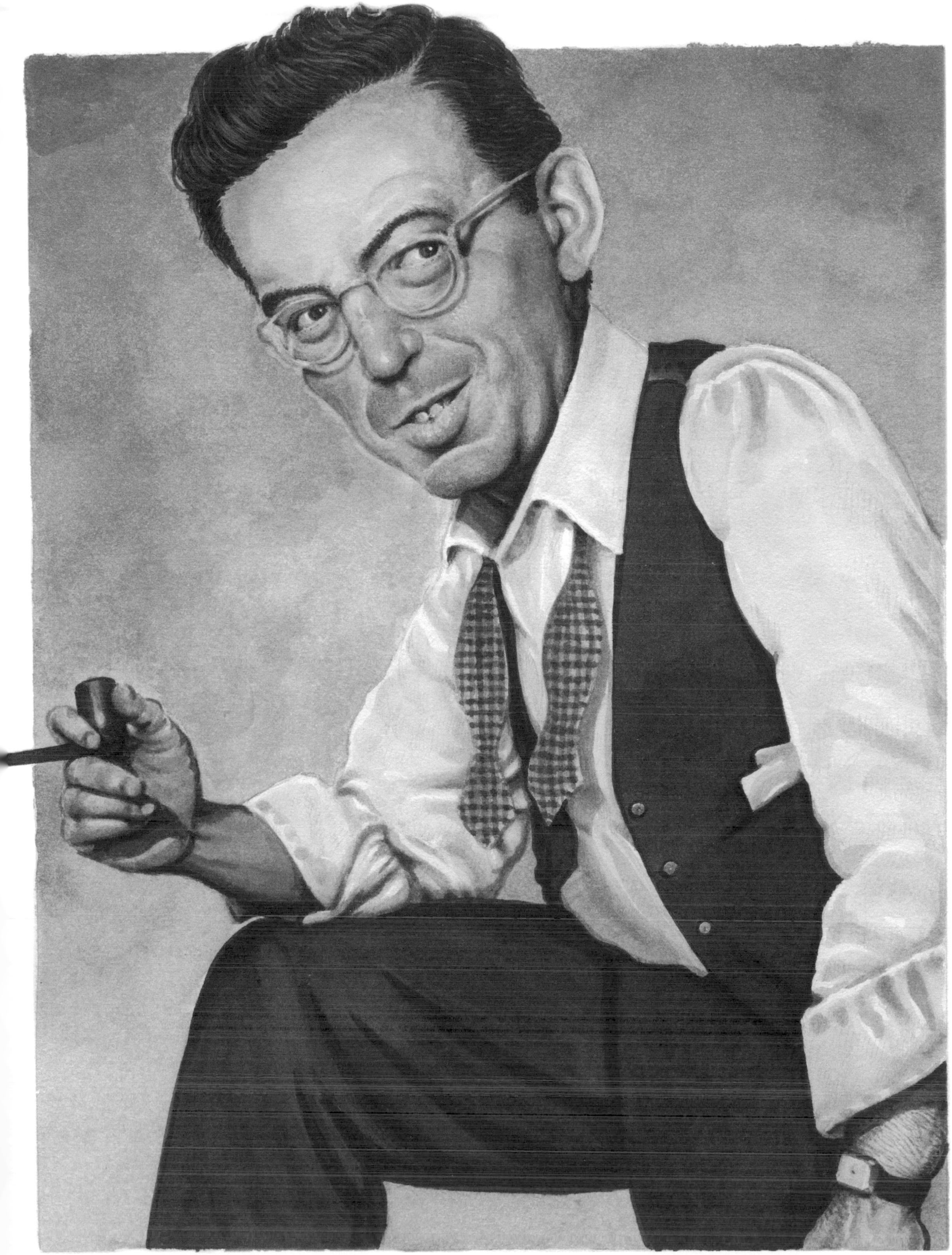

CREIG FLESSEL

1912–2008

plate
5

Creig Valentine Flessel was an early comic book artist who enjoyed a long and prolific career as an illustrator and/cartoonist, although much of his work went uncredited. In 1935 Flessel was drawing for pulp magazines when he saw an ad placed in the *New York Times* by publisher Major Malcolm Wheeler-Nicholson seeking artists to work for his new company, National Allied Publications. Flessel answered the ad, and his first published comics work appeared in 1936's *More Fun Comics*. The next year the Major's *Detective Comics* made its debut, with the first cover depicting a menacing Asian villain drawn by the comic's editor, Vin Sullivan. Flessel took over the cover duties starting with issue #2, and today he is probably best remembered for his bold, pulp-like presuperhero covers created for the pre-Batman *Detective Comics* #2–19, which depicted stark murder scenes, evil villains, and earnest, square-jawed detectives. Flessel wrote and drew many features for the Golden Age of comics, including the early adventures of the Shining Knight and the Sandman. The versatile journeyman artist continued drawing comics throughout the fifties, including *Superboy*, and also worked on the "hip" title *Prez* for DC in the seventies. He also ghosted for several syndicated comic strips, including Al Capp's *Li'l Abner*, created advertising work, and drew illustrations and cartoons for *Boy's Life* and *Playboy*.

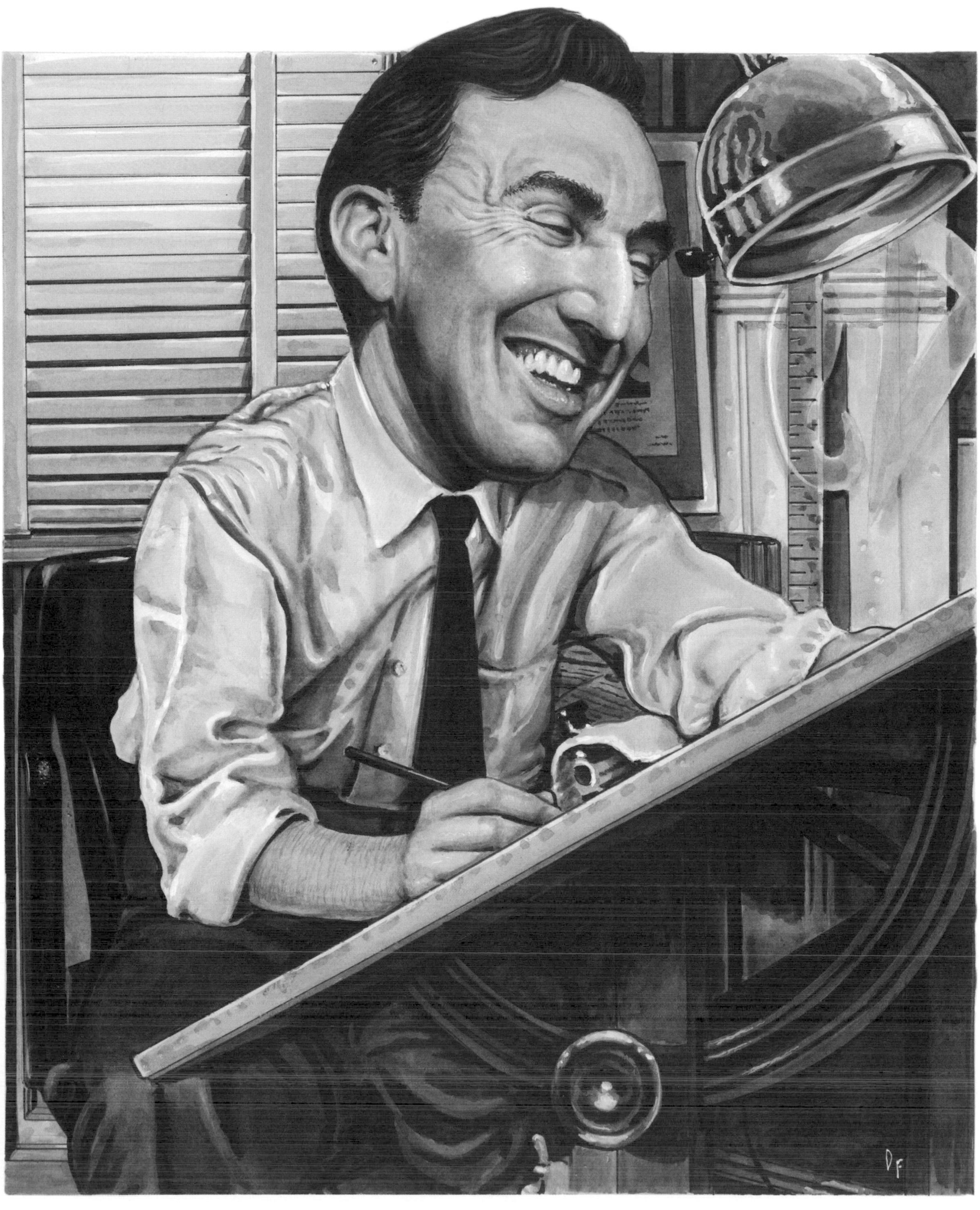
DF

JERRY IGER

1903–1990

plate
6

Samuel Maxwell "Jerry" Iger began his career as a newspaper cartoonist. In 1935 he contributed several humor strips to what is now regarded as the first comic book, *Famous Funnies*, which was composed mostly of reprinted newspaper comic strips in the new comic book format. Iger became the editor of the comic *Wow, What a Magazine!* the following year, and although it would only last four issues, it included early work by Bob Kane as well as Iger's future partner, nineteen-year-old Will Eisner, who drew the strip *Scott Dalton*. After *Wow* folded, Iger and Eisner anticipated the demand created by the newly flourishing comics publishers entering the new medium, who were seeking newly created material to fill their comic books. Following the lead of the Harry "A" Chesler comics packaging assembly-line shop, they opened their own shop, Syndicated Features Corporation, commonly referred to as the Eisner and Iger Studio. Their comics factory was an instant success, and they soon employed an assembly line of young, eager artists, writers, and letterers, including future comics legends Jack Kirby, Bob Kane, Lou Fine, and Wally Wood. The studio supplied completed comic books to publishers Fox, Fiction House, and Quality Comics, among others. Working under various pseudonyms, Iger also wrote many comics scripts. By 1939 the studio had fifteen employees on staff. Eisner later boasted that he was rich before he turned twenty-two. He split off from Iger in 1940 to concentrate on his character the Spirit, and Iger continued to package comics under the name S. M. Iger Studio until 1955.

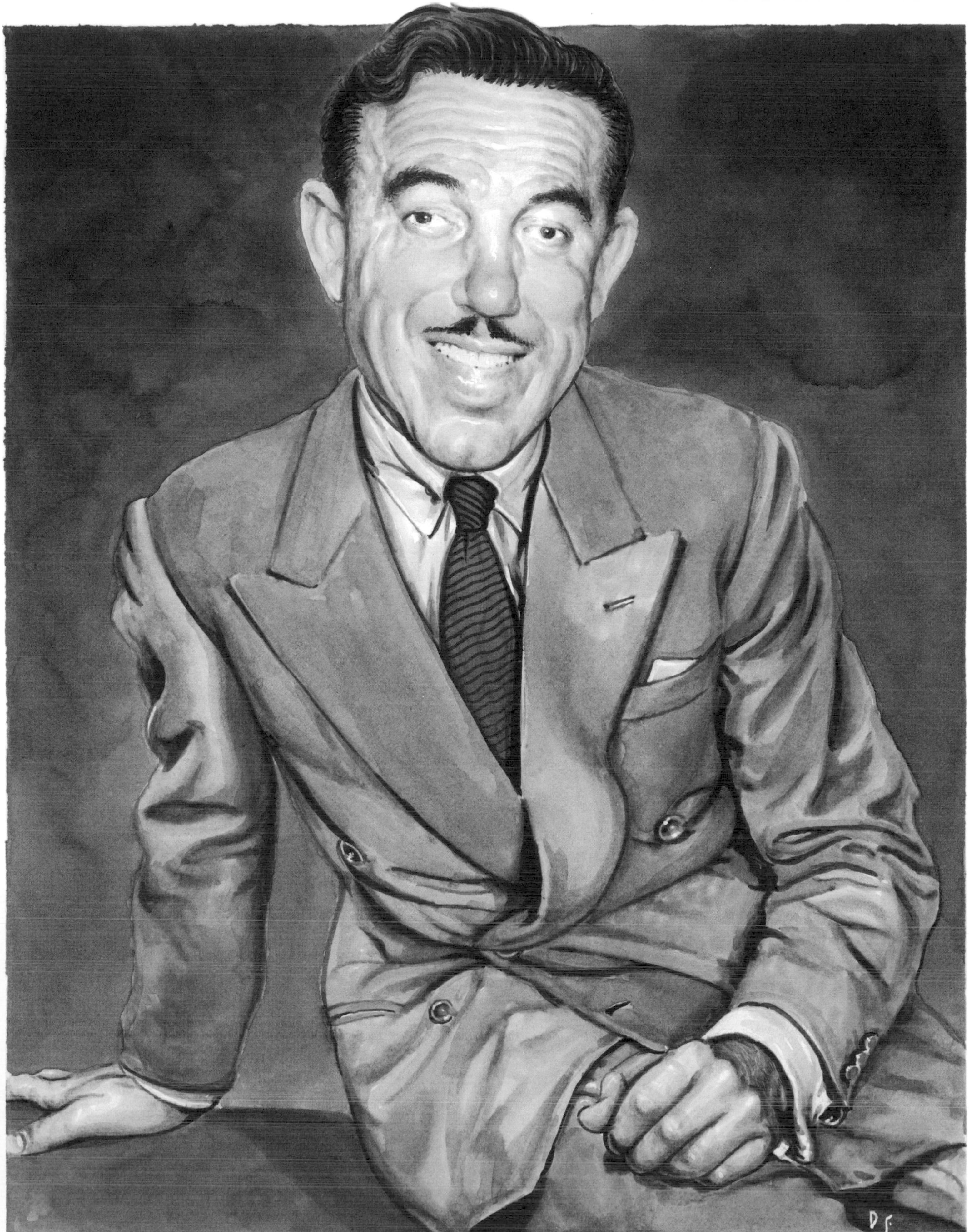

WILL EISNER

1917–2005

plate
7

William Erwin "Will" Eisner grew up in the Bronx dreaming of someday becoming a successful cartoonist. In 1936 Eisner's friend from Dewitt Clinton High School Bob Kane suggested he sell some of his cartoons to a new tabloid-sized magazine that was running comics called *Wow, What a Magazine!*, edited by cartoonist and letterer Jerry Iger. Eisner created the adventure strip *Captain Scott Dalton* as well as several covers for *Wow*. Although Iger was twelve years older than the nineteen-year-old Eisner, they clicked, and each anticipated the call for publishers looking for brand-new material for the infant comics industry. Together they opened the Eisner and Iger studio, a mass production comic book factory, in New York in 1937. Eisner roughed out layouts for young comics artists to finish, among them Lou Fine, Bob Kane, Bob Powell, and Reed Crandall. The studio produced finished comics primarily for Quality, Fiction House, and Fox, including the titles *Sheena, Queen of the Jungle* (created by Eisner), *Jumbo*, *Planet*, and *Wonderworld*. Eisner also created the characters Dollman and Blackhawk while working at the shop.

The "sweatshop" proved to be a huge financial success for the two partners, but Eisner, finally more interested in concentrating on his own writing and drawing, sold his interest in the shop in 1939 to pursue an offer to create a syndicated newspaper comics section of his own, aimed at a more adult audience. His first sixteen-page *The Spirit* episode ran in 1940. The urban, crime-fighting nonsuperhero the Spirit caught on big, and Eisner's stories stood out in part to his innovative, almost cinematic artwork, writing, and panel composition, which combined dynamic action, tongue-in-cheek humor, and glamour (an Eisner specialty was drawing sexy women with features based on Carole Lombard). Some of Eisner's assistants on *The Spirit* were Lou Fine, Bob Powell, and Jules Feiffer (who strongly objected to Eisner's stereotypical black character, Ebony).

At its height, *The Spirit* insert appeared in twenty major market newspapers with a combined circulation of five million readers on Sundays. Eisner was called into service in 1942 and was given the job of editing *Fire Power*, the official army magazine. After his discharge in 1945, he returned to drawing *The Spirit* for another six years. In 1951 he hired artist Wally Wood to draw *The Outer Space Spirit*, an attempt to relaunch the floundering series, but Wood finally couldn't meet the deadlines, and *The Spirit* was canceled in 1952. Eisner spent most of the next twenty-five years with his American Visuals Corporation, which created educational comic books for the government and military. He later enjoyed a resurgence of *The Spirit* via reprints by Harvey Comics, Warren Publications, and Kitchen Sink Press. Eisner became a comics instructor at New York's School of Visual Arts in the early seventies (as did Harvey Kurtzman) and was a frequent and popular guest at comic book conventions. In 1978 he created the first of his many graphic novels, *A Contract with God*.

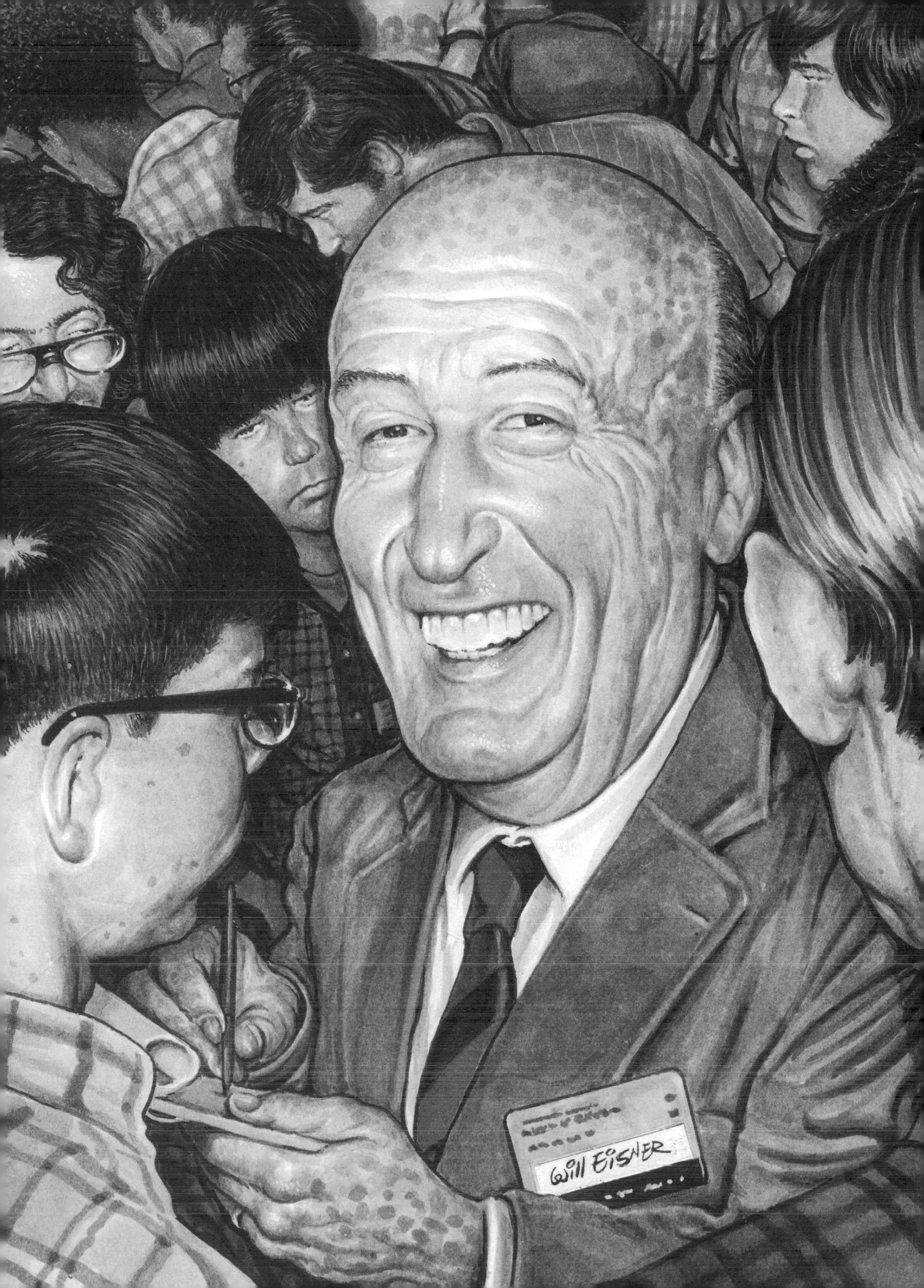
Will Eisner

JERRY SIEGEL

JOE SHUSTER

1914–1996

1914–1992

plate

8

Jerome "Jerry" Siegel and Joseph "Joe" Shuster met each other at Glendale High School in Cleveland, Ohio. The two shy Jewish teenagers discovered they shared much in common. The writer/artist team broke into comics by creating work for National Allied Publications' early comic book *New Fun*. Among their earliest characters were the musketeer swashbuckler Henry Duval and the supernatural crime fighter Doctor Occult. Their character Slam Bradley debuted in National's *Detective Comics* #1 in 1937, edited by Vin Sullivan.

In 1938 Max Gaines implored National's new publishers, Harry Donenfeld and Jack Liebowitz, to publish Siegel and Shuster's character Superman. The character finally debuted as the cover feature for National's *Action Comics* #1 (June 1938). Superman was an instant sensation, heralding the beginning of the superhero craze and the Golden Age of comics. By accepting a payment of $130 along with the assurance that they would be the primary artist and writer for *Superman* and the upcoming syndicated *Superman* newspaper comic, Siegel and Shuster, without any legal advice, forever signed away all their rights to the character.

The pair continued to oversee the *Superman* comic books and newspaper strip for close to a decade, collecting a decent salary, while Donenfeld and Liebowitz grew rich. In 1946, when the company refused to compensate them to the degree they felt was fair, Siegel and Shuster sued National over rights to the characters. They accepted a $94,000 settlement, although the courts agreed that National had validly purchased the rights to Superman when they bought that first story. After all the legal wrangling, Siegel and Shuster were basically severed from the company, and their byline was removed from all comic books and newspaper strips.

In 1947 the team was hired by Superman's original editor, Vin Sullivan, to create the short-lived character Funnyman for his company, Magazine Enterprises. In the early fifties, Siegel became the editor at Ziff-Davis. He returned to DC to write (uncredited) Superman stories until the midsixties, when he once again unsuccessfully sued DC over the Superman rights.

In 1975, after the announcement that DC's parent company Warner Communications was producing a multi-million-dollar *Superman* film, Jerry Siegel, who had been working as a file clerk, and the near-blind Joe Shuster, along with artists Neal Adams, Jerry Robinson, and others, helped launch a public-relations campaign to protest DC's treatment of them. After mounting public pressure, a shamed Warner Communications awarded the duo $20,000 a year for the rest of their lives as well as a guarantee that the credit "created by Jerry Siegel and Joe Shuster" would be added to all future Superman comics, TV shows, and films.

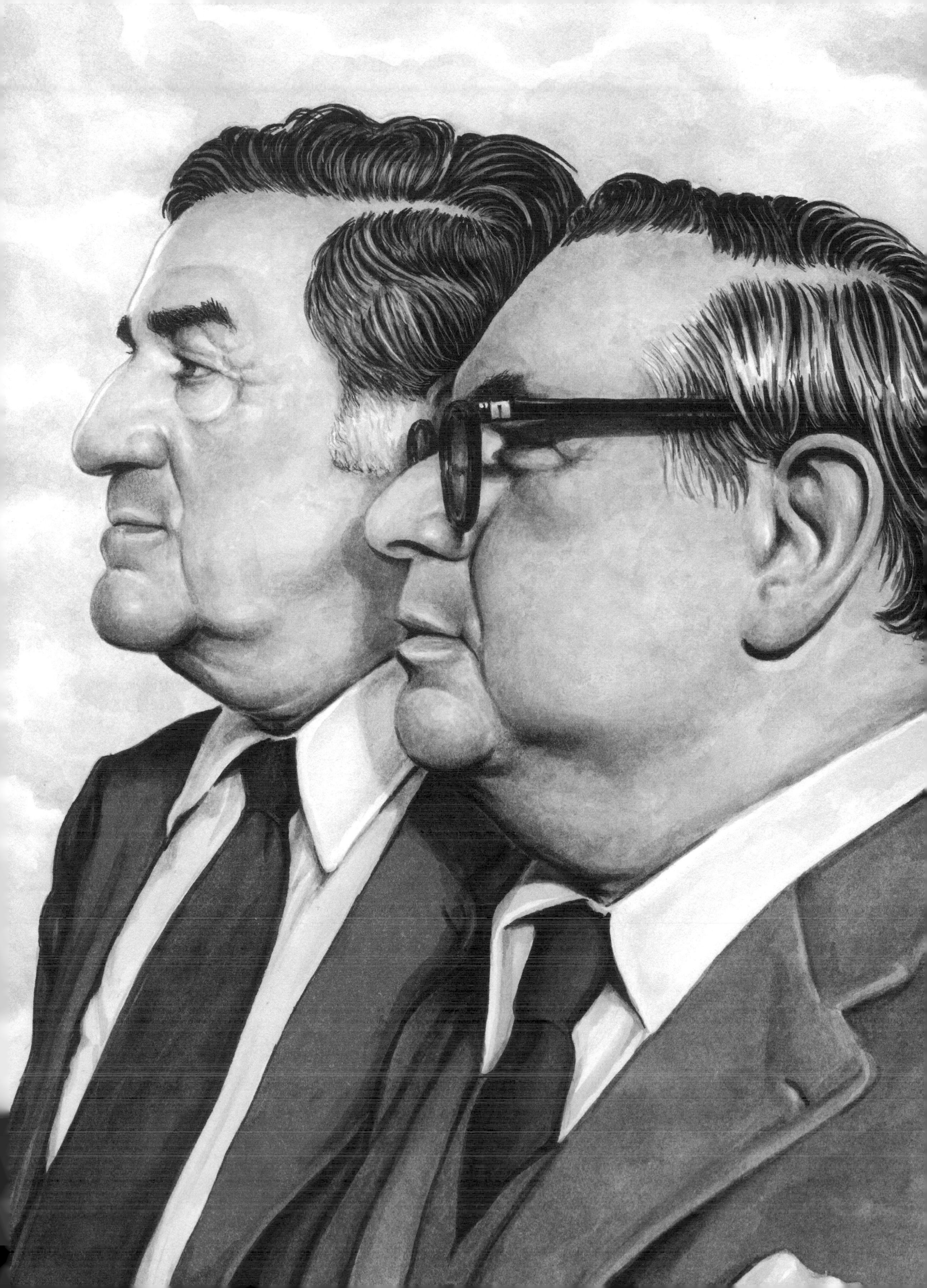

BOB KANE

1915–1998

plate
9

Bob Kane (born Robert Kahn) was the disputable artist who posed for almost half a century as the sole creator of Batman. Kane joined the Fleischer cartoon studio in 1934 as a trainee animator, but decided to switch careers and enter the new medium of comic books instead. In 1936 he contributed to several of editor Jerry Iger's comics and then was asked to join the new Eisner and Iger comics shop. Kane created several funny animal features, including *Peter Pup* for National Periodical Publications' *More Fun* and *Oscar the Gumshoe* for *Detective Comics*.

In 1938, after Superman caused a sensation in *Action Comics* #1, National sought more superheroes to add to their roster, and Kane soon conceived a character he called "The Batman." He showed his flimsy conception drawings to writer Bill Finger, whom he had hired to work for him, and Finger suggested specific changes to redesign the character into the now familiar Dark Knight persona. Finger also wrote the debut Batman story, with Kane supplying the crude art. The completed Batman debut finally appeared in *Detective Comics* #27 (May 1939). The character became a breakout hit and was soon starring in his own series, featuring his sidekick Robin, who was created by Finger and artist Jerry Robinson. Kane worked out a cozy deal with National under which he would receive sole credit as the writer and artist behind *Batman*, even though the character was essentially created by Bill Finger. Soon Kane assembled his "Batman Team": Bill Finger, Jerry Robinson, inker George Roussos, and later artist Dick Sprang, among others, all of whom worked as ghosts for Kane, creating, writing, and drawing the familiar and iconic cast. What Bob Kane actually did on the *Batman* comics, if anything, is still debated by comics historians and comics fans.

In 1943 Kane left the *Batman* comic book to focus on "penciling" the *Batman* newspaper strip. He later received credit for creating the popular series of TV cartoons channeling Batman and Robin for toddlers, *Courageous Cat and Minute Mouse*, and proudly took full credit (never disputed by a soul) for writing the 1960s "comedy" album *The Adventures of Batman & Rubin (Jewish Boy Wonder)* for Allen & Rossi. Steve Rossi later said that that particular album essentially derailed their careers. Kane also found time to pose as a fine artist, until it was revealed that he had employed ghost artists. Bob Kane enjoyed his charade of masquerading as the sole creator of Batman till the end. The true story continues to unfold, and only recently has Bill Finger received his long overdue credit as the true cocreator of Batman.

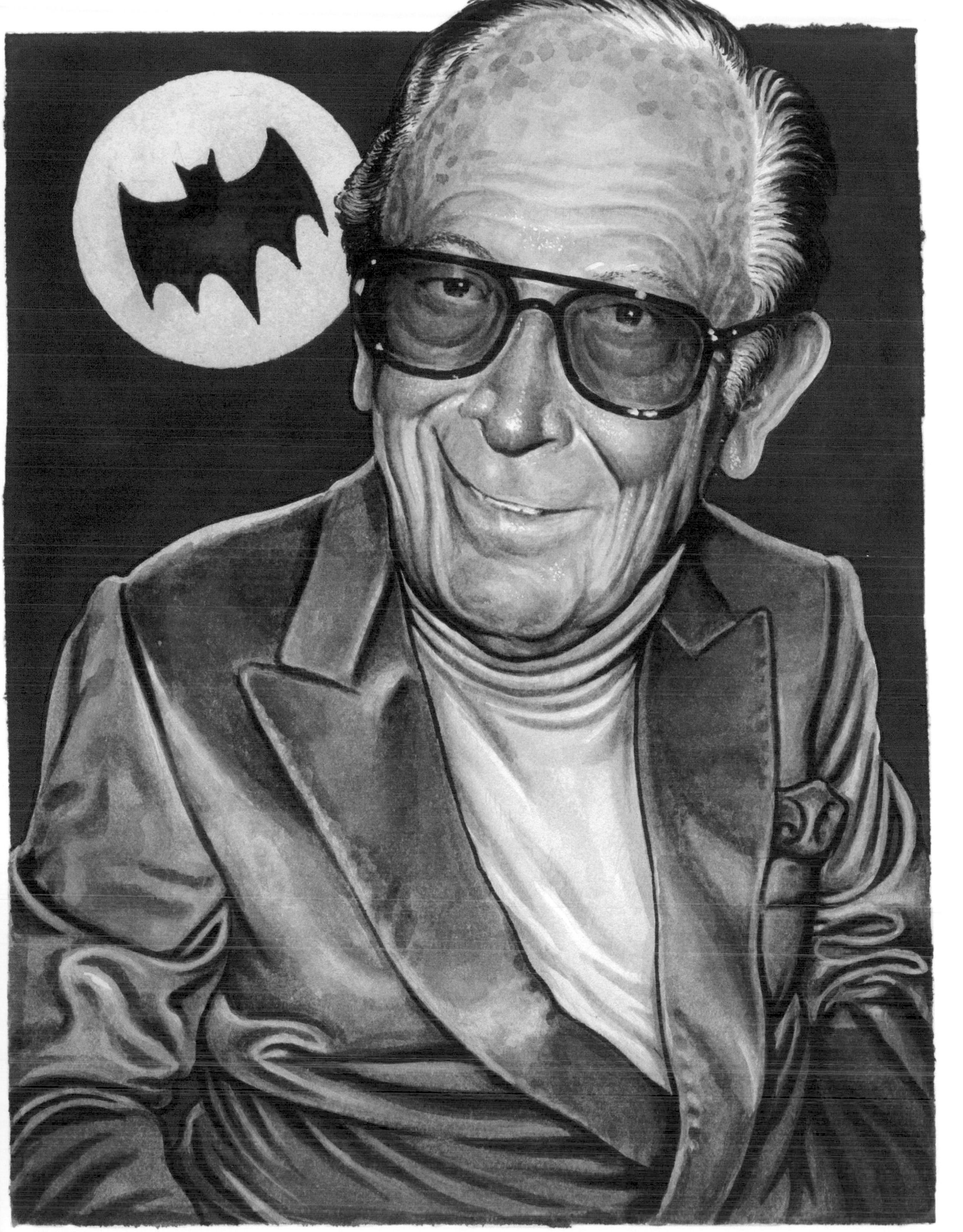

BILL FINGER

1914–1974

plate
10

Milton "Bill" Finger was the uncredited cocreator of Batman and one of the most influential writers to ever work in comics. Bill Finger met artist Bob Kane at a cocktail party in 1938 and soon joined his studio, ghostwriting for several of Kane's adventure strips. The following year, after the huge success of Superman in *Action Comics* #1, National put out the word that it was looking for more superhero titles, and Kane conceived a character he called "The Batman." He showed some of his character sketches to Finger, who thought the character looked too much like Superman, with reddish tights and boots, so he helped create the character's costume, suggesting a cowl instead of a domino mask, a cape instead of two stiff wings, a black costume as opposed to red tights, and gloves and gauntlets—an appearance based more on Lee Falk's popular character the Phantom than on Superman. Finger also had the idea to make Batman a millionaire named Bruce Wayne.

Finger wrote the initial script and Kane provided art for the debut Batman story, which appeared in National's *Detective Comics* #27. Kane negotiated a contract with National that granted it ownership of the character in exchange for large financial compensation and a mandatory byline for Bob Kane—and Bob Kane alone—on every Batman comic and newspaper strip. Batman became a winner and was soon featured in his own solo comic, while Bill Finger and the Batman team, including artist Jerry Robinson and inker George Roussos, went completely uncredited. Finger, who also cocreated National's (DC's) Green Lantern and Wildcat, made major contributions to Batman, including cocreating Batman's young sidekick, Robin, and the smiling villain the Joker, suggesting to Bob Kane that his appearance be based on Conrad Veidt's portrayal of Gwynplaine from the 1928 silent horror classic *The Man Who Laughs*. Finger eventually left Kane's studio to work directly for DC, while also freelancing for other companies, including Fawcett, Quality, and Timely. He also wrote several films, such as *The Green Slime*, and TV scripts, including two episodes of the 1966 *Batman* TV series. Several years after Finger's death, Bob Kane finally acknowledged him as a "contributing force" in the creation of Batman and admitted he never received the fame and recognition he deserved. That slight continues to be remedied as Bill Finger's name is now officially mentioned alongside Bob Kane's as one of the two creators of the Dark Knight, Batman.

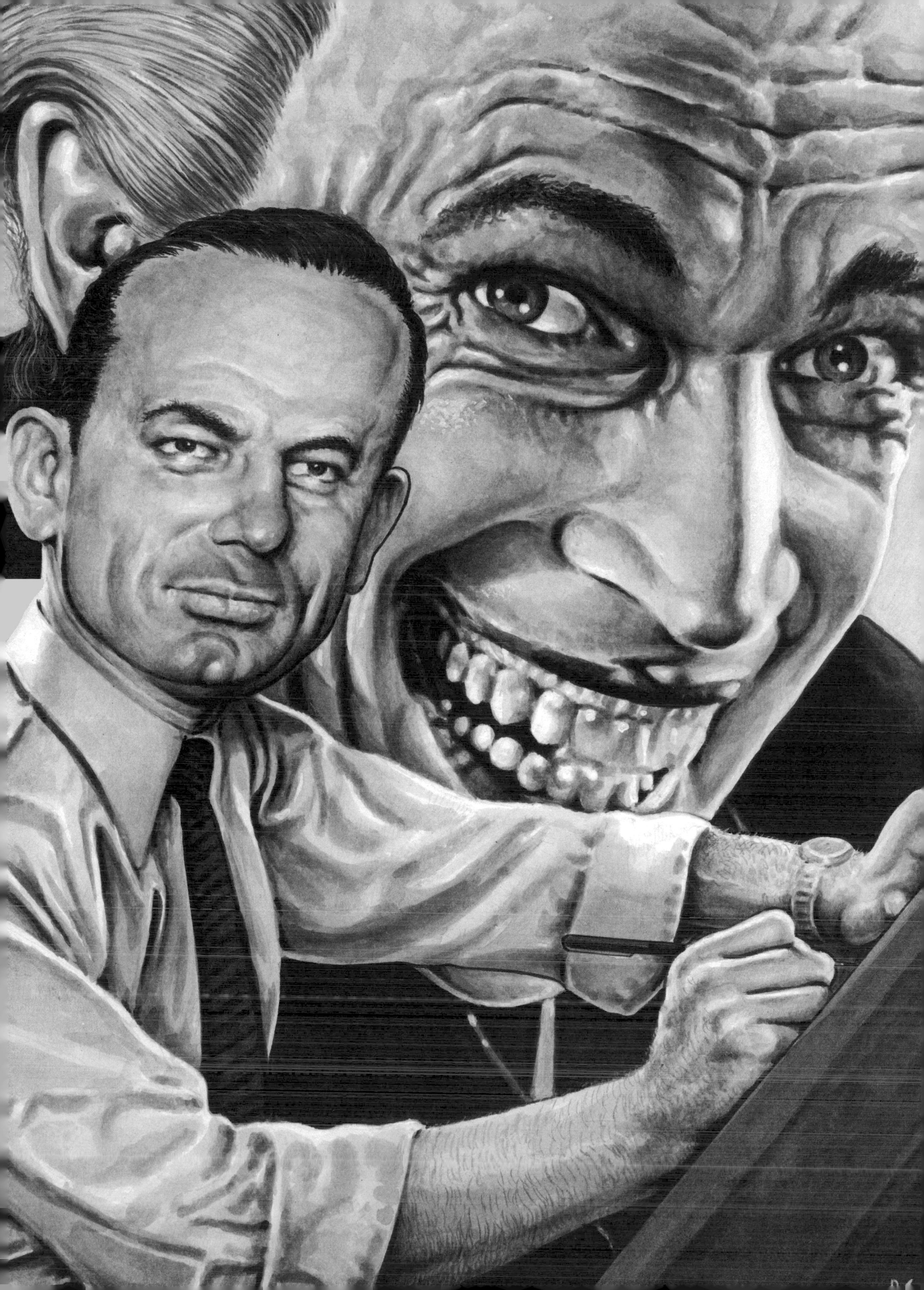

MARTIN GOODMAN

1908–1992

plate
11

Martin Goodman (born Moses Goodman) was the elusive pioneering publisher of Timely, Atlas, and finally Marvel comics. His company introduced seminal characters such as Captain America, the Sub-Mariner, the Fantastic Four, and Spider-Man. Goodman began his career publishing pulp magazines in the early thirties. In 1939 he released a test comic book, *Marvel Comics* #1, which featured mostly reprint material, but also the debuts of both Carl Burgos's the Human Torch (featured on the cover) and Bill Everett's Prince Namor, the Sub-Mariner. The comic sold out instantly and Goodman soon launched Timely Comics, an umbrella title for his comics division, which was instrumental in ushering in the Golden Age of comic books. Soon after the war began, he published the patriotic Captain America, created by the team of Joe Simon and the brilliant Jack Kirby, and it became an instant hit. Goodman's wife's cousin Stanley Lieber, a.k.a. Stan Lee, had been hired by the company at age seventeen in 1939, and at age nineteen he became the top editor of the comics division, a position he would hold for decades.

After the war, superhero titles were on the wane, and Timely evolved into Atlas, publishing a wider variety of the most popular comics genres, including horror, crime, western, romance, and teenage titles. The comic book industry suffered through lean years in the fifties, and Goodman slowly cut the department down to one in-house employee, Stan Lee, and Lee's secretary. In the early fifties Goodman also started what would become a vast magazine empire under the banner Magazine Management, publishing humor, cheesecake, and men's adventure titles. Atlas Comics would eventually struggle back from the dead and evolve into Marvel. In 1961 writer Stan Lee and artist Jack Kirby created *The Fantastic Four*, introducing the naturalistic superhero with superhuman problems, and forever changed the industry. Martin Goodman would remain on as Marvel's publisher until 1972.

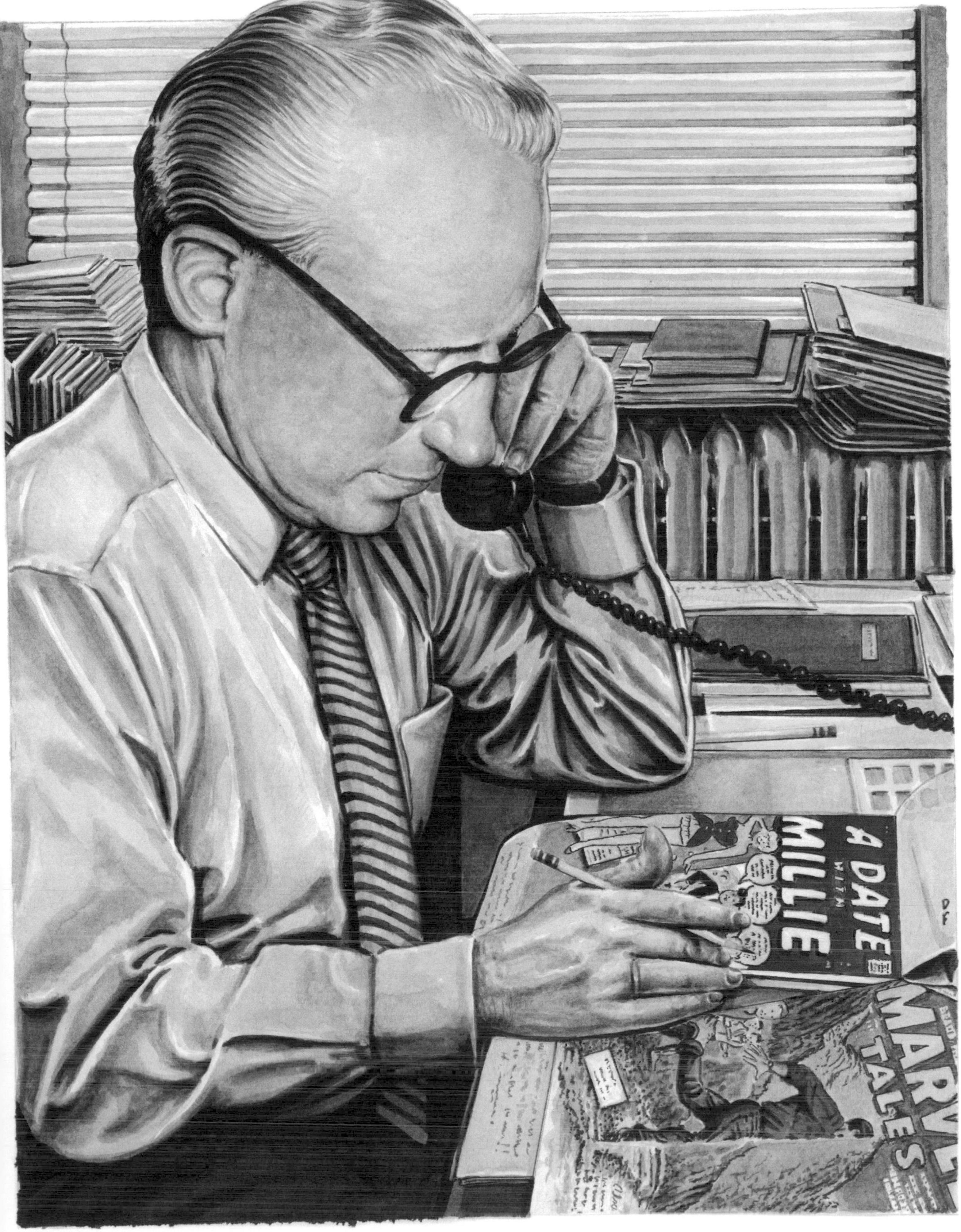
A DATE WITH MILLIE
MARVEL TALES
DF

JOE SIMON

plate
12

Joseph Henry "Joe" Simon, together with his partner of two decades, Jack Kirby, was a major creative force during the Golden Age of comic books. In the 1930s Simon began his career as a newspaper cartoonist and was later hired by Lloyd Jacquet, who ran Funnies Inc., which packaged finished comics to publishers in the late thirties. Funnies Inc.'s first job was packaging *Marvel Comics* #1 for pulp magazine publisher Martin Goodman, who was looking to expand into the comics field after the huge success of National's Superman the year before. *Marvel Comics* was a hit, and Goodman was soon looking for a hero similar to the Human Torch, who had been featured on the first cover. Joe Simon got the assignment and created the Fiery Mask. Simon also met his future partner, artist Jack Kirby, around this time, while both were doing work at Fox Publications.

When Goodman launched Timely Comics, he hired Simon as his first editor. One of Simon's first assignments was to create (with Kirby) a patriotic superhero who would be called Captain America. The first issue of *Captain America Comics*, featuring a cover with the star-spangled character punching Hitler in the jaw, came out in December 1940, an entire year before the United States entered World War II, and was a hit for Timely, selling over a million copies. Simon asked Kirby to join him at Timely as art director, and the team remained with *Captain America* for ten issues, until they were abruptly fired from the company over a disagreement with Goodman about promised percentage of profits. Captain America stayed with Timely (the future Marvel Comics), but his two creators left. Simon and Kirby were instantly snapped up by National and given free reign, proving themselves to be instant hit makers. They revamped National's characters the Boy Commandos and the Sandman, and created Manhunter and the Newsboy Legion. They were the busiest and most successful partnership of the Golden Age of comics.

Simon took time off to serve in World War II, and after his discharge he found superhero comics dwindling in popularity. Simon and Kirby expanded to other genres, including horror, crime, and romance, a genre they pioneered with their title *Young Romance*. Their partnership ended in 1955 as comic book sales slumped and work dried up due to the aftermath of the senate hearings on crime and horror comics. Kirby stuck with comics, while Simon branched out into advertising and commercial art. In 1960 Simon founded and edited the *Mad* magazine imitation *Sick*, which he would stay with for over a decade. In 2003, after Kirby's death, Simon and Marvel reached an agreement that granted him royalties for merchandising and licensing of Captain America and ensured that he and Kirby would forever be recognized as the creators of the character.

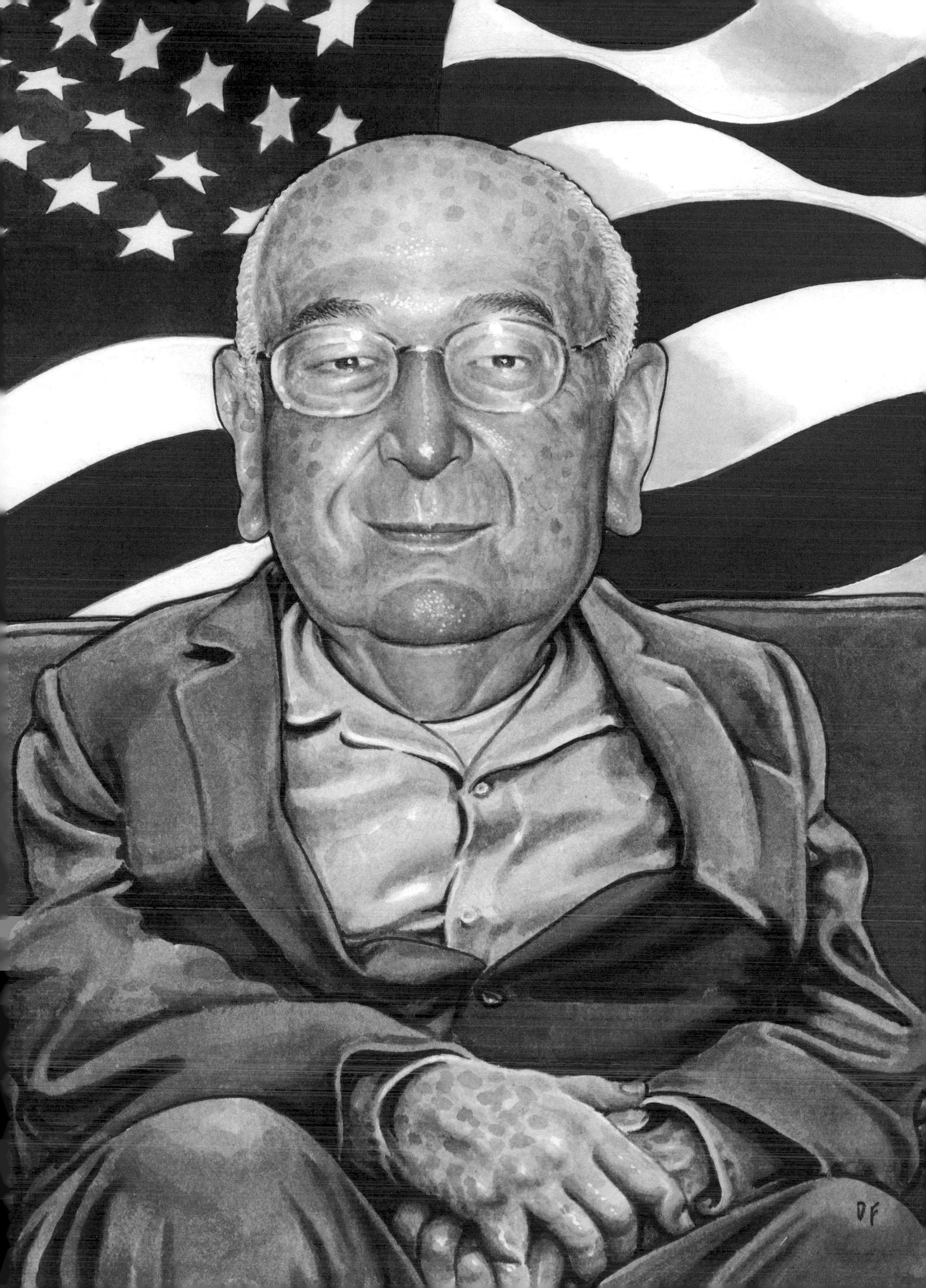
DF

JACK KIRBY

1917–1994

plate
13

Jack Kirby (born Jacob Kurtzberg), a towering figure in comic books, was born on the Lower East Side of New York. Growing up he worshipped the comic strips of Hal Foster, Alex Raymond, and Milton Caniff. Kirby began drawing for newspapers in the midthirties, then worked briefly as an inbetweener at the Fleischer studio before joining the Eisner and Iger comics shop. He moved on to freelance for Fox Feature Syndicate, where he hit it off with editor and artist Joe Simon, with whom he collaborated on *Blue Bolt Comics*. Simon was hired as an editor at Martin Goodman's new company Timely, where he and Kirby created the comics character Captain America. Simon asked Kirby to join him at Timely as art director, but after a dispute with Goodman over profits, Simon and Kirby left the company and were hired by National Comics, where they enjoyed instant success revamping the character Sandman and creating the superhero Manhunter and the kid crime fighting gangs the Boy Commandos and the Newsboy Legion.

Kirby was drafted in 1943 and discharged in 1945, and he returned to work with Simon on multiple genres. Simon and Kirby had their biggest success with *Young Romance*, the prototype romance comic book. By the midfifties, following the senate hearings on juvenile delinquency and the establishment of the self-imposed Comics Code, comic book sales were down to an all-time low and work was drying up. Simon left to work in advertising, while Kirby forged on in comics.

Freelancing for both DC and Atlas (formally Timely), Kirby began to specialize in action-packed stories and covers featuring giant, unearthly monsters created for Atlas's various anthology series including *Tales to Astonish*, *Amazing Adventures*, and *World of Fantasy*. By 1961, taking note that DC was having success with several of its revised superhero titles, Atlas (soon to be Marvel) publisher Martin Goodman gave his editor Stan Lee carte blanche to create a new superhero team title. Lee conceived *The Fantastic Four*, and with Kirby plotting out and drawing the series, it became an instant smash, a landmark title that helped to revolutionize the comics industry and launch the Silver Age of comics. Lee and Kirby repeated the successful formula, cocreating character after character, including The Incredible Hulk, Thor, Iron Man, the X-Men, the Silver Surfer, and Galactus.

Kirby created what was essentially Marvel's house style, designing dynamic visual motifs and creating a template that comics artists have been following ever since. By the late sixties, Kirby, the most important figure in Marvel's success, was making a mere $35,000 a year freelancing for the company. He finally grew dissatisfied and left Marvel in 1970 to work for DC. In 1987, under mounting pressure from comics journalists, creators, and fans, Marvel returned close to two thousand pages of original art to Kirby (it was customary for comics publishers to keep original artwork) out of the estimated ten to thirteen thousand pages he had created for the company over the years, enabling him to sell the pages to collectors and enjoy his final years in a little more comfort.

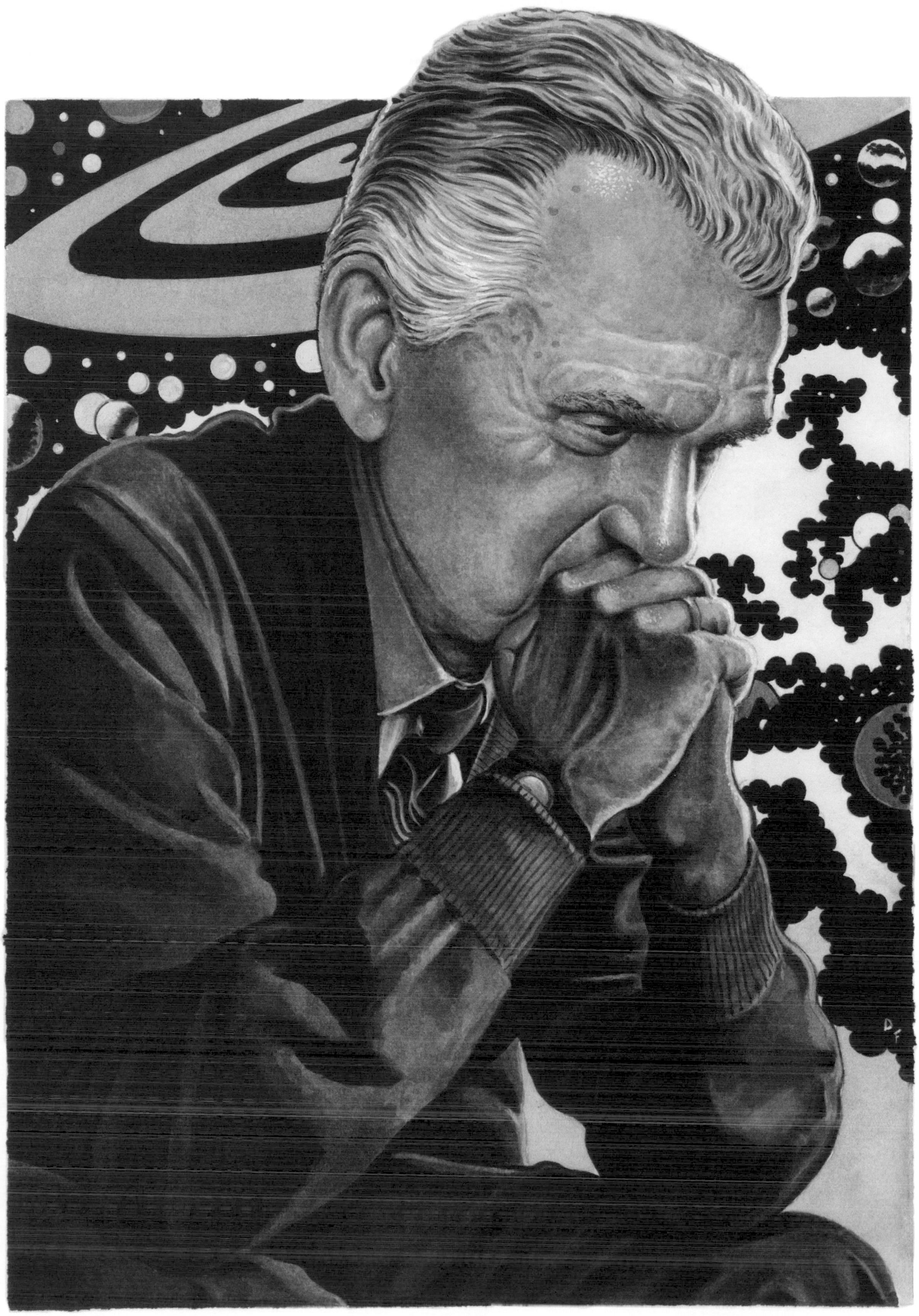

STAN LEE

b. 1922

plate
14

Just as Walt Disney was the face of the Disney company, Stan Lee (born Stanley Martin Lieber) was and still is the face of Marvel Comics. Seventeen-year-old Stanley Lieber was hired as an assistant at Timely Comics in 1939. Timely's publisher Martin Goodman's wife, Jean, was Lieber's cousin. At first Lieber worked odd jobs, but he was soon asked to write filler copy and eventually entire comics stories. Lieber's childhood ambition was to be a serious novelist, so for his comics writing he created the pseudonym "Stan Lee." When Timely editor Joe Simon and his creative partner Jack Kirby, who had recently created the successful Captain America, left the company over a dispute with Goodman in 1941, Lee was hired as interim editor and soon rose to editor in chief, taking over all of Simon's editorial duties. Lee entered the US Army in 1942 and returned to Timely in 1945 to continue working as an editor and writer.

By the early fifties Timely, now called Atlas, had phased out most of its superhero titles in favor of following the popular trends in comics, including romance, westerns, sci-fi, crime, and horror. Lee continued to write and edit for Atlas, but by 1955, following the senate hearings on juvenile delinquency, comic sales plunged, page rates were slashed, and smaller publishers shut down. Martin Goodman's once vast comics department was down to just Stan Lee and his secretary. Lee considered switching careers so he could finally concentrate on his literary ambitions.

In the late fifties, with nothing to lose, National/DC decided to update several of its dormant superheroes (Batman, Superman, and Wonder Woman had never gone away; they had just become bland), among them the Flash. His costume was updated to a bright, snazzy red, and the comic caught fire. Martin Goodman gave the OK to his editor Stan Lee to create a new superhero team for Atlas (soon renamed Marvel). Lee, in collaboration with artist Jack Kirby, conceived *The Fantastic Four*, combining science fiction; fantasy; naturalistic, flawed superheroes; and cheeky, literate dialogue. The title exploded. Using the same template, Lee duplicated the process and, with artists such as Kirby, Bill Everett, and Steve Ditko, unleashed a cavalcade of superhero icons, including the Hulk, Thor, Iron Man, X-Men, Dr. Strange, the Avengers, and Marvel's most successful character, Spider-Man. By the 1970s Lee's involvement with the actual comic books had declined, yet he became a tireless celebrity spokesman for Marvel. He is both worshipped and vilified, having been described as an imperious comics writer and editor, a persistent self-promoter, a credit and publicity hog, and probably the most famous man to have ever worked in comics.

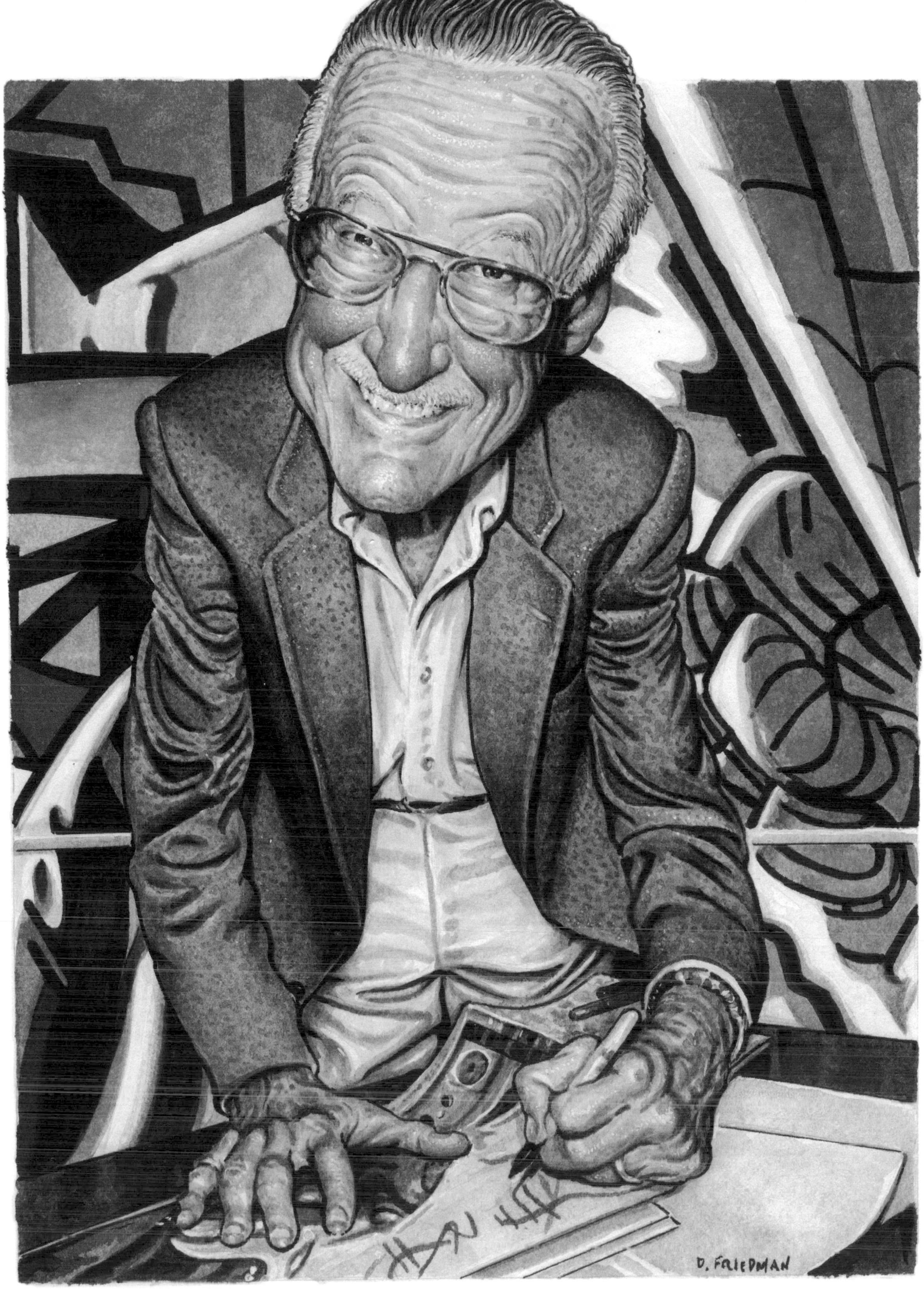
D. FRIEDMAN

BILL EVERETT

1917–1973

plate
15

Bill Everett was a renowned viruoso of the comic book medium. He did his first comics work in the late thirties for Centaur and soon followed its art director to his new comics packaging shop Funnies Inc., which created complete comics on demand for publishers. Funnies Inc.'s first client was pulp publisher Martin Goodman, who, seeking to duplicate National Periodical Publications' huge success with its new character Superman, wanted to get into the burgeoning superhero comic book market. The first comic Funnies created for Goodman's newly titled company Timely was *Marvel Comics* #1 (October 1939), featuring Carl Burgos's new character the Human Torch and Bill Everett's eight-page debut of his aquatic antihero, half man, half sea creature Prince Namor, the Sub-Mariner. The issue proved to be a knockout, and the Sub-Mariner and Human Torch joined Simon and Kirby's Captain America as Timely's three peaks of superherodom, leading to the Golden Age of comics.

Soon the Sub-Mariner was starring in his own series created by Everett. The character began to focus his anger more toward the Nazis, rather than the entire human race. Everett entered the war in 1942 and returned four years later, picking up where he had left off on the *Sub-Mariner* comic. But postwar, as Timely evolved into Atlas, the once popular superheroes, including the Sub-Mariner, found themselves with less tangible villains to battle than Nazis and faded in popularity. Everett continued freelancing in comics, proving himself adept at every popular genre, including western, funny animal, romance, crime, and particularly horror. He became one of the preeminent horror comics artists of the fifties, until the strict new Comics Code enforced their end. The versatile Everett was also adept at humor, creating the first cover for *Cracked* magazine in 1957, which also featured work by other veteran comics artists seeking employment, among them John Severin and Carl Burgos. Everett continued doing work for Marvel Comics as the Silver Age emerged, cocreating Daredevil in 1964, and drew new adventures of his own revived, more humanized Sub-Mariner. Everett, a lifelong chain smoker who also struggled with alcoholism, died in 1973 at age fifty-four.

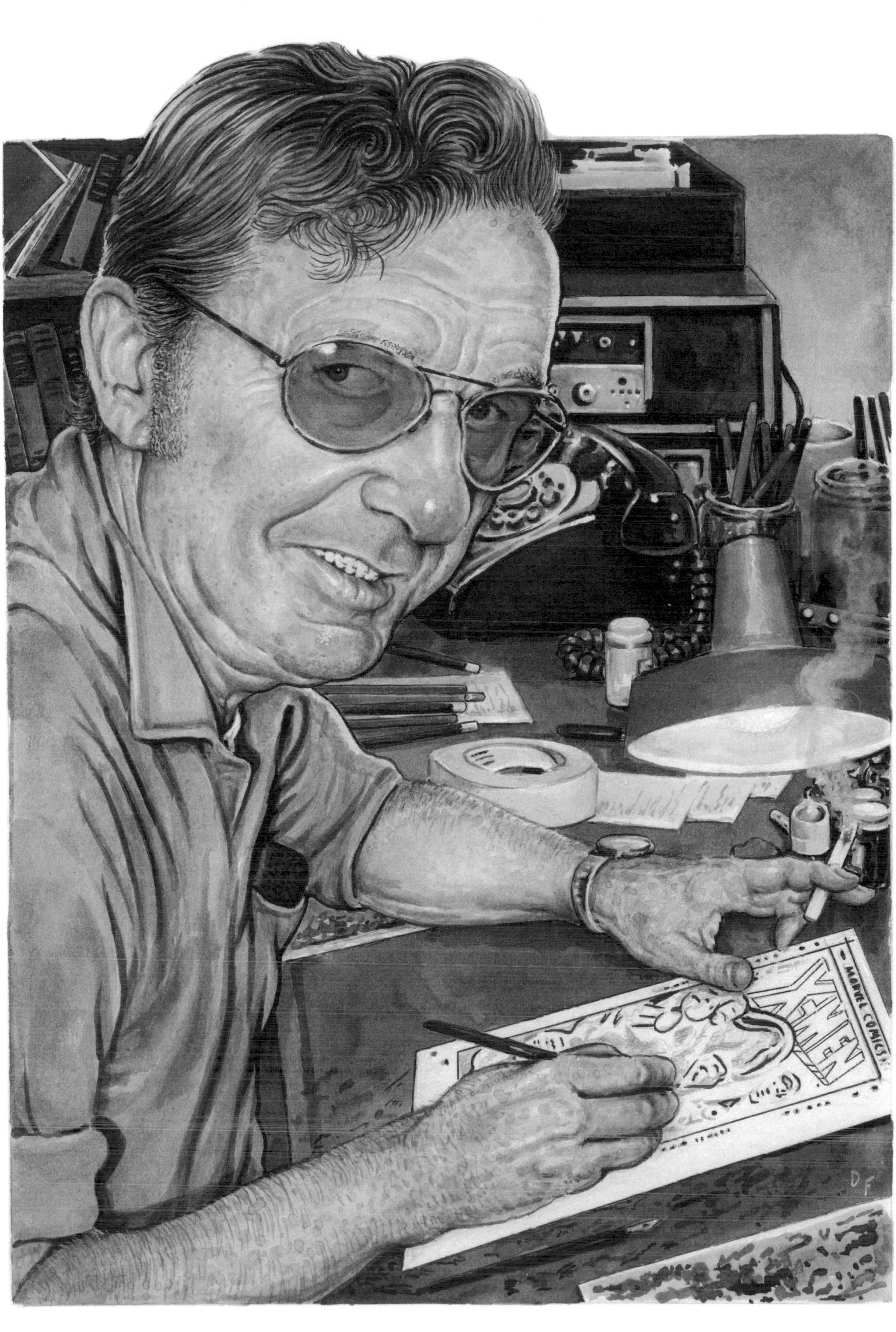
MARVEL COMICS
X-MEN
DF

CARL BURGOS

1916–1984

plate
16

In 1938 Carl Burgos (born Max Finkelstein) began working at the Harry "A" Chesler comics packaging shop as an apprentice, drawing backgrounds and panel borders, and inking other artists' pencils. Burgos drew his first solo story the following year, an eight-page pirate comic for *Star Comics* published by Centaur Publications. The art director at Centaur asked Burgos to join him at his new comics packaging shop, Funnies Inc. Funnies' first sale was to publisher Martin Goodman at Timely Comics, supplying the contents of *Marvel Comics* #1 (October 1939). Burgos created and drew the character the Human Torch for the issue (the cover featuring the Torch was painted by pulp artist Frank R. Paul), and Bill Everett's new character the Sub-Mariner also made his debut in the issue. *Marvel Comics* was an instant hit, and the Human Torch was soon given his own solo title, which debuted in 1940, with Burgos handling the scripting and drawing.

Burgos left to serve in the US Air Force in 1942 and returned in 1946, when superhero comics were on the decline, so he enrolled at the City College of New York to study advertising. But he eventually returned to drawing comics for Timely and was later hired to be on staff at Atlas (formally Timely), where editor Stan Lee kept him busy with cover and interior assignments, primarily for horror and humor titles, and with a brief attempt to reactivate several dormant superhero characters, among them Burgos's own creation the Human Torch. Burgos also drew for early issues of the *Mad* imitation magazine *Cracked*. In the early sixties Atlas, now Marvel, ushered in the Silver Age with its hit comic *The Fantastic Four*, created by Stan Lee and Jack Kirby with art by Kirby. Carl Burgos was distressed to see that although the Human Torch was now one-forth of the hugely successful new title, he received no credit. He eventually launched a lawsuit that proved unsuccessful. Burgos was bitter and heartbroken that the character he created had been revived without his participation and that he didn't receive any financial compensation, but he continued to do occasional work for Marvel into the midsixties. He was also hired to edit and draw covers and interior art for publisher Myron Fass's notorious and delightfully depraved Eerie Publications, including *Weird*, *Tales of Voodoo*, and *Tales from the Tomb*.

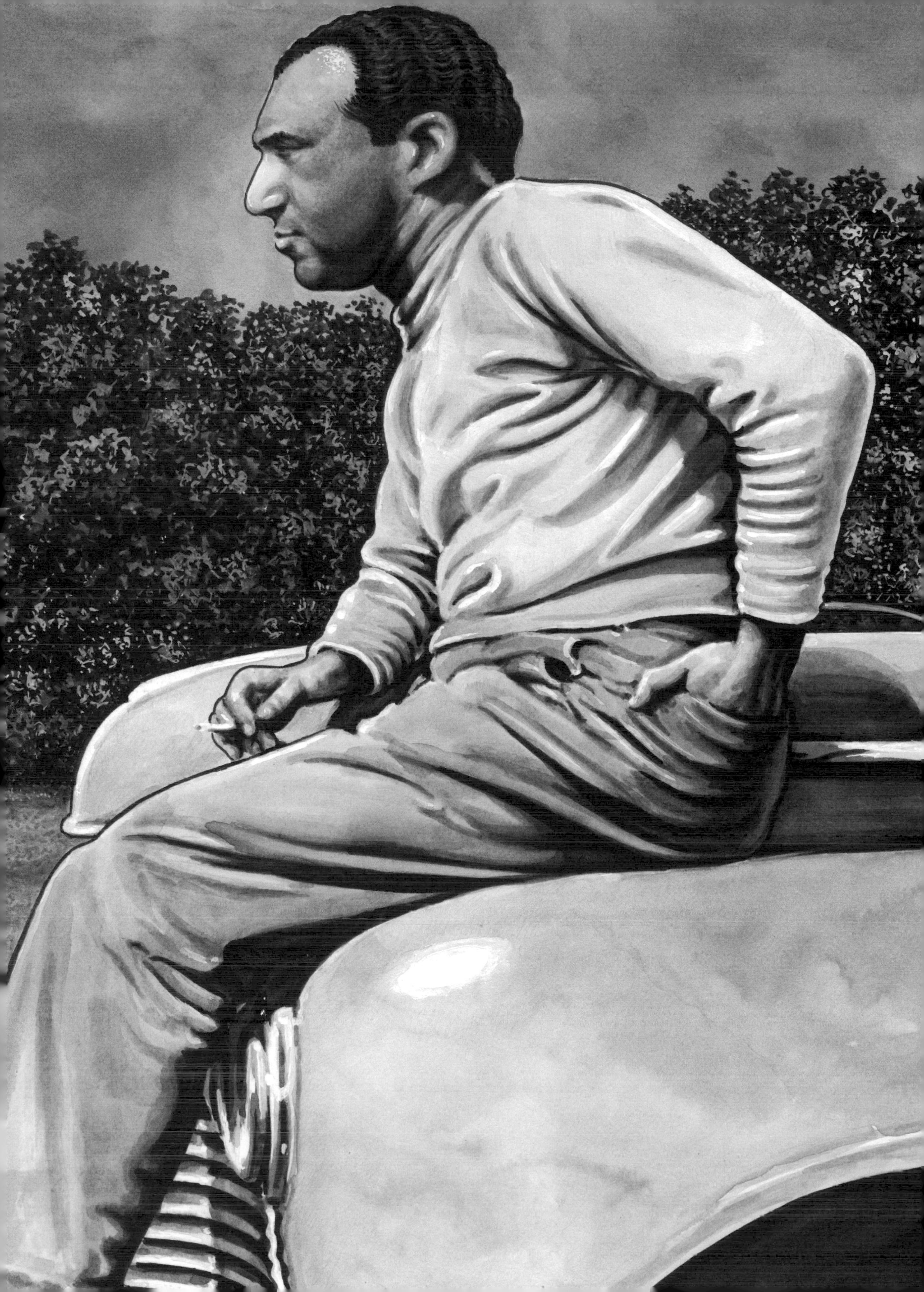

JERRY ROBINSON

1922–2011

plate
17

In 1939 Sherrill David "Jerry" Robinson, a seventeen-year-old journalism student and cartoonist, met comics professional Bob Kane on a tennis court at a Poconos summer camp. Kane invited him to work as a penciler and inker for his brand new character Batman (cocreated with Bill Finger), who had recently made his debut in *Detective Comics* #27. Robinson joined the original Batman team as the primary inker, and was soon hired to work directly in the bullpen at National Comics, Batman's publisher. Batman was a huge sensation, and Robinson and writer Bill Finger conceived a sidekick for Batman, whom Robinson is credited with naming "Robin" based on his love of the Robin Hood books of his youth. In 1940 the first issue of Batman's solo comic was published, introducing his nemesis the Joker. Only Bob Kane was given credit for *Batman*, but over the years there has been controversy over who actually conceived what. Robinson claimed he created the Joker, basing the villain with the painted evil clown face on a joker playing card, but Bob Kane credits Bill Finger with showing him a still photo of German actor Conrad Veidt from the 1928 film *The Man Who Laughs*, inspiring the iconic villain. Success has many fathers and failure is an orphan, so the true version will continue to be debated among comics fans and historians. What is clear is that Jerry Robinson and Bill Finger conceived, wrote, and drew the majority of the early Batman adventures and were the true architects of the series, yet Bob Kane received sole credit.

Robinson broke away from the *Batman* team and, along with his friend and fellow comics artist Mort Meskin, formed a studio that produced material for the short-lived Spark Publications. Robinson also created his own superheroes, including London and Atoman. After leaving superhero comics, he became a newspaper cartoonist, creating the adventure strip *Jet Scott* for the *New York Herald Tribune* and later the political satire feature *Still Life*, which featured inanimate objects in conversation. He also wrote and drew the syndicated strip *Flubs & Fluffs*, which ran in the *New York Sunday News* for years. Jerry Robinson taught comics for many years at New York's School of Visual Arts, was a prolific comics historian, and became a leading champion of artists' rights.

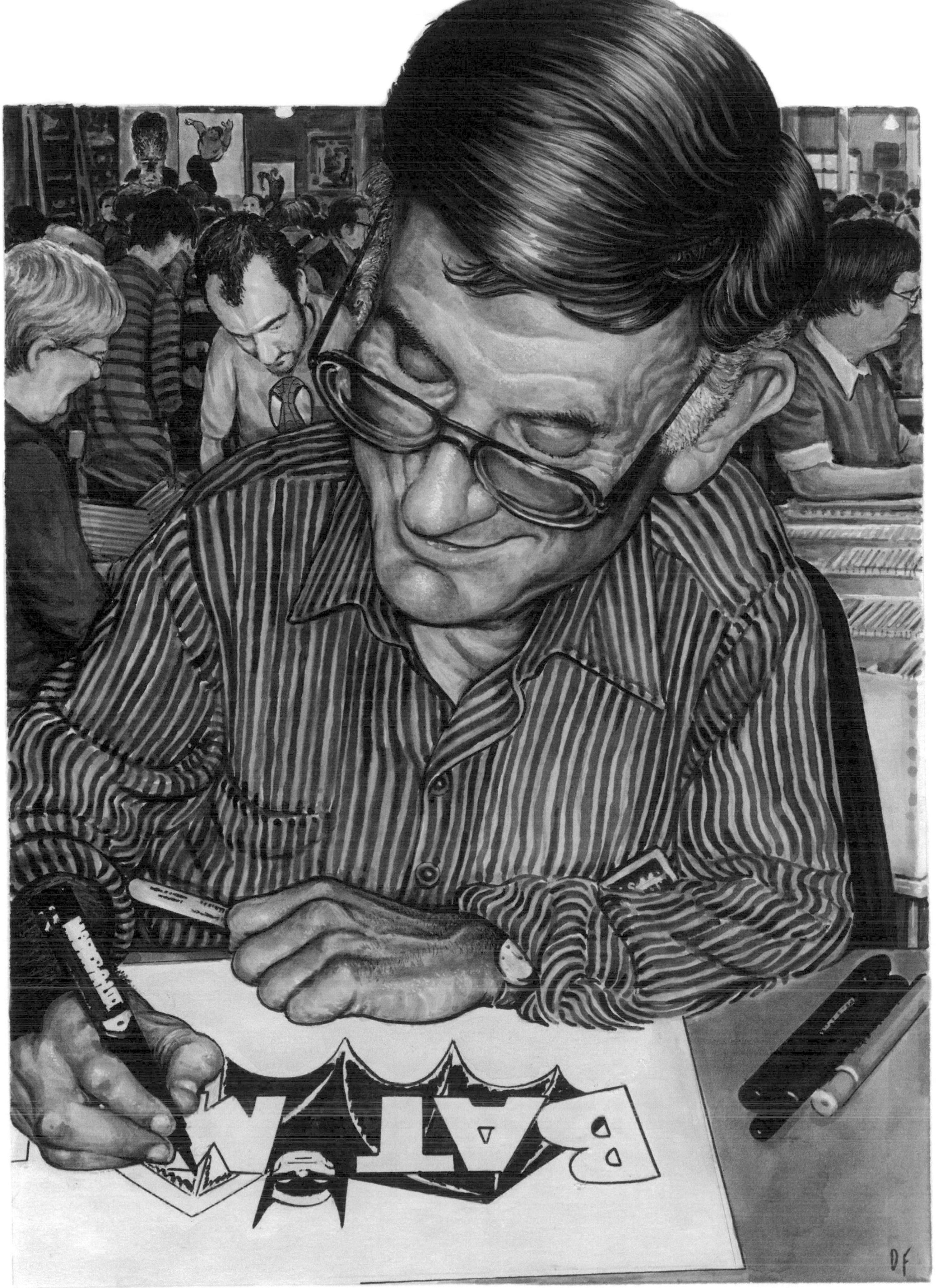
BAT

GEORGE ROUSSOS

1915–2000

plate
18

George Roussos earned the nickname "Inky" because he was so skilled with a brush, using heavy, thick black brushstrokes that gave his figures uncommon weight. Roussos's first work in comics came when Batman creators Bob Kane and Bill Finger hired him to assist artist Jerry Robinson on the second issue of *Batman* by drawing backgrounds, lettering, and inking. Roussos and Robinson eventually left the Kane studio to work directly for National (DC) on *Batman*, *Superman*, *Starman*, and other new Golden Age superhero titles. Roussos branched out and did inking, penciling, and coloring work for Timely, Avon, Lev Gleason Publications, and EC. Roussos also worked on various syndicated comic strips, including assisting Dan Barry on *Flash Gordon*. Roussos didn't receive an actual comic book credit until the early 1960s, when, working under the pseudonym George Bell, he became Jack Kirby's inker on early issues of *The Fantastic Four*. He also worked on other hugely popular Marvel Silver Age titles, including *The Incredible Hulk*, *The Avengers*, and the newly revitalized *Captain America*, and finally became known to comics fans. He later became Marvel's full-time staff colorist and finally its production chief.

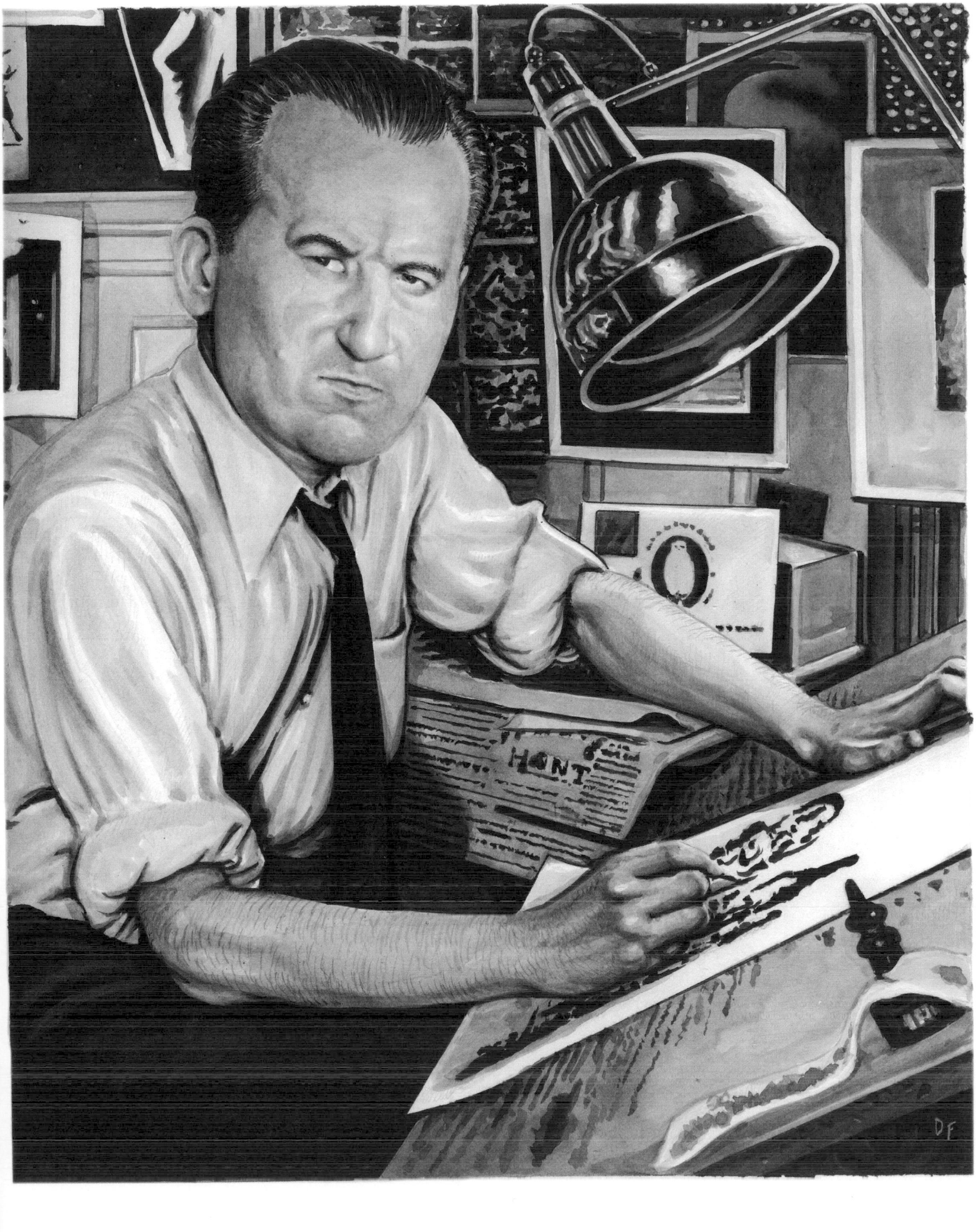
DF

JOHN GOLDWATER

1916–1999

plate
19

In 1939 John L. Goldwater, along with Louis Silberkleit and Maurice Coyne, founded MLJ Comics (named after the first initial of each partner), following the great success of National's *Superman* and *Batman*. MLJ's first offering was *Blue Ribbon Comics*, followed by other underwhelming superhero titles, including *Pep Comics*. In 1941 the crosshatch-haired teenage redhead Archie Andrews made his debut in the back of *Pep*, conceived by Goldwater (who based the typical teenage boy on the then popular Andy Hardy films and Henry Aldrich films and radio show) and written and drawn by Bob Montana. Archie quickly caught on and became so popular that MLJ scrapped all its superhero titles in place of nothing but Archie and his pals and changed the name of the company to Archie Comics. Archie Comics became a publishing empire, expanding to newspaper strips, radio, and television, including a #1 bubblegum pop song, "Sugar Sugar."

In 1954, in response to Dr. Fredric Wertham's book *Seduction of the Innocent* and the public outcry and senate hearings that followed, Goldwater helped found the Comics Magazine Association of America, which introduced the strict Comics Code Authority. The Comics Code weeded out all of what they deemed offensive material from comic books and helped to drive EC Comics, among others, out of business. Goldwater served as president of the Comics Magazine Association for twenty-five years.

In 1973 Goldwater licensed out Archie's characters to his former Archie artist Al Hartley for evangelical Christian comics publications. Although Jewish, Goldwater said the sentiments were in line with his wholesome family message. He retired as the head of Archie Comics in 1993.

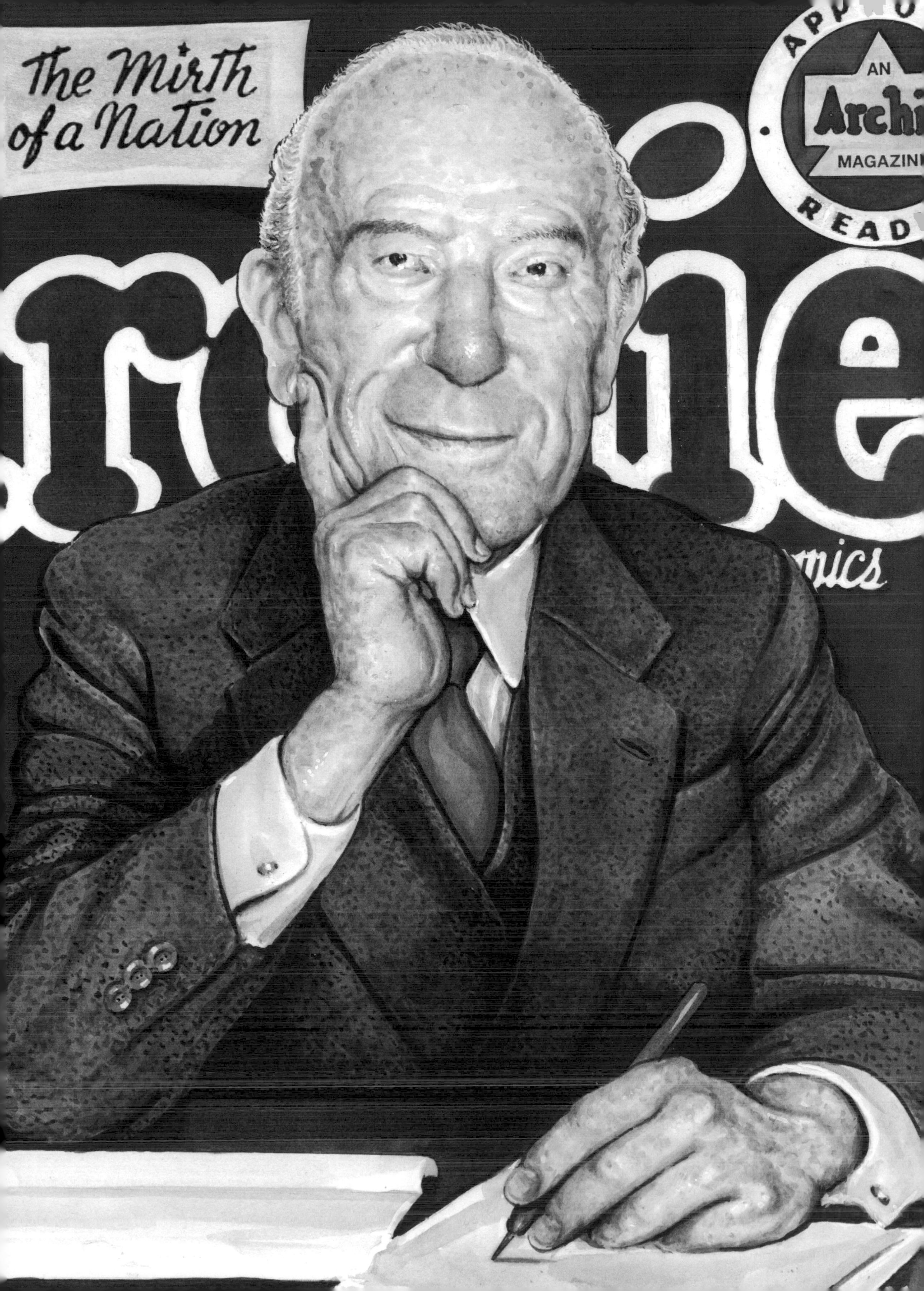
The Mirth of a Nation
AN

BOB MONTANA

1920–1975

plate
20

Robert William "Bob" Montana created and drew the still-enduring characters for *Archie* comics, basing the characters on classmates and teachers from his own high school experiences in Massachusetts. In 1941 John Goldwater, publisher of the MLJ comic book line, conceived *Archie* to cash in on the success of Andy Hardy and Henry Aldrich, the then popular teenage everyman character appearing on radio and in movies. Montana had been drawing superhero comics for MLJ when he was asked to develop the characters for *Archie*, which first appeared in the back of *Pep Comics*. The *Archie* characters would prove to be so popular that eventually all of MLJ's comics were dedicated to Archie and his friends, and the company changed its name to Archie Comic Publications. Montana was a talented artist who had an animated flair for humor, creating an exaggerated, sexy, and in some cases grotesque (Mrs. Grundy) world inhabited by the peppy, freckled, red-headed Archie Andrews and his cohorts and rivals. Eventually the entire Archie format was streamlined and its artists (including Abe Vigoda's brother Bill Vigoda), were instructed to follow a more watered-down Archie comics template. Bob Montana drew and wrote the original *Archie* comic book for only one year before he joined the Army Signal Corps. Returning to civilian life, he took over the *Archie* newspaper daily and Sunday comic strip, which he drew for the next thirty-five years, never working on comic books again.

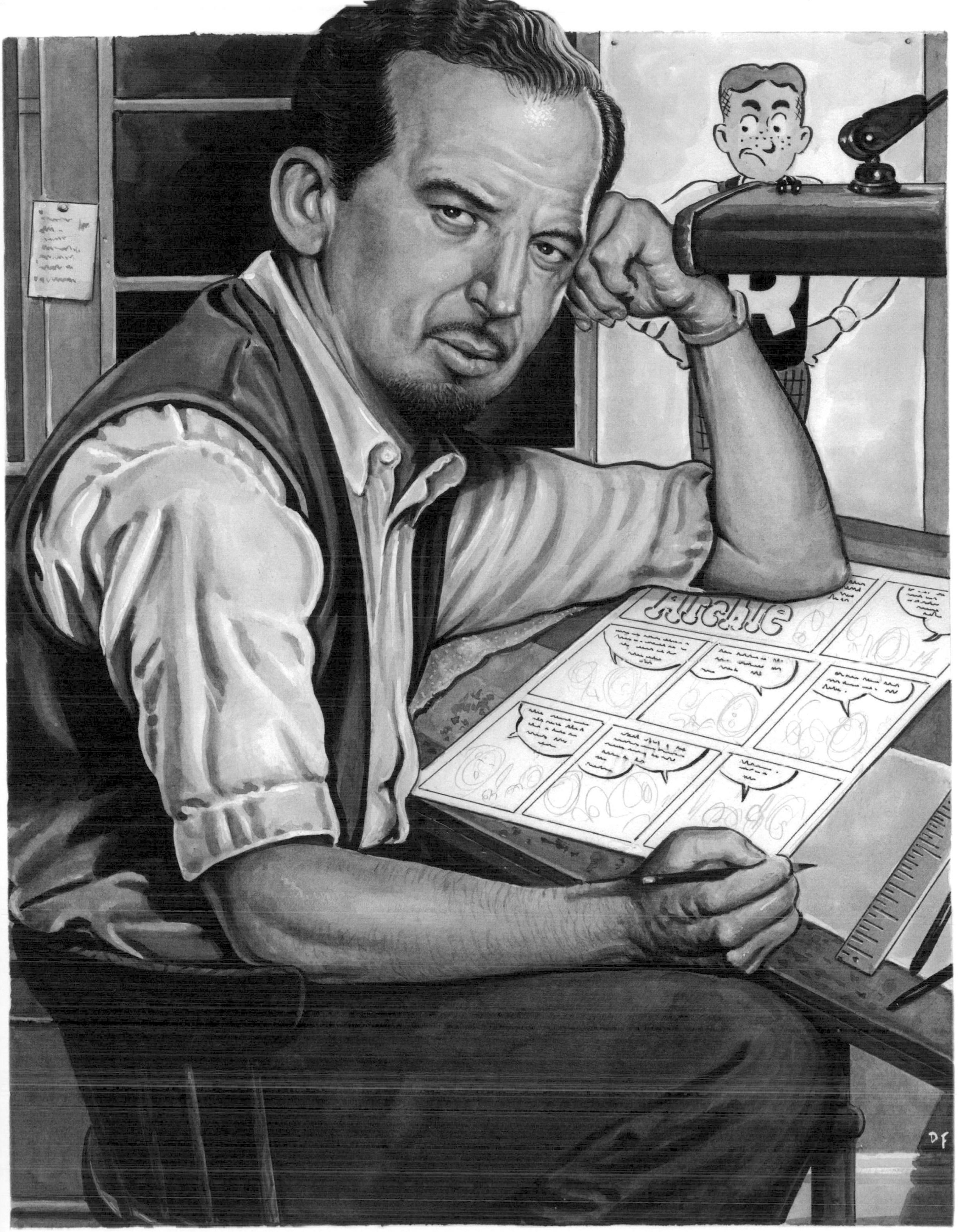
Archie
DF

LEV GLEASON

1898–1971

plate **21**

Leverett Stone "Lev" Gleason, a Harvard dropout, started working at *Open Road for Boys* magazine as an artist, and by the early 1930s he became advertising director. He then took a position as advertising manager for Eastern Color Printing, an early pioneering comic book company that launched in 1933. Next Gleason became an editor at United Feature and introduced *Tip Top Comics*. In the early 1940s, while working as the treasurer for New Friday Inc., he purchased its series *Boy*, *Daredevil*, and *Silver Streak*, and then he created his own company, Comic House, a.k.a. Lev Gleason Publications. An early Gleason comic book, *Daredevil Battles Hitler* (July 1941), was an overt political message calling for US intervention in Europe.

Under the guidance of his newly hired employee, the talented artist, writer, and editor Charles Biro, who was tired of working on superhero titles and envisioned creating comics aimed at a more intelligent audience, *Silver Streak* was transformed into *Crime Does Not Pay*. *Crime Does Not Pay* was the first and most successful crime comic, populated with hard-edge, sometimes lurid real-life situations based on actual stories of convicted criminals, told in a bold, rapid documentary style that had not been seen in the superhero and funny animal comic books that came before. *Crime Does Not Pay* was a comic book for grown-ups, although children happily bought it up too, and it spawned dozens of imitators, including EC's two crime comics, *Crime SupenStories* and *Shock SupenStories*. When a postwar spike in juvenile delinquency was reported, crime (and horror) comics became the convenient target, and Gleason, as president of the Association of Comics Magazine Publishers (which would later evolve into the industry's self-censorship Comics Code), came to his industry's defense, asserting that "Comics can actually help mold young readers into happier, more intelligent adults." But the die was cast, and psychiatrist Dr. Fredric Wertham's 1954 best seller *Seduction of the Innocent*, which blamed juvenile delinquency on crime and horror comics, was the final nail in the coffin. *Crime Does Not Pay* was doomed, and like EC, Lev Gleason Publications went out of business.

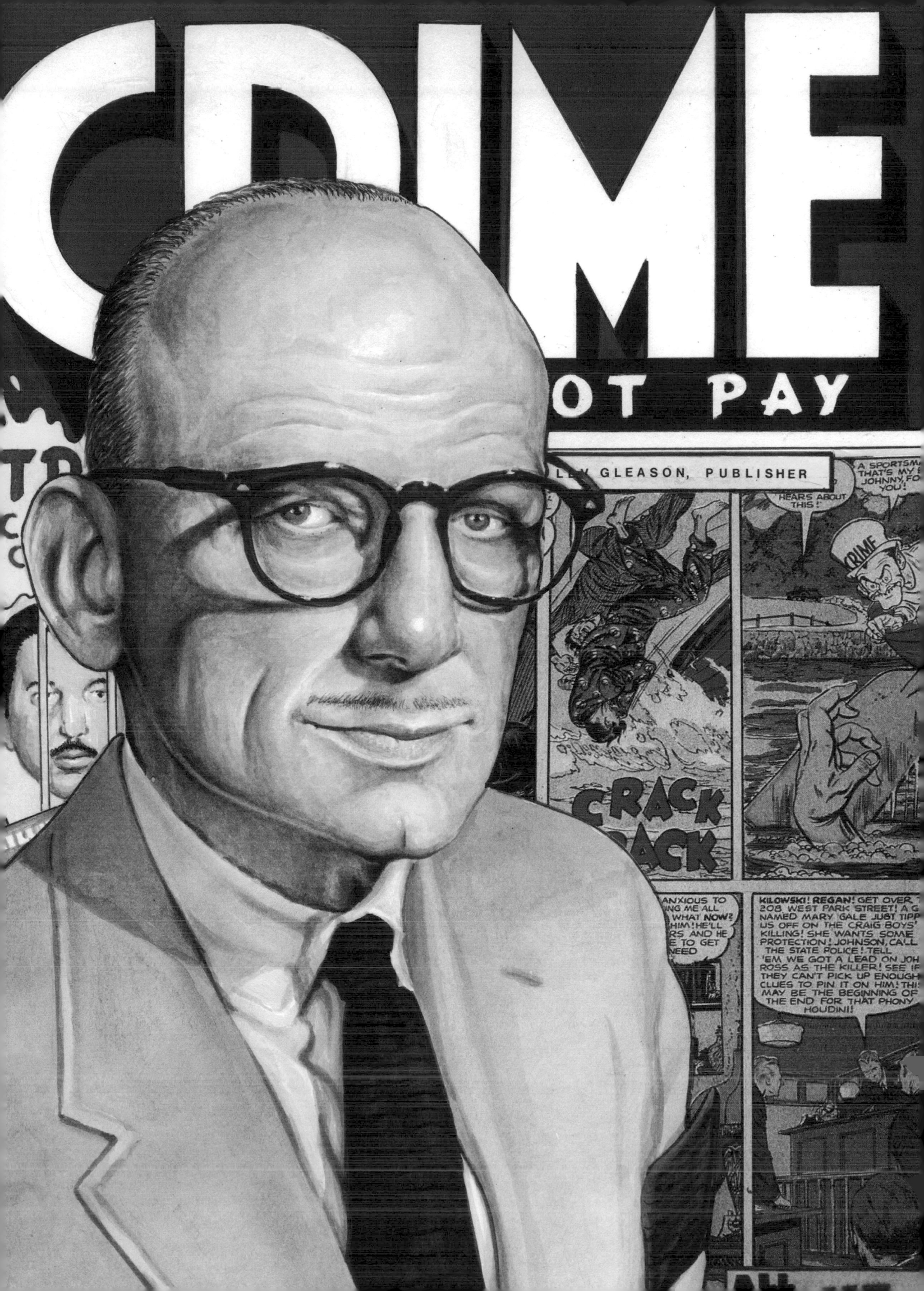

GLEASON, PUBLISHER
HEARS ABOUT THIS!
CRIME
CRACK
KILOWSKI! REGAN! GET OVER
208 WEST PARK STREET! A
NAMED MARY GALE JUST
US OFF ON THE CRAIG BOYS'
KILLING! SHE WANTS SOME
PROTECTION! JOHNSON, CALL
THE STATE POLICE! TELL
'EM WE GOT A LEAD ON
ROSS AS THE KILLER! SEE IF
THEY CAN'T PICK UP
CLUES TO PIN IT ON HIM!
MAY BE THE BEGINNING OF
THE END FOR THAT PHONY
HOUDINI!

CHARLES BIRO

1911–1972

plate
22

A tall, ruddy, and jovial man, Charles Biro was a "larger than life" character. He joined the Harry "A" Chesler comics packaging shop in 1936 as a writer and artist, and soon moved up to supervisor. In 1939 he joined MLJ Publications, taking on a similar role before being hired by Lev Gleason Publications in 1941 as editorial director, cover artist, and writer, primarily for *Boy Comics*, *Daredevil*, and *Silver Streak*, which in 1942 he evolved into *Crime Does Not Pay* (basing the title on a series of popular MGM shorts of the 1930s). Biro, an idealist and a visionary, was tired of the superhero comics he had been mired in and imagined more realistic comic books aimed at a more adult audience. He and coeditor Bob Wood (also a Chesler shop alum) wanted to portray criminals and gangsters in real-life situations, rather than the expected adolescent fantasies of most current comics. *Crime Does Not Pay* was the first comic book crime title, putting the genre on the map and spawning dozens of imitators, yet it remained the best-written, best-drawn (particularly those issues by artist Dan Barry, though Biro also drew fifty-seven covers for the series), and best-edited crime title, thanks to the obsessive perfectionist Charles Biro. Biro researched his shocking and sometimes lurid stories firsthand and based his scripts on fact, telling them in a brisk, hard-edge documentary style new to comics, narrated by the moralizing Mr. Crime (whom the three EC GhouLunatics were later based on).

Crime Does Not Pay (as well as the other Gleason titles edited by Biro) became one of the most popular and best-selling titles of the forties and early fifties, until horror and crime titles came to a crashing end thanks to the comic book witch hunts and the formation of the strict Comics Code. *Crime Does Not Pay*, the least excessive and gory of all the other crime comics it spawned, finally folded in 1955, and Biro left Lev Gleason Publications the following year to work in television graphics. Reflecting on Biro's *Crime Does Not Pay*, Harvey Kurtzman said, "I remember how Biro's stories affected me. I felt the same excitement about them that I felt about underground comic books of twenty years later."

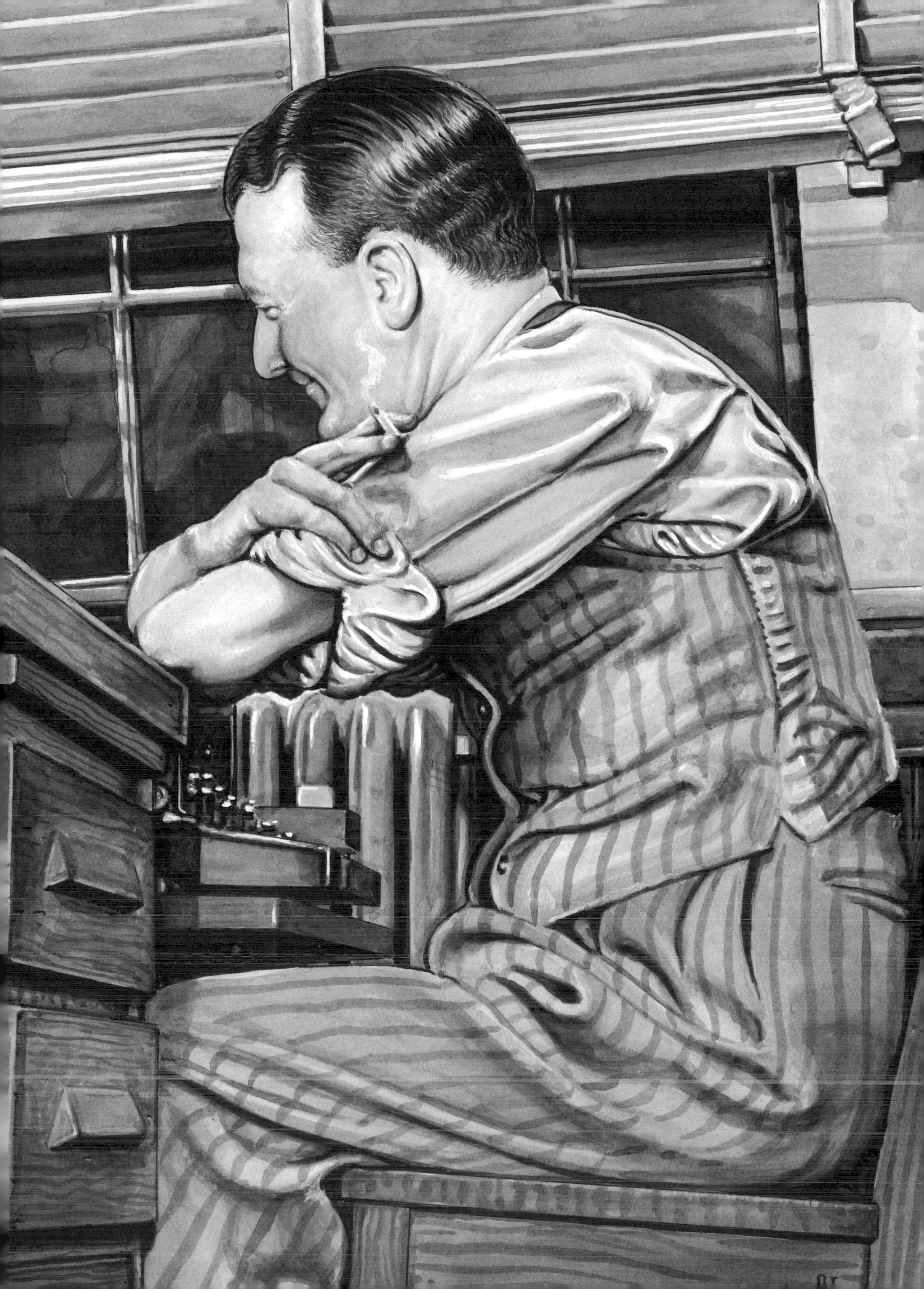

C. C. BECK

1910–1989

plate
23

Charles Clarence "C. C." Beck joined Fawcett Publications as a staff artist in 1933, turning out illustrations for various pulp magazines. In 1939, after National Periodical Publications' debut of Superman became an instant hit, Fawcett got into the comic book game and asked Beck to draw a character called Captain Thunder, soon renamed Captain Marvel, who debuted in *Whiz Comics* #1 (1939). Beck's rendering of Billy Batson, a.k.a. Captain Marvel, was slightly more cartoony than realistic, unlike other emerging superheroes. Beck based the character's face on the likable Hollywood actor Fred MacMurray. The scripts by former pulp writer Otto Binder were whimsical and distinctive, introducing the words *Shazam!* and *Zap!* into the vernacular, and Beck's style was clean, humorous, and simple, turning Captain Marvel into a huge hit. Fawcett produced several spin-offs of the popular series, and Beck opened his own comics studio in New Jersey to oversee and supply most of the artwork for the Marvel Family line of comic books (the exception being Captain Marvel Jr., whom Mac Raboy drew in his more realistic manner).

After years of litigation due to a suit lodged by DC against Fawcett for copyright infringement, claiming that Captain Marvel was a copy of Superman, Fawcett reached a settlement with DC in the early fifties in which it agreed to discontinue the Marvel Family comics (sales were lagging anyway). Beck left the comics industry to focus on commercial illustration and opened the Ukelele Bar & Grill in Florida, where he tended bar. He eventually returned to comics, and in 1973 he drew the first ten issues of (ironically) DC's revival of Captain Marvel. After his retirement, Beck was a popular and lively guest at comic book conventions and wrote the "Crusty Curmudgeon" column for the *Comics Journal*.

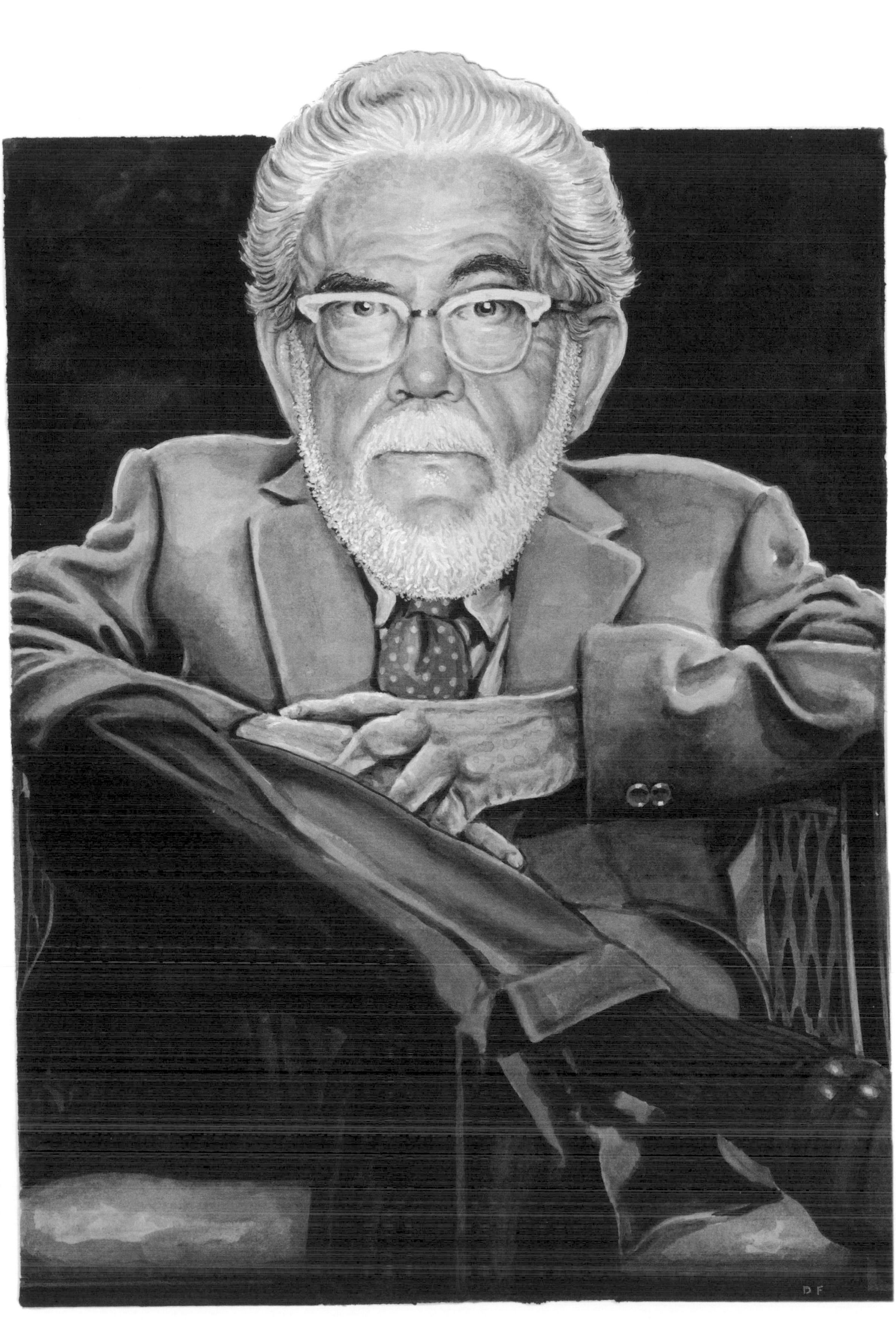
DF

WILLIAM MOULTON MARSTON

1893–1947

plate
24

Dr. William Moulton Marston's relatively short life was filled with compelling, at first seemingly unrelated accomplishments. He attended Harvard, received a PhD in psychology, and became a teacher. In 1929 he briefly served as the director of public services for Universal Studios in Hollywood. Marston was also a lawyer and inventor, and is credited as the creator of the systolic blood pressure test, which helped lead to the invention of the modern polygraph machine. He also authored several self-help books and was a champion of women's causes, writing that he was convinced that women were "more honest and reliable then men, and could work faster and more accurately." Marston also recognized and wrote about the "great educational potential" of the new medium of comic books, and in the early forties he was hired by publisher Max Gaines (who later founded Educational Comics) to be an "educational consultant" for National Periodical Publications and All-American Publications, which merged into DC Comics soon thereafter.

Marston's wife, Elizabeth, gave him an idea to create a female superhero in the then male-dominated world of comics, and he pitched the idea to Gaines, who gave it the go-ahead. Marston developed the character Suprema, soon renamed Wonder Woman, basing her to an extent on his wife and on his polyamorous partner Olive Bryne, a former student of his who lived with the couple in an open marriage. The warrior princess Wonder Woman was created to be a liberated, powerful superwoman. She made her debut in *All Star Comics*, and the next year she starred in her own title, *Wonder Woman*. Marston wrote the early adventures of Wonder Woman, and the art was drawn by former newspaper artist Harry (H. G.) Peter. Wonder Woman was a hit, with her crime-fighting superhuman strength, her ability to force villains to confess the truth by binding them with her magic lasso, her indestructible silver bracelets used to deflect bullets, and her tiara serving as a projectile. She became one of the most iconic, enduring, and sexiest characters ever created for comic books and is considered by many to be a feminist icon.

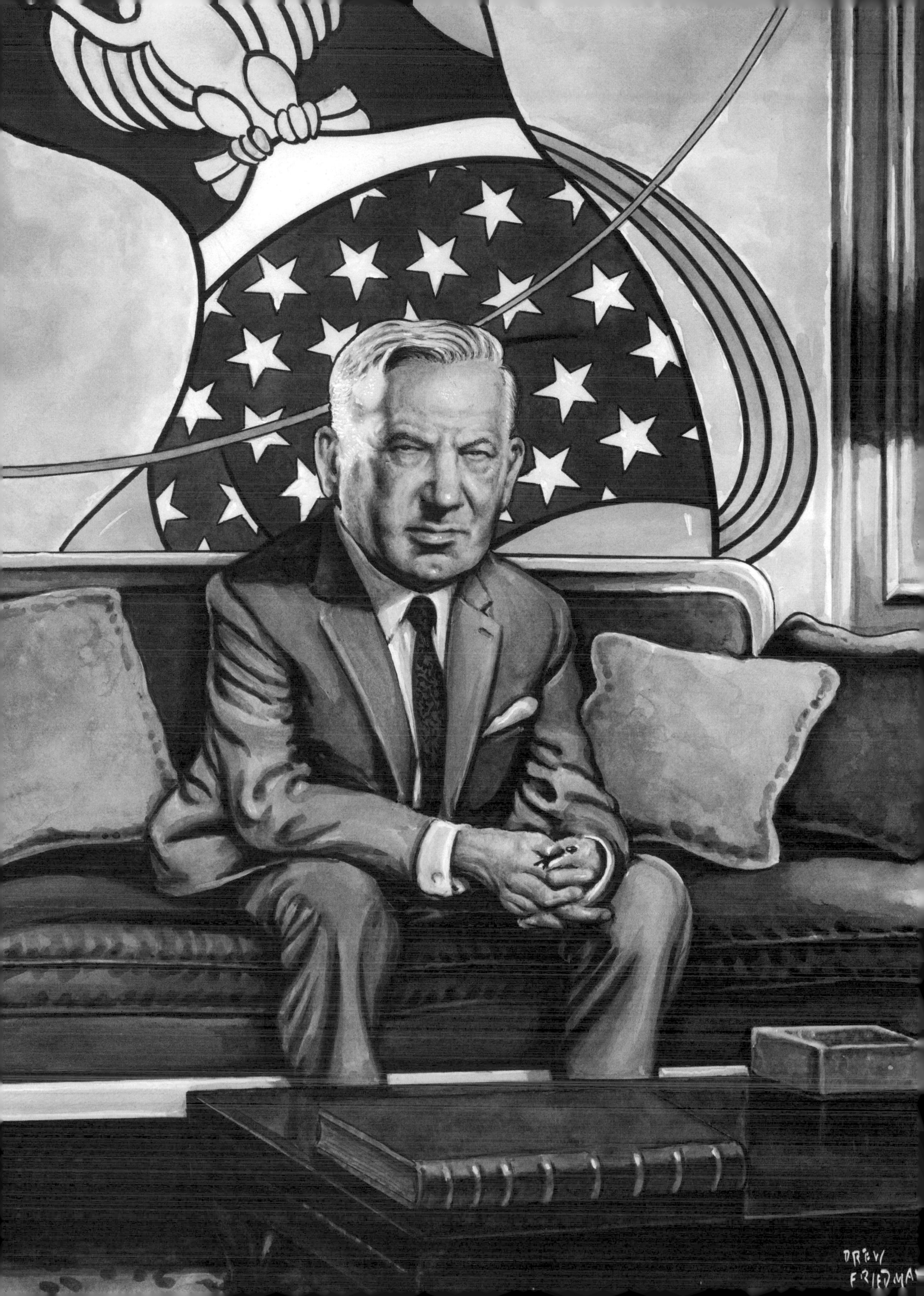
DREW
FRIEDMA

IRWIN HASEN

b. 1918

plate **25**

Irwin Hasen, who was enamored with the work of Alex Raymond and Milton Caniff, studied at the Art Students League of New York before entering the world of comics just as its Golden Age was in full swing. Like so many of his fellow young artists, he first found employment working on the assembly line at the Harry "A" Chesler shop, turning out pages for the burgeoning superhero market, including art for *The Green Hornet*, *The Fox*, and *Cat-Man*. In 1941 Hasen contributed to the first issue of *Green Lantern*, and soon he was creating the title's covers. In 1942 he and writer Bill Finger (the cocreator of Batman) created "Wildcat," the final story included in the first issue of *Sensation Comics*, which featured the debut of Wonder Woman on its cover. During World War II, Hasen worked for the *Fort Dix Post* newspaper as editor, publisher, and art director, and dreamed of someday creating his own syndicated newspaper comic strip. After his discharge, Hasen was hired to draw the syndicated comic strip based on the popular radio show *The Goldbergs* featuring Gertrude Berg. The strip only lasted for a year, and he then returned to work mainly for DC on titles like *Johnny Thunder* and *The Flash*. In 1954, along with writer Gus Edson, whom he had met while on tour in Korea, Hasen created the adorable button-eyed jug-eared war orphan Dondi. The comic strip *Dondi* appeared in over one hundred newspapers and kept Hasen busy for the next three decades.

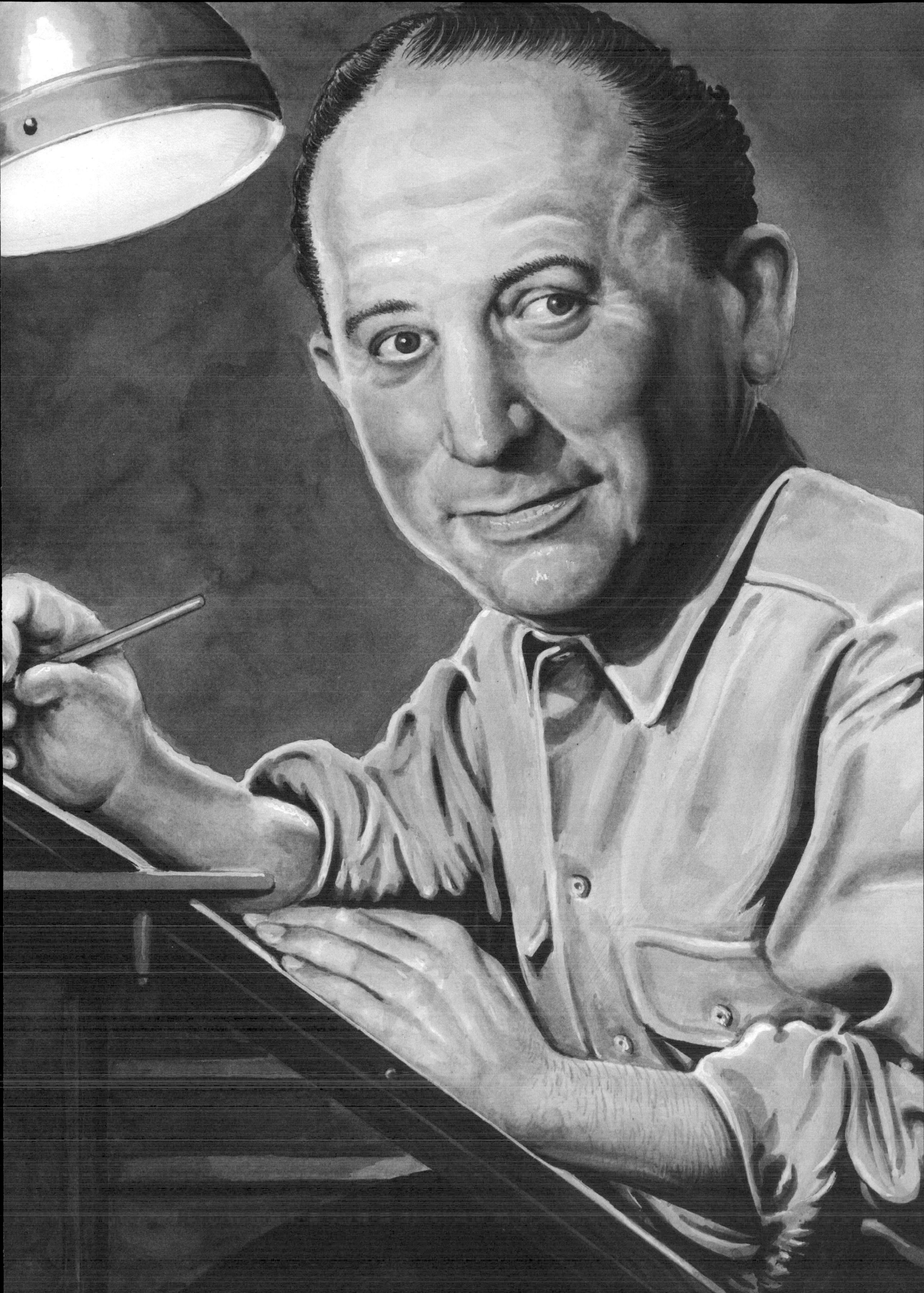

MORT MESKIN

1916–1995

plate
26

Morton "Mort" Meskin began his career in comics like so many other young and motivated artists, working at the new comic book assembly-line sweatshops in the late 1930s. Meskin first worked at the Eisner and Iger shop, penciling *Sheena, Queen of the Jungle* for Fiction House's *Jumbo Comics*, then at the Harry "A" Chesler shop, creating art for the MLJ line of comics. In 1941 he moved on to National Periodical Publications (DC) and drew stories for titles featuring their new superheroes Vigilante (featured in *Action Comics*), Wildcat, and Starman. That same year Meskin saw the new film directed by Orson Welles, *Citizen Kane*, and he was mesmerized. He went back to watch it thirteen times during its initial run, fully absorbing Welles's brilliant visual storytelling and groundbreaking noirish use of shadow and light, which had a profound effect on his comics work. Soon the low-key Meskin was considered a comic book stylist by his peers, and his work from the Golden Age of comics, created for a wide variety of genres, still stands out for its clean, dignified, and stunning graphic storytelling.

In the postwar forties Meskin teamed up with a friend, *Batman* artist Jerry Robinson, to open their own studio, producing work for the short-lived Spark Publications. Later Meskin created work for the Simon and Kirby studio. In the late fifties comic book work dried up for many, but he continued to freelance, mainly for DC. Meskin finally left comics altogether in 1965 to concentrate mainly on illustrations and storyboards for advertising. His work continues to be rediscovered by new fans, who are taken away by his stylish and breathtaking visual storytelling.

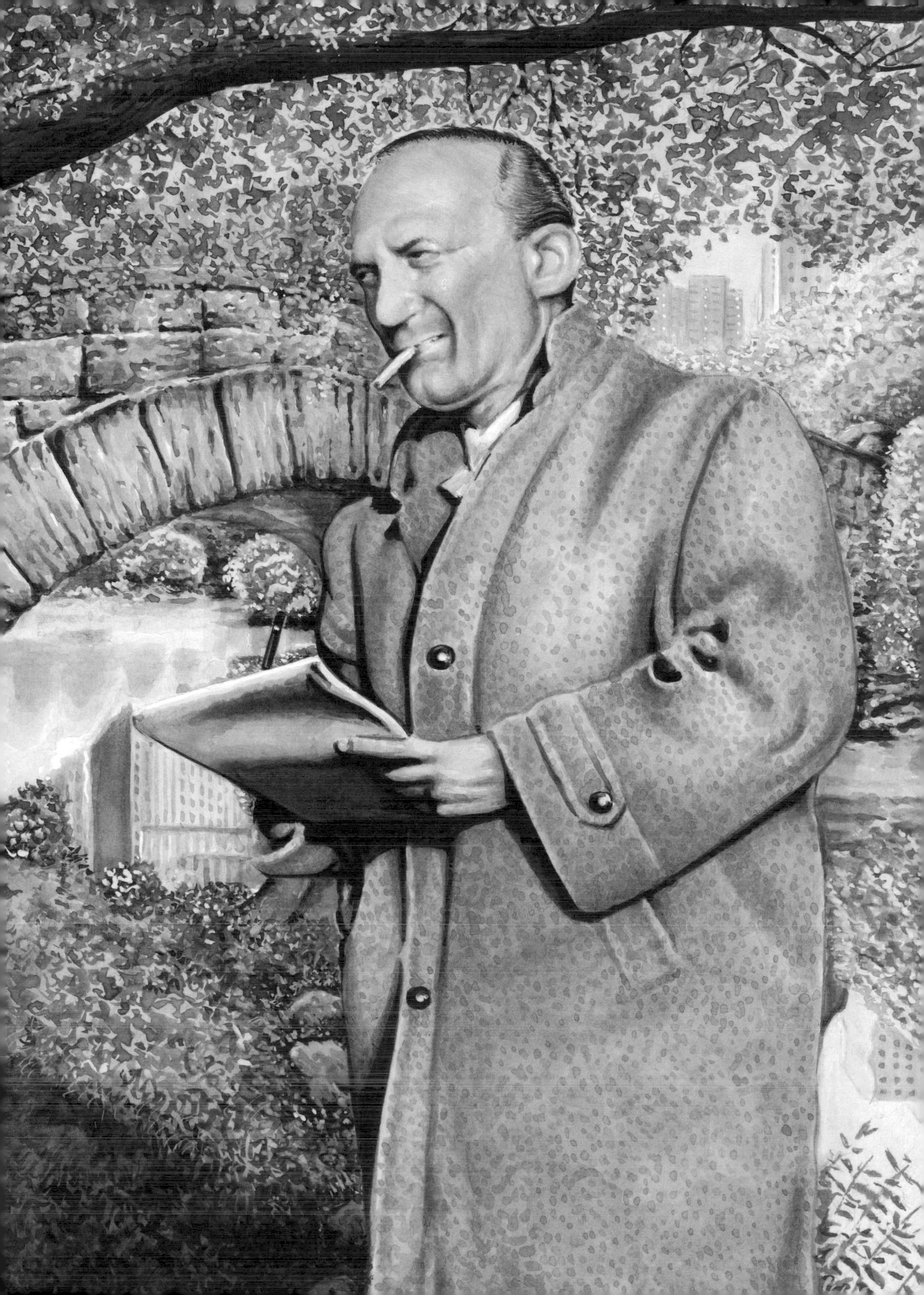

SYD SHORES

1913–1973

plate
27

Sydney "Syd" Shores began his comics career as an apprentice at the Harry "A" Chesler comics shop in the late thirties and drew his first published work for *Mystic Comics* #5 in 1941, for Martin Goodman's fledgling company Timely. Timely's editor, Joe Simon, was impressed with Shores's skills and hired him as the company's third employee, following Simon himself and Stan Lee. Shores inked the early covers of the new *Captain America* comic, which were penciled by Jack Kirby. When the team of Simon and Kirby left Timely in 1942, Stan Lee was promoted to editorial director and writer of *Captain America*, and he hired Shores and artist Al Avison to become the regular pencilers and inkers of the immensely popular title. Shores soon became one of the busiest, most highly regarded inker/pencilers during the Golden Age of comic books. He continued as the regular penciler for *Captain America* and other titles while Avison served in the military. Shores was inducted into the army in 1944, and after he was discharged in 1946, he returned to Timely, where he was promoted to art director. He also freelanced for other comics companies, and when comic books were in recession in the late fifties and the work virtually dried up, he switched over to illustration work, creating Nazi and bondage images for Martin Goodman's Magazine Management men's adventure magazines. He also contributed to the *Mad* imitation *Cracked*. Shores, rarely seen without a cigarette, resumed his comics career in 1967 during the height of Marvel's Silver Age and kept busy until he finally succumbed to lung cancer at age sixty.

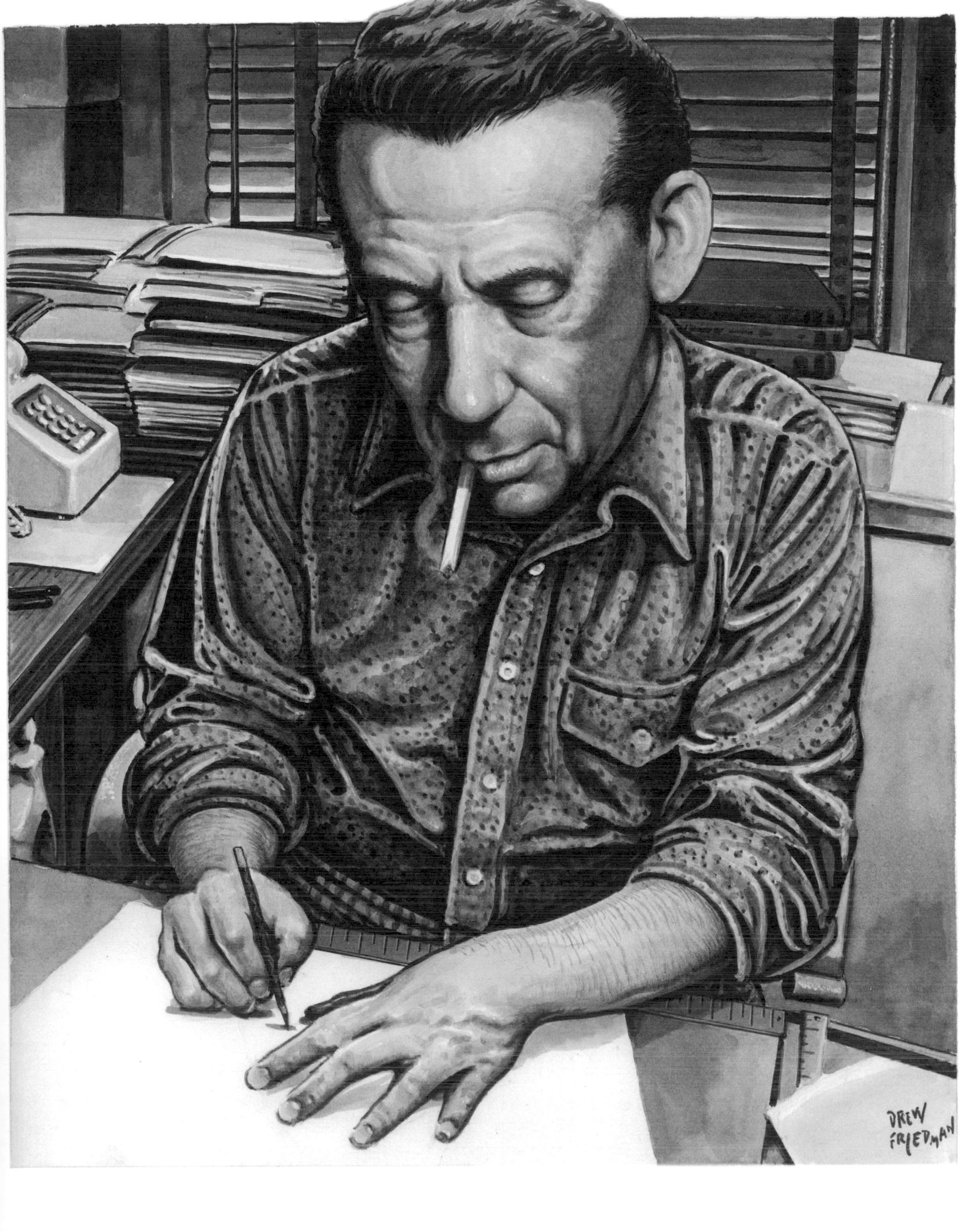
DREW FRIEDMAN

LOU FINE

1914–1971

plate
28

Lou Fine began his career in comics at the Eisner and Iger comics packaging shop in the late thirties, using various pseudonyms to give the appearance that the shop had a large stable of artists. Fine, continuing with his various pen names, was soon considered one of the finest draftsmen and designers of the Golden Age of comics among his peers, creating outstanding work for Quality, Fiction House, and Fox Feature Syndicate, where he drew the feature *The Flame*. He was an artist's artist, turning out exquisite comic book artwork achieved via his painstaking attention to detail and the introduction of his highly influential, standard-setting feathering technique, which used rows of wedge-shaped brushstrokes to achieve an effect of changing tones. He also created many radiant, exciting covers for *Hit Comics*, *Fantastic Comics*, and *Wonderworld Comics*, among others. His career in comic books was breathtaking yet brief, and soon he would be ghosting for Will Eisner's Sunday-supplement newspaper comic book *The Spirit*, as Eisner was serving in the military. From the late forties on Fine worked full-time on syndicated comic strip work. Jack Kirby claimed Lou Fine was his favorite artist, and Will Eisner said about Fine: "He was the epitome of the honest draftsman. No fakery, no razzle-dazzle."

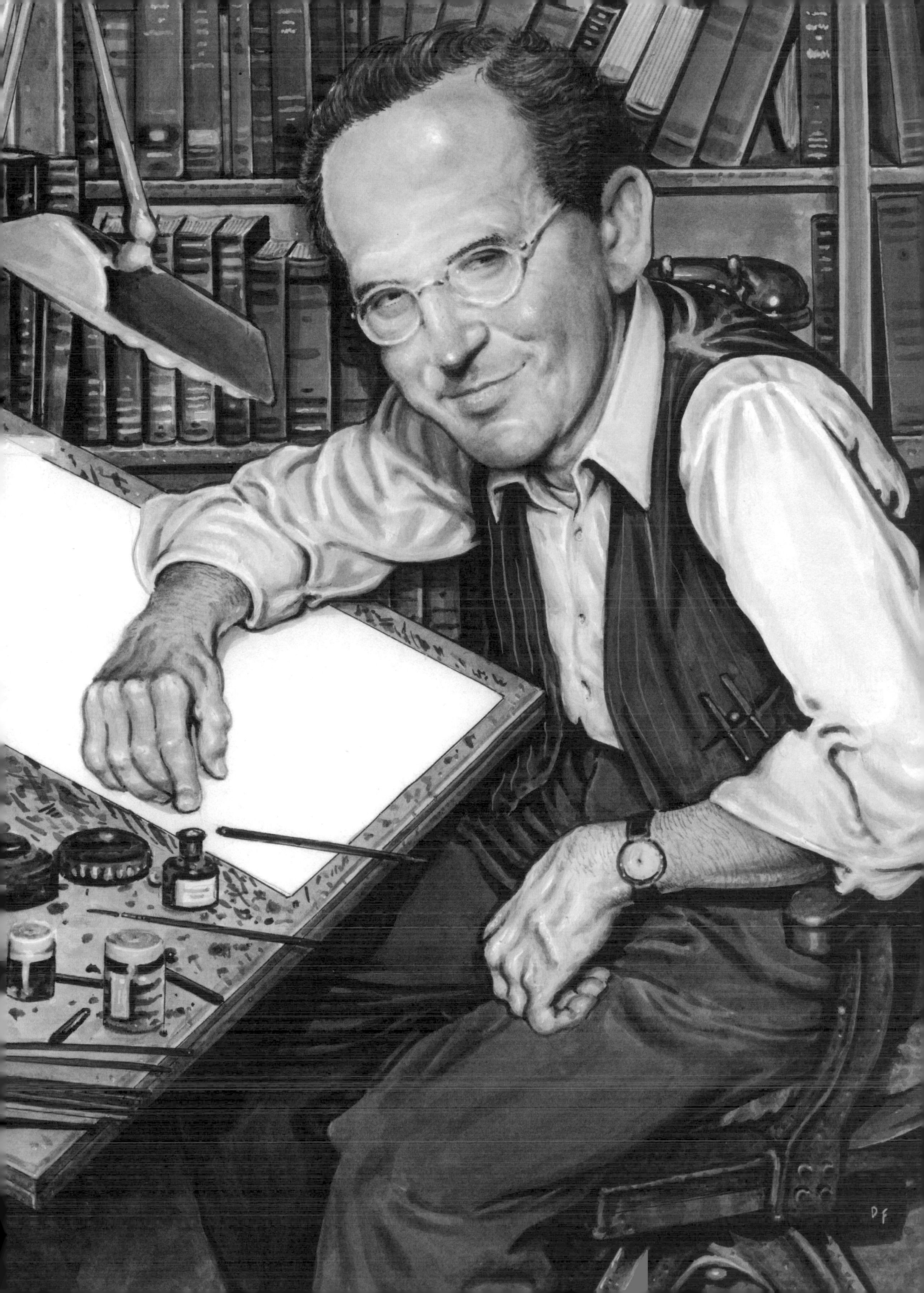
DF

ALEX SCHOMBURG

1905–1998

plate
29

Alex Schomburg was born in Puerto Rico and moved to New York as a teenager. He started out working as a commercial artist, forming a partnership with his three brothers. He was soon freelancing and finding work in pulp magazines, and he emerged in the late thirties as a talented science fiction pulp cover illustrator, especially skilled at drawing anything mechanical, such as spaceships. In the early forties he began creating covers under editor Stan Lee at Timely Comics for *Captain America*, *The Sub-Mariner*, and *The Human Torch*. His stylized and dynamic covers, with their action-packed tableaux, instantly stood out. Schomburg filled every square inch of his covers with excitement, weapons, explosions, machines, and patriotic flag-waving. Later he mastered the use of the airbrush and, under the pseudonym "Xela" (Alex backwards), created some of the sexiest pinup girls ever drawn for comic book covers. Schomburg created more than five hundred covers during the Golden Age of comics in the forties. In the early fifties he began to create covers and illustrations mainly for science fiction and astrology publications. Stan Lee wrote of Alex Schomburg: "He was to comic books what Norman Rockwell was to the *Saturday Evening Post*."

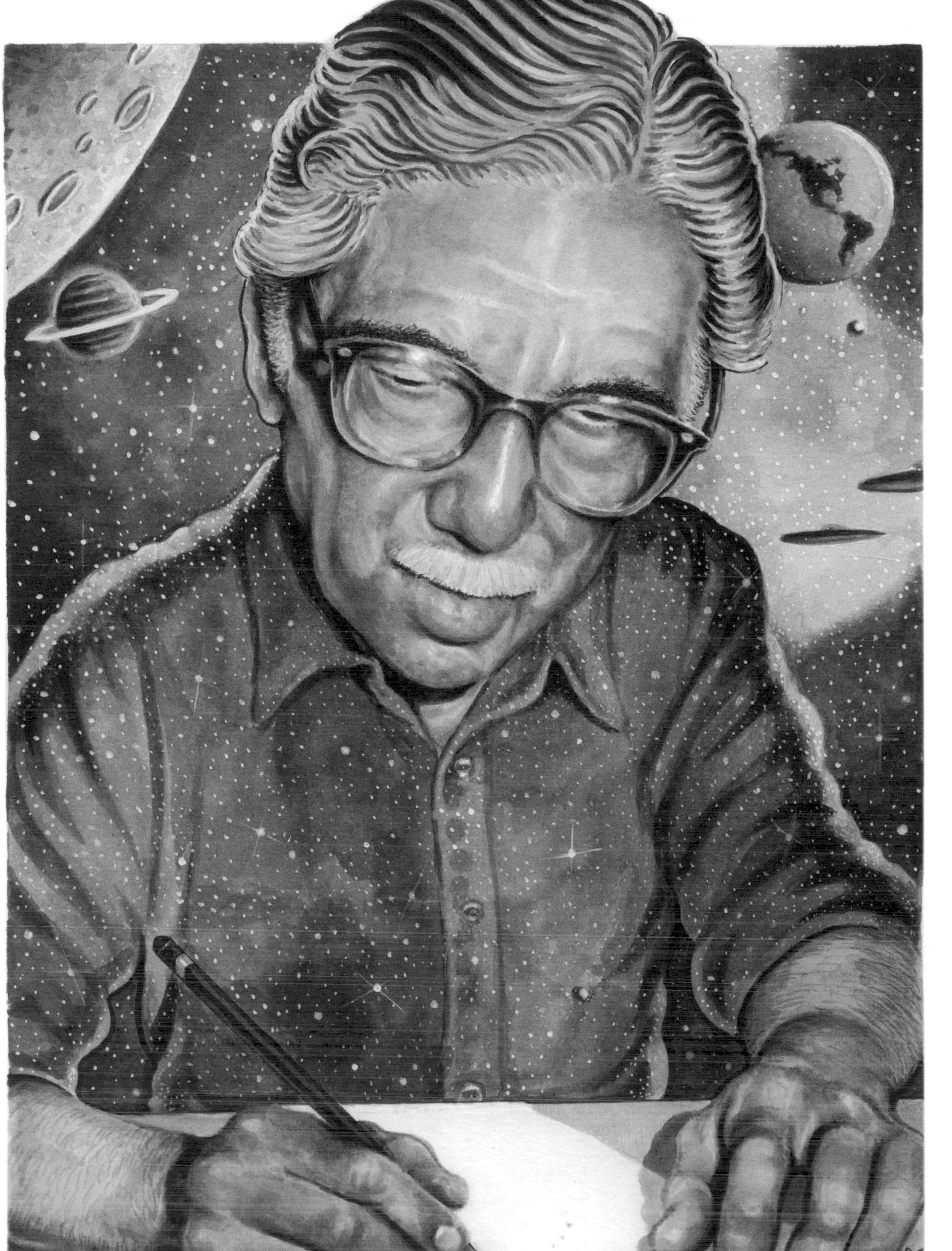
DF

CARMINE INFANTINO

1925–2013

plate
30

As a twelve-year-old, Carmine Michael Infantino spent his summer working at the Harry "A" Chesler comics shop for a dollar per day in order to learn the ropes of working on comic books. Learning from his early internship, Infantino went on to draw *The Human Torch* and *Angel* for Martin Goodman's Timely Comics in 1940, then freelanced for various companies before joining DC Comics, where he drew *The Green Lantern* and other superhero titles during the Golden Age of comics. Infantino drew *Charlie Chan* for Joe Simon and Jack Kirby's company Prize Comics and worked for DC in the fifties, drawing stories for various western, mystery, and science fiction titles. Infantino made his mark in the late fifties, when editor Julius Schwartz of DC asked him to resurrect the speedy superhero the Flash. Infantino reinvented the Flash with a sleek, spare, modern look and a bright red costume. The new Flash became a hit for DC and helped to spur on the Silver Age of comics in the early sixties. Infantino was hailed as one of the industry's finest pencilers, a dynamic artist, and a master of motion. When the poorly selling *Batman* comics were being threatened with cancellation in 1964, Schwartz again hired Infantino to revive the series. Infantino gave the comic a streamlined, modern vitality and replaced Batman and Robin's silly superhero antics with more detective-oriented stories (after all, they were featured in *Detective Comics* for twenty-five years), leading to the beginnings of "Batmania," which swept across the country two years later. The well-liked Infantino enjoyed a particularly long career with DC, rising from artist to art director to editor and finally to publisher.

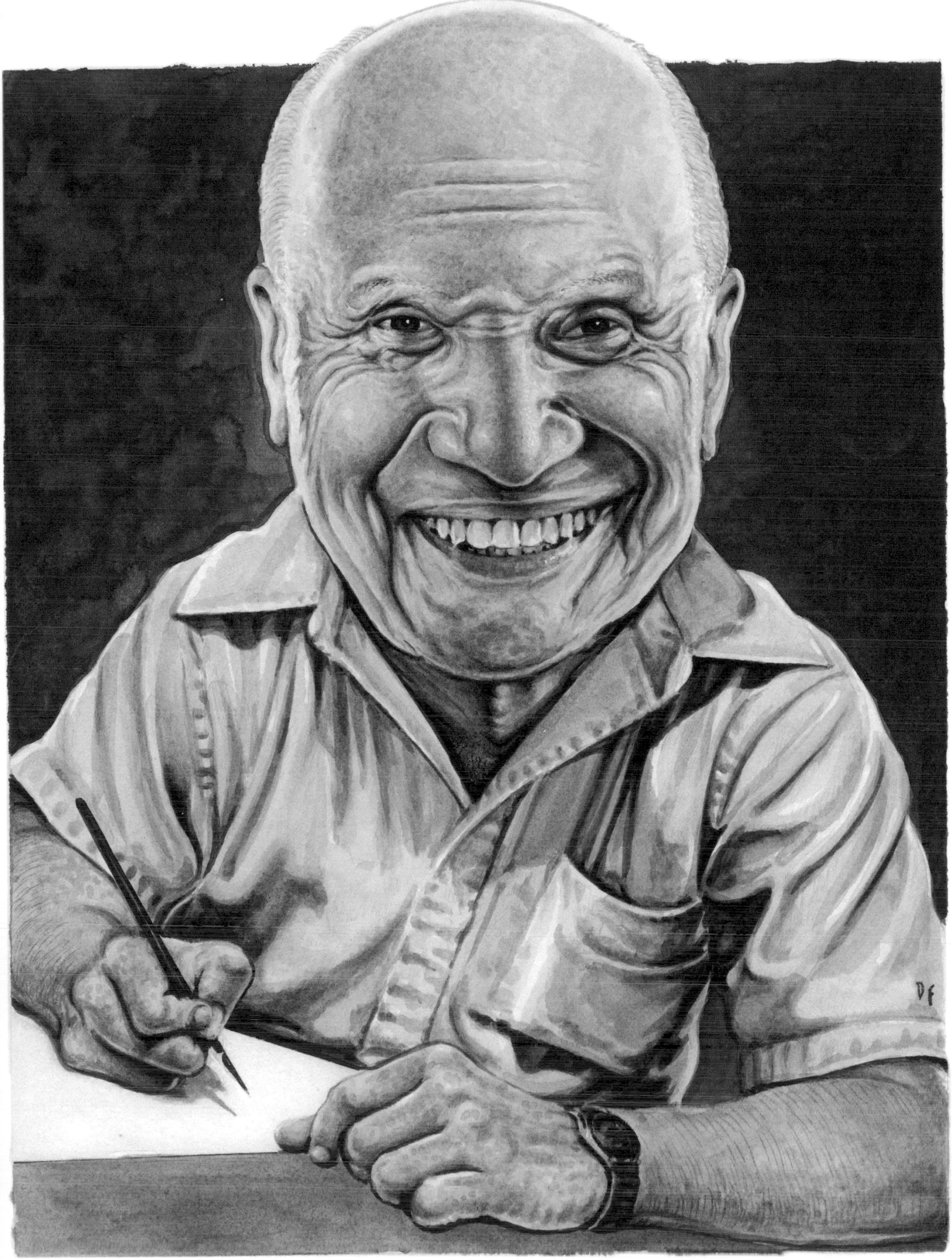

REED CRANDALL

1917–1982

plate
31

Reed Crandall was a master comics craftsman, clearly influenced by the great illustrators of his youth, including Howard Pyle and N. C. Wyeth. When he first arrived at EC in 1953, he was already a well-respected veteran of the comics business. Like so many other young, eager comics artists, he began his career by working at the Eisner and Iger comics shop in 1940, where his work was packaged to appear in various comic books, among them *Doll Man*, *Hit Comics*, and *Police Comics*, but soon he began working directly for Quality Comics. After serving in the Army Air Forces in World War II, Crandall returned to Quality and became the main artist on its popular title *Blackhawk* until Quality ceased operations in 1953. That same year, seeking new employment, he walked through the doors of EC on Lafayette Street. Al Feldstein, who had long admired Crandall's elegant draftsmanship, instantly hired him and kept him busy for the next three years, mainly on science fiction, crime, and horror comics, and later on New Direction comics, including *Valor* and *Piracy*. Like George Evans, Crandall specialized in realistically illustrated depictions of ordinary people caught up in horrific situations. After EC went under, Crandall again freelanced, and again like George Evans found work with Classics Illustrated comics, Dell's adaption of *Twilight Zone*, and Warren's two horror comics magazines *Creepy* and *Eerie*, where he would create some of his most meticulous and stunning crosshatched work to date.

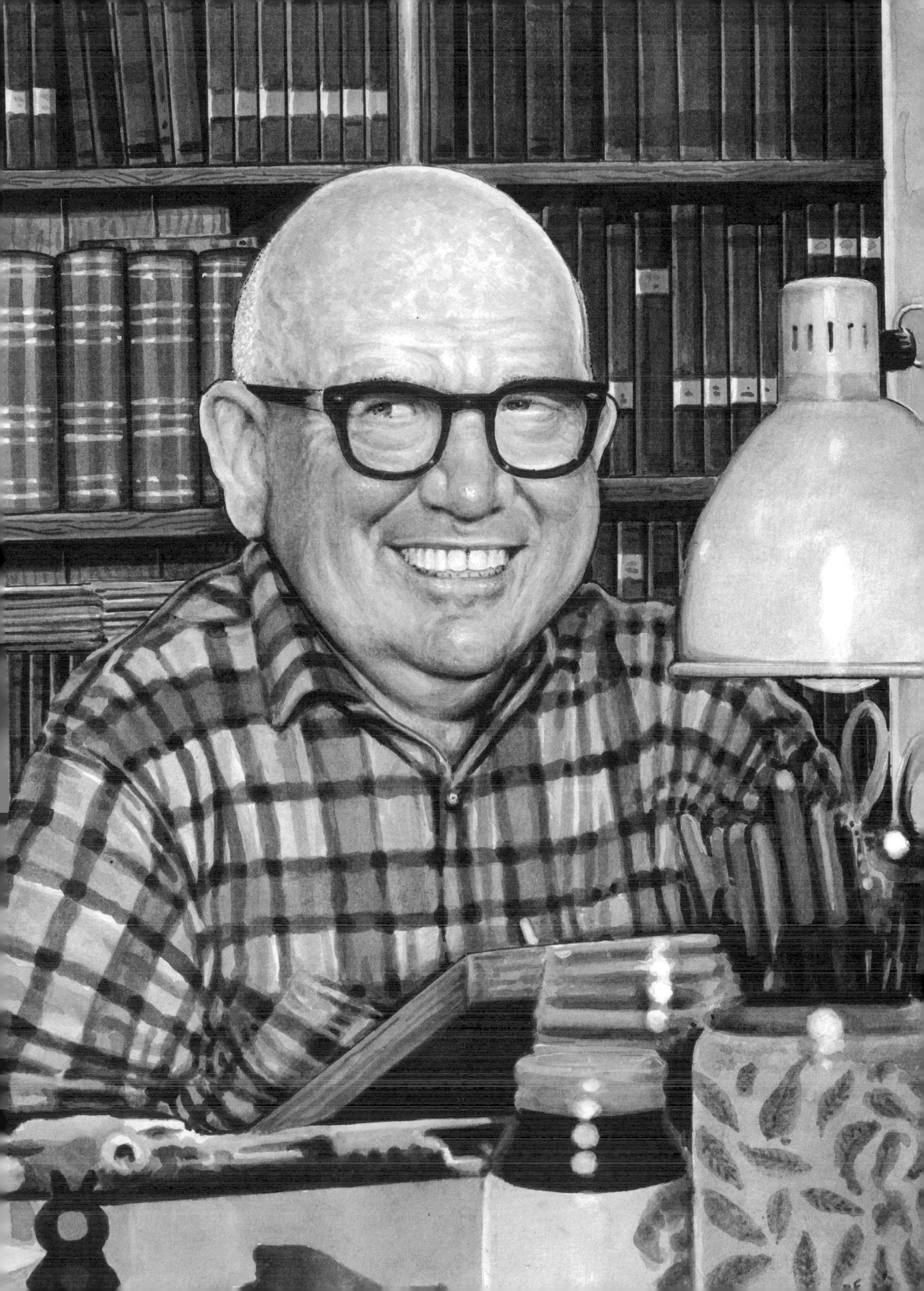

BOB POWELL

1916–1967

plate
32

Bob Powell (b. Stanislav Robert Pawlowski) found work in the late 1930s as an artist at the new Eisner and Iger comics packaging shop. Powell's earliest published comics appeared in 1938, and he was soon creating comic art for Fox, Fiction House, Timely, and others. While with Eisner and Iger, he drew the early adventures of the Will Eisner–created *Sheena, Queen of the Jungle* for *Jumbo Comics*. When Eisner split off from his partner, he took Powell with him and had him cowrite (uncredited) his new character Blackhawk. Powell, using many pseudonyms, kept busy during the Golden Age of comics, doing work for *Captain America* and various jungle titles.

Following his discharge from military service, Powell formed his own studio and continued freelancing for most of the comic book publishers. He created work for every popular comics genre throughout the fifties, be it superheroes, romance, crime, or especially horror, which he relished, until the horror comics purge of the midfifties. In 1961 Powell became the art director for and chief contributor to the new humor magazine *Sick*, an imitation of *Cracked* (which was itself an imitation of *Mad*), a job he held till his death. He also drew the tight pencil sketches (based on roughs supplied by Wally Wood, among others) for the iconic 1962 Topps trading card series *Mars Attacks*, which was painted by Norman Saunders. He continued freelancing for comics, mainly for Marvel during their Silver Age, drawing a handful of stories featuring Daredevil, the Hulk, and the Human Torch.

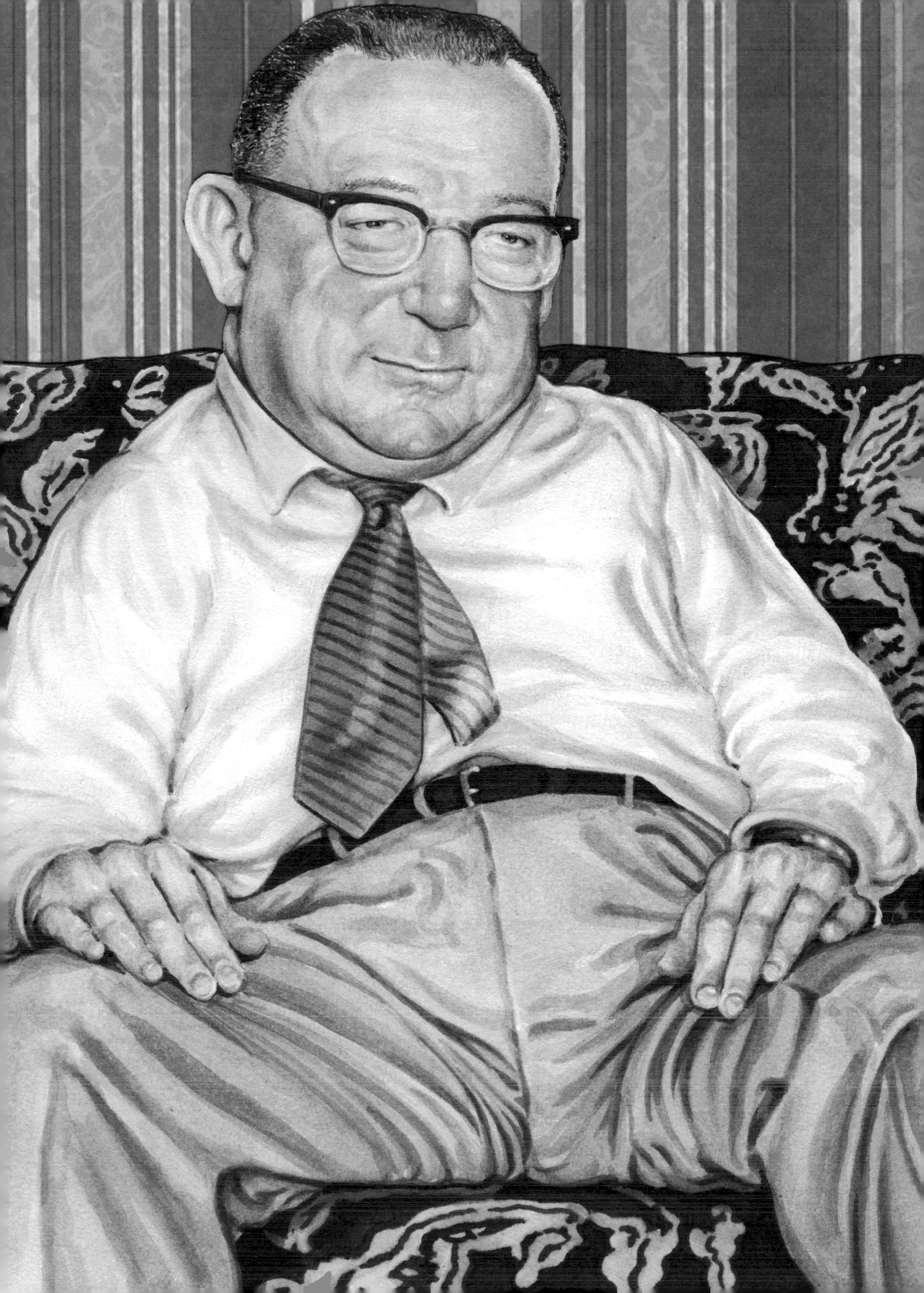

MAC RABOY

1914–1967

plate
33

Emmanuel "Mac" Raboy started his art career as a Works Progress Administration (WPA) artist, creating wood engravings that were exhibited around the country. Inspired by his idol Alex Raymond to draw comics, he joined the Harry "A" Chesler shop in 1940 and began turning out work mainly for Fawcett Publications, the publisher of the hugely popular Captain Marvel. Fawcett editor Ed Herron was so impressed with Raboy's polished, graceful art that he hired him as a permanent staff artist in 1941 to illustrate the adventures of the crippled teenage newsboy Freddie Freeman, a.k.a. Captain Marvel Jr. The new series was written by Otto Binder, who was also the writer for *Captain Marvel*. Raboy was an expert technician with pen and brush, and his lush covers for the series are some of the most unusually beautiful to ever grace comic books. He kept a portfolio of Alex Raymond's *Flash Gordon* comics by his side for inspiration and guidance as he worked, but unlike Raymond, who drew quickly using models, Raboy was slow and meticulous, and finally needed assistants to help him get his deadlines completed on time. After one too many clashes with his editors over missed deadlines, he left Fawcett and joined Spark Publications, where he would draw *Green Lama* comics for several years. In 1948 Raboy finally received his dream job, illustrating the *Flash Gordon* Sunday strip for King Features, which he continued doing for the rest of his life.

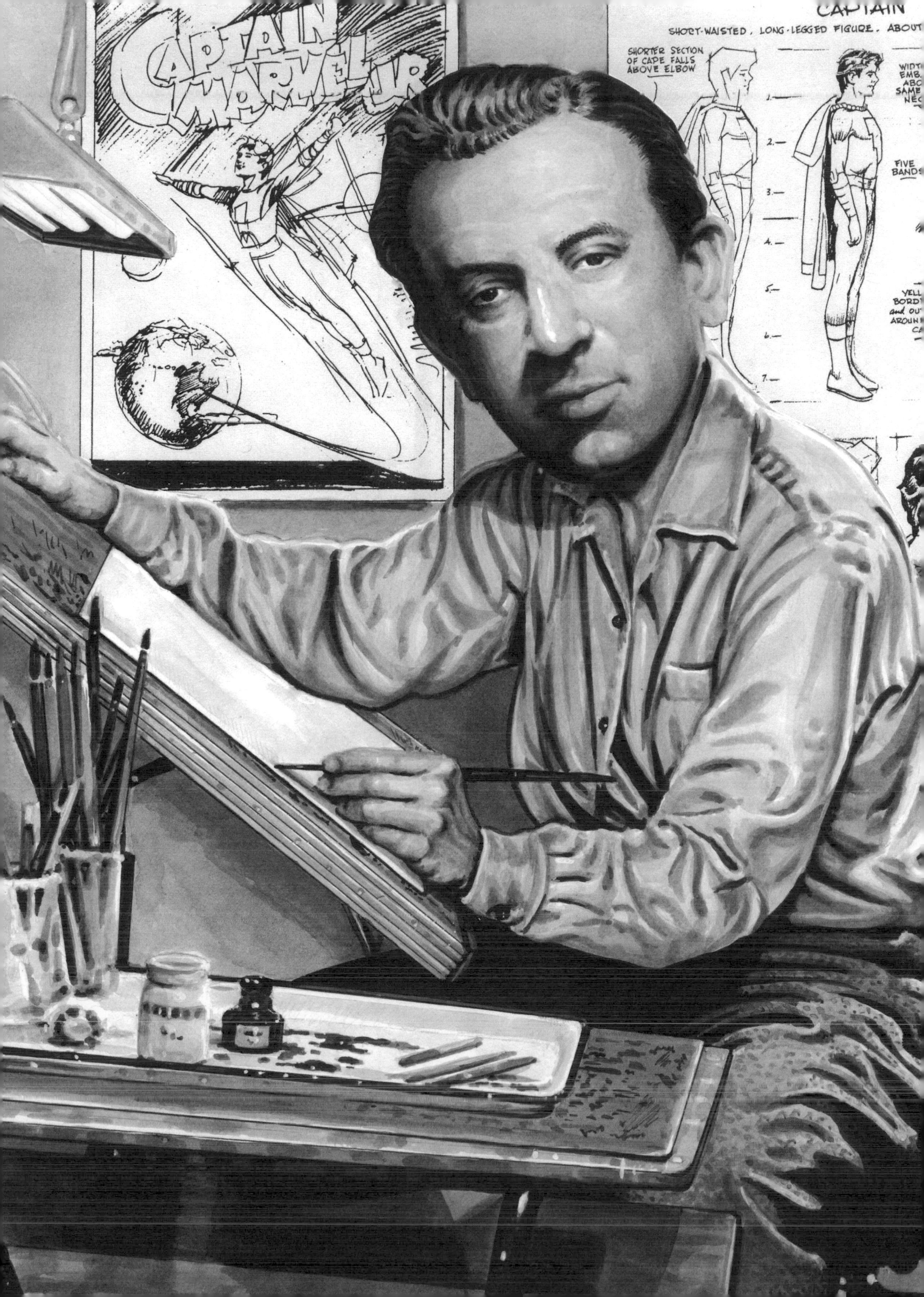
CAPTAIN MARVEL JR
CAPTAIN
SHORT-WAISTED, LONG-LEGGED FIGURE. ABOUT
SHORTER SECTION OF CAPE FALLS ABOVE ELBOW
FIVE

DICK SPRANG

1915–2000

plate
34

Richard W. "Dick" Sprang was a longtime Batman ghost artist, referred to by many as "the good Batman artist." Sprang began drawing for pulp magazines in the thirties, but as interest in pulps began to wane, he switched to comic book work. His drawing abilities caught the attention of DC/National editor Whitney Ellsworth, who hired Sprang to draw *Batman* in 1941. Sprang's earliest *Batman* stories weren't published immediately, but rather were held in storage for two years to prevent schedule delays in the event that Batman creator Bob Kane was drafted into World War II. His first published *Batman* work finally appeared in 1943 on the cover of *Batman* #18, and his first interior stories were published in *Batman* #19 later that year. Sprang, whose work, like that of all early artists drawing "Bob Kane's *Batman*," appeared uncredited (to give the appearance that Bob Kane actually drew and wrote the stories himself), became one of the character's main artists, both in the comic books and in the syndicated newspaper strip. Sprang's Batman stood out because of his highly stylized, clean, bold line; his innovative comic page breakdowns; and the Dick Tracy–like square jaw and the massive barrel chest he endowed the Caped Crusader with. He's also credited with several other Batman innovations, including redesigning the Batmobile and drawing the debut of The Riddler. Sprang later became the primary artist on the unlikely team-up of Batman and Superman in *World's Finest Comics*. Sprang's wife, Pat Gordon, was his chief letterer.

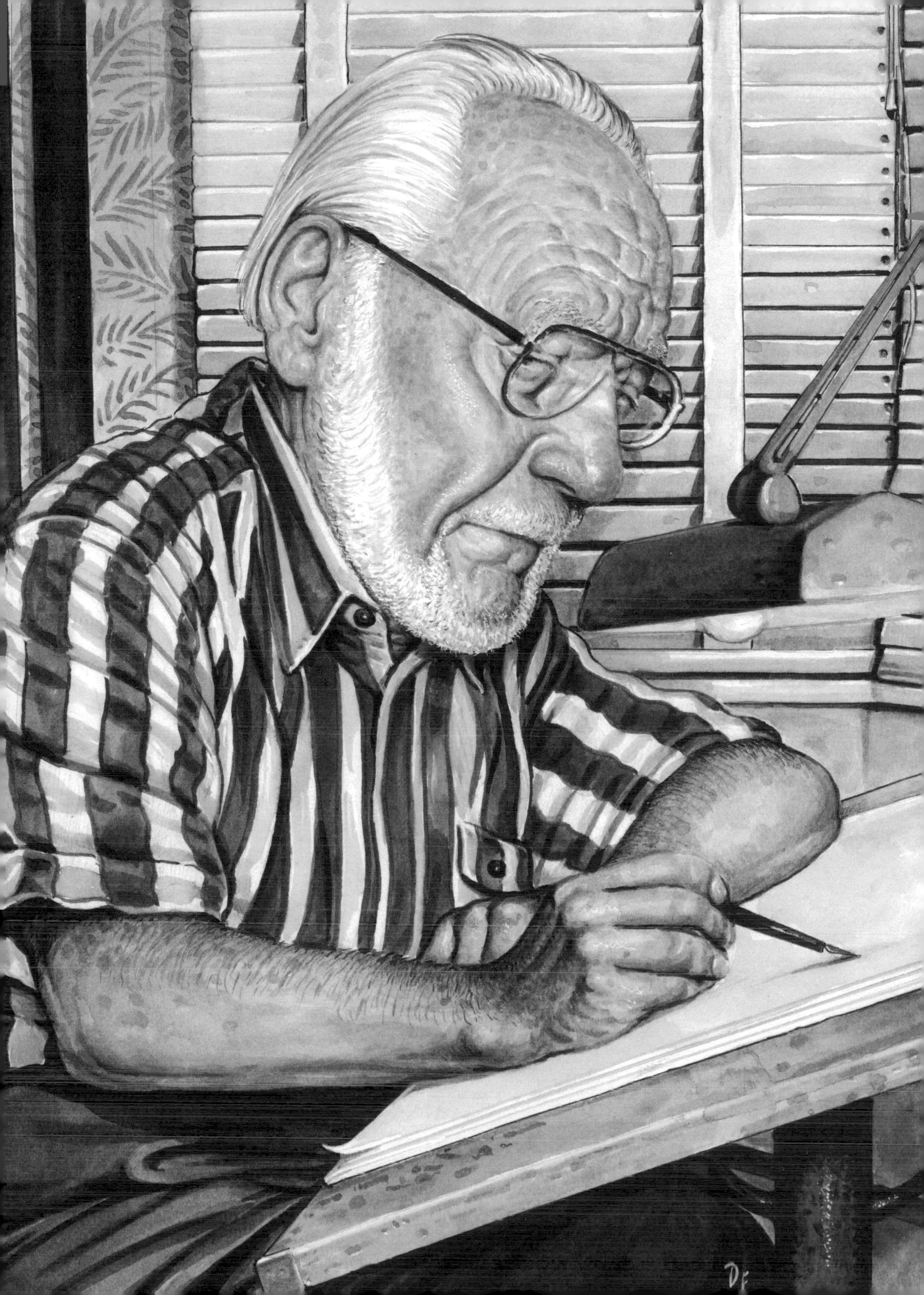

WAYNE BORING

1905–1987

plate
35

Like so many other young artists of the day, Wayne Boring worshipped Alex Raymond's heroic *Flash Gordon* comic strip. The red-headed Boring began his comics career in the midthirties by ghosting for writer Jerry Siegel and artist Joe Shuster on the pre-Superman comics they created for National, including *Slam Bradley*. After Superman burst onto the scene, Boring continued ghosting for Siegel and Shuster, now for their *Superman* comic strip, and absorbed Joe Shuster's techniques as an artist. In 1942 National hired Boring as a full-time staff artist, and by the end of the decade, he was drawing the *Superman* comic book after Siegel and Shuster finally departed over a rights issue concerning the new character Superboy. As the primary *Superman* artist throughout the fifties, Boring helped redefine the character's look by giving him a more earnest and wooden facial expression; a more powerful, menacing, and imposing body; and a massive torso, jutting jaw, and small cranium, creating an odd, distorted Bizzaro effect, which Superman fans seemed to love. Boring drew Superman throughout the fifties and continued working off and on in comics, at one point working as a bank security guard.

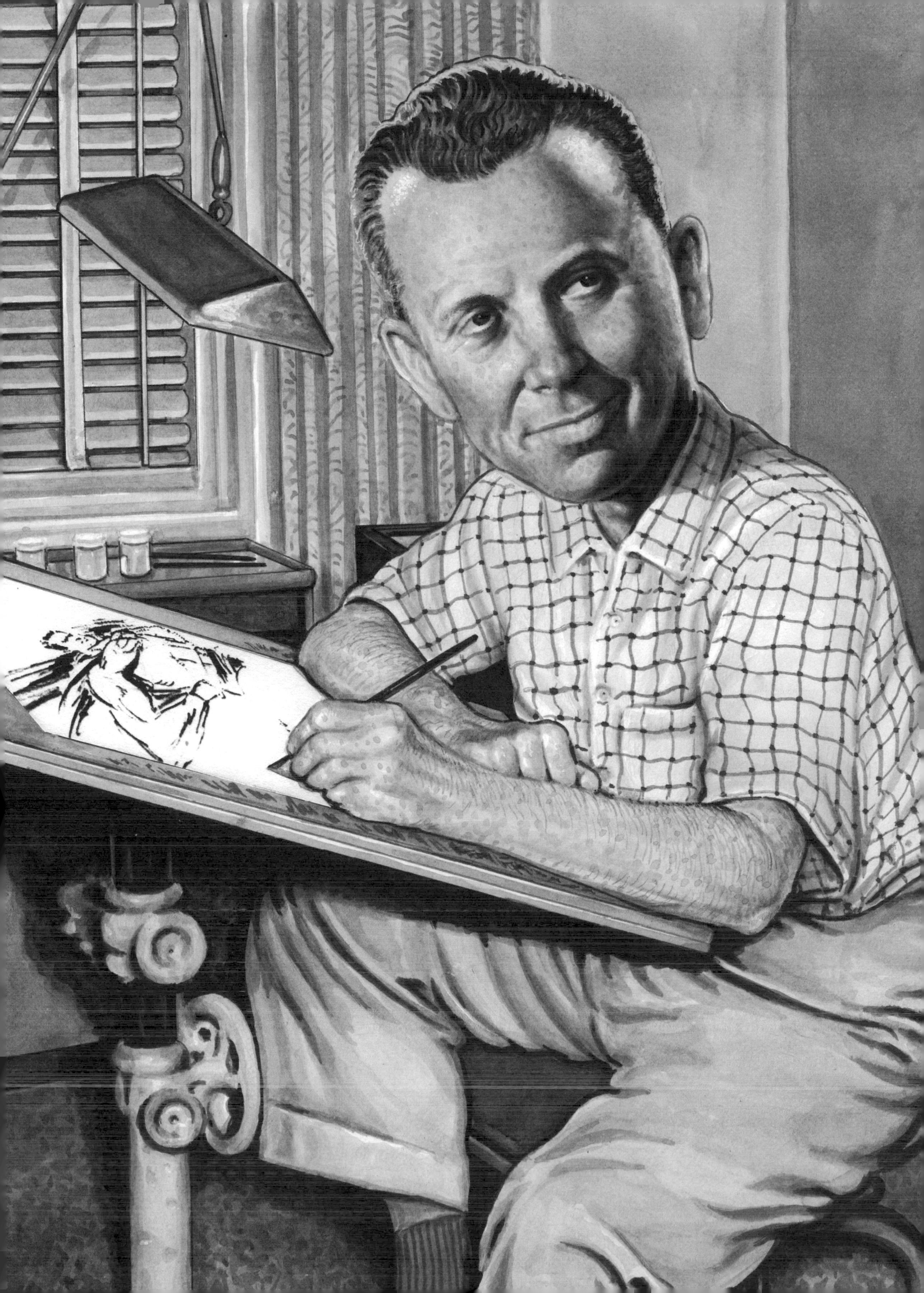

L. B. COLE

1918–1995

plate
36

Leonard Brandt "L. B." Cole was a rotund, smiling, pleasant looking comic book artist who created some of the most freakishly twisted and bizarre horror covers ever. He began in comics in the early forties and soon established himself with his distinctive, colorful covers. Cole became one of the most in-demand cover artists during the Golden Age of comics in the prewar 1940s. In 1942 he opened his own comics packaging studio, and later he became a comics publisher and editor himself, creating Star Publications, where he drew the popular *Blue Bolt Comics*. In the late forties and early fifties, when horror comics were at their zenith, Cole created his most vibrant and memorable work. His startling, swirling, colorful horror covers, which were like proto–psychedelic posters, remain some of the most eye-popping comics covers of all time. Unfortunately the interiors of the comics rarely lived up to Cole's insane covers. When the horror comics disappeared from the landscape in the midfifties, giving way to the strict new comics code, Cole switched gears and happily found work as an art director at the family-friendly Dell comics. In the midsixties he left comics altogether to create industrial materials and audiovisuals for university films. His work has been rediscovered and celebrated in recent years.

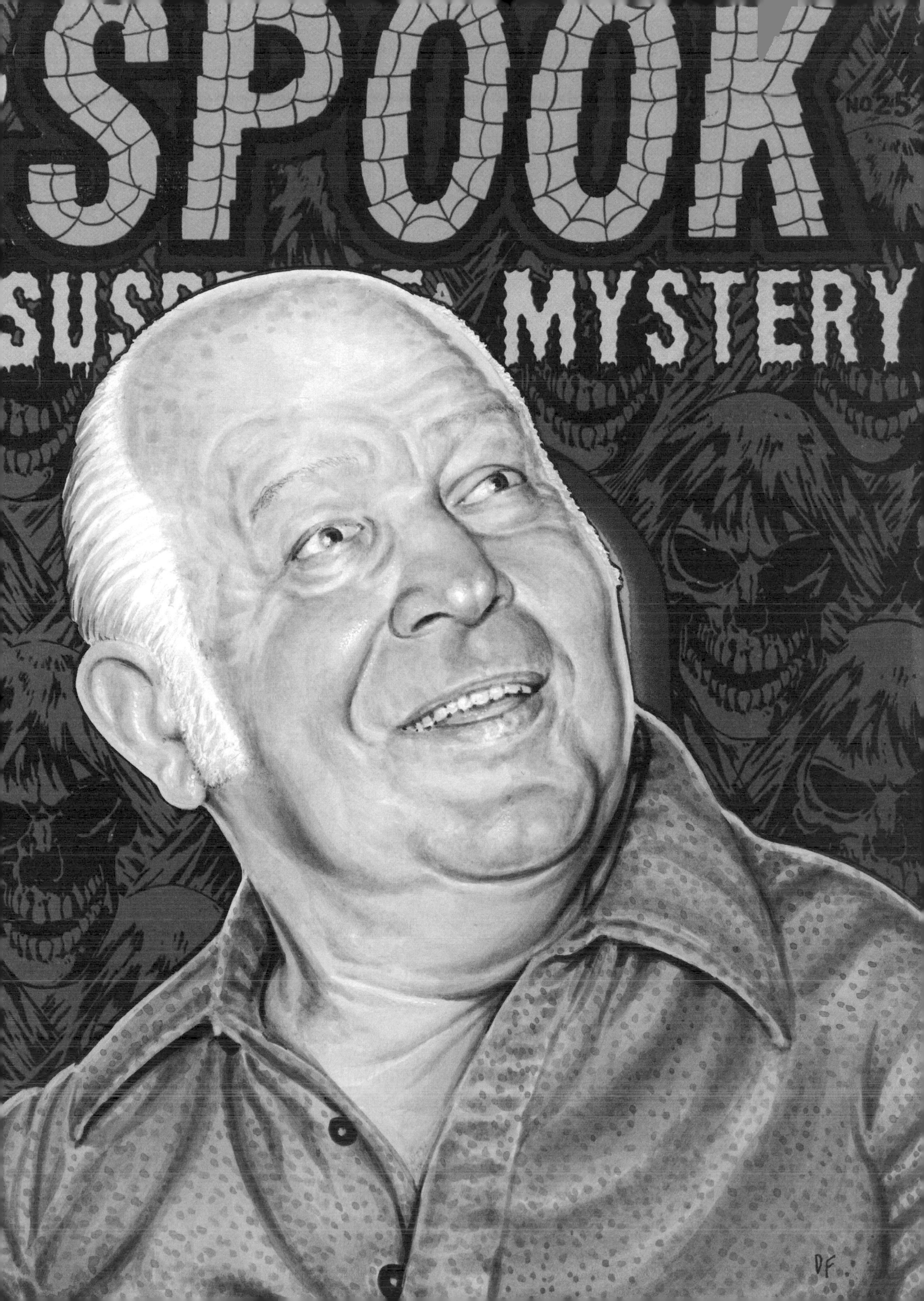
SPOOK
MYSTERY
DF.

DICK BRIEFER

1915–1980

plate
37

Richard "Dick" Briefer did his first work in comics in 1936 for editor Jerry Iger's *Wow, What a Magazine!*, an early prototype tabloid-sized comic. He then joined the Eisner and Iger comics packaging shop and created work for various new comics publishers, drawing cowboy, sci-fi, and superhero comics for Fiction House, Fox, and Timely, among others. In 1940 Briefer introduced his *New Adventures of Frankenstein* for *Prize Comics* #11, an updated version of the Mary Shelley monster story, which had become public domain. Briefer's version featured a bizarre, maniacal creature actually named Frankenstein, who, after being created by a scientist, rampages through 1930s New York, tearing innocent bystanders apart in what was perhaps the first official horror comic book series. During the war the monster turned his angry attentions to fighting Hitler and the Nazis.

Following the war, Briefer updated the series for *Frankenstein* #1, which featured a more cartoony, humorous monster settled into postwar small-town life. The kid-friendly "Merry Monster" shared madcap, whimsical adventures with Dracula, the Wolfman, and other creatures. In his book *Art out of Time*, comics historian Dan Nadel writes that Briefer was "one of the few guys in the 1940s who had that loose, gestural art style that's funny. The drawing is inherently funny." Briefer continued his best-selling humorous *Frankenstein* series into the late forties, later reviving his original, grim, horrific, rampaging version before the title was canceled due to the midfifties purge of horror and crime comics. Briefer retired from the comics industry to work in advertising.

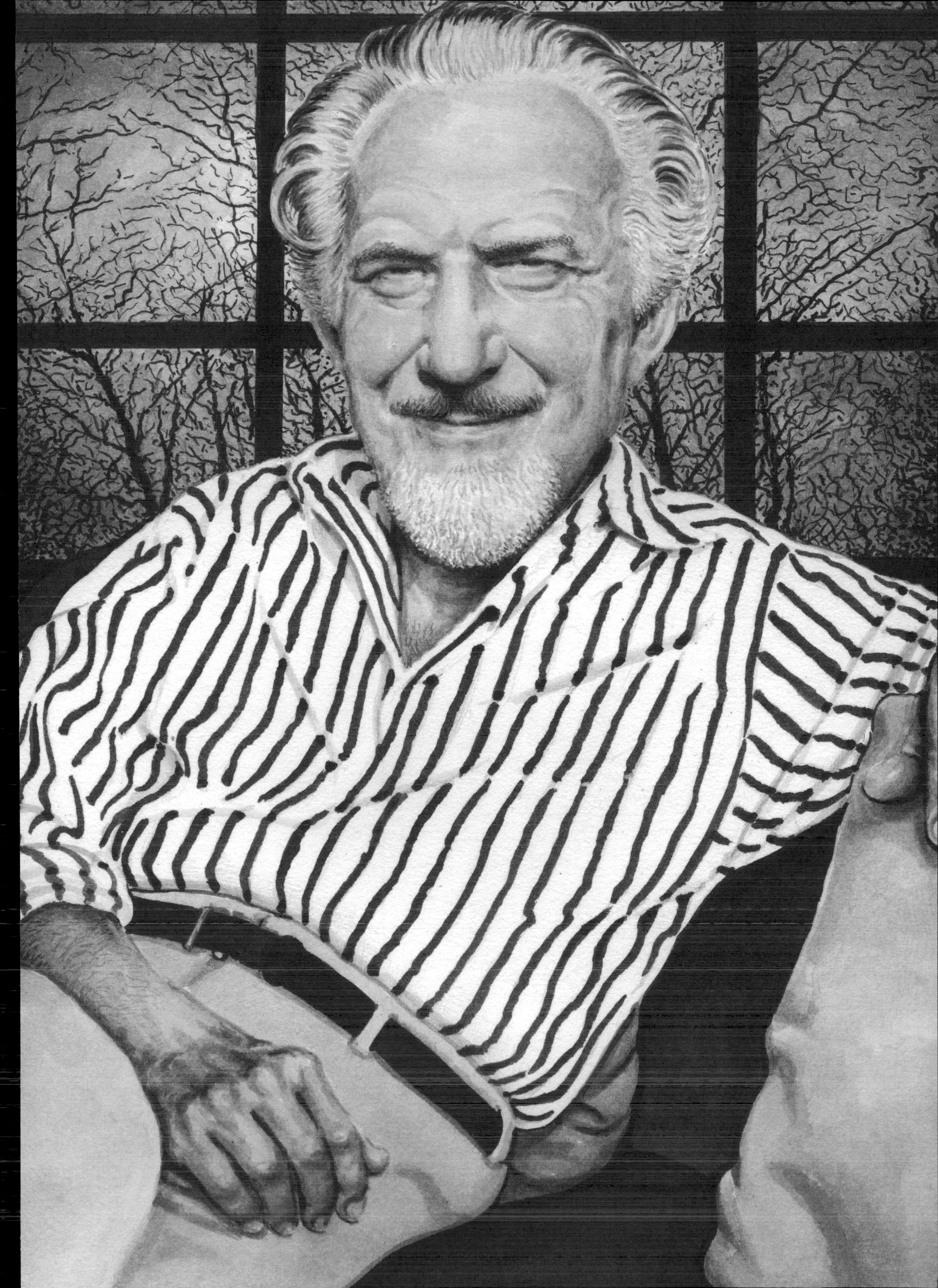

BASIL WOLVERTON

1909–1978

plate

Basil Wolverton, a "producer of preposterous pictures of peculiar people," was a unique, never to be duplicated screwball cartoonist. In fact, he invented his particular style of cartooning, which featured icky, otherworldly humans with exposed organs and glands (which some found grotesque) and unique, inventive creatures with painstakingly sculpted, crosshatched features, spaghetti-like hair (*Life* magazine wrote that he invented the "Spaghetti and Meatball school of design"), and wacky, rhyming, poetic cartoon captions and names (Leanbean Green, Nell No-Smell). In the late thirties Wolverton began drawing for his first comic book, *Circus Comics*. He then created the intergalactic superhero Spacehawk, but after the war switched gears and leaned toward the absurd, creating the adventures of Powerhouse Pepper, a not-so-bright boxer and "superhero," for Timely Comics. Featuring alliterating, rhyming dialogue, it became his most successful comic book feature, running for ten years.

In 1946 Wolverton entered a contest for Al Capp's *Li'l Abner* comic strip, rendering "Lower Slobbovia'a ugliest woman, Lena the Hyena." His horrifyingly funny portrait beat out five hundred thousand entries and brought him brief international fame. Wolverton created horror and science fiction comic book work into the 1950s and occasionally did work for his admirer Harvey Kurtzman at *Mad*, including a Lena-like cover for *Mad* #11. In his later years he produced five hundred incredibly detailed illustrations depicting the New Testament's book of Revelation. He'd also create memorable (uncredited but instantly identifiable) work for Topps Ugly Stickers and for the covers of DC's early seventies humor comic book *PLOP!* Basil Wolverton continues to have a huge influence on young cartoonists, who always seem to remember the jolt of first seeing his amazing work.

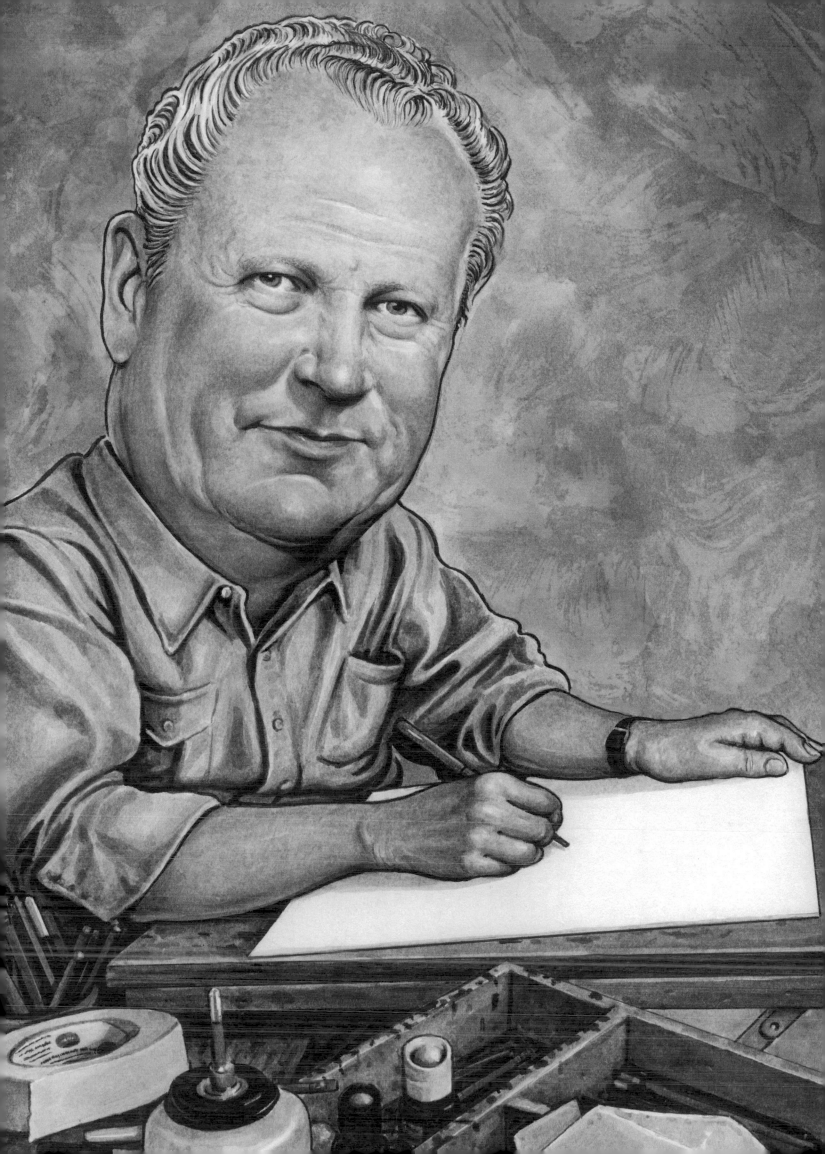

JACK COLE

plate
39

Jack Ralph Cole rode a bicycle across the country at age seventeen, was married to his high school sweetheart at nineteen, and began working in comics at twenty-four, creating one-page fillers at the Harry "A" Chesler comics packaging shop for several titles published by Centaur Publications. Cole was hired by Lev Gleason Publications in 1939 to edit *Silver Streak Comics* and help revamp the new superhero character Daredevil. From there he moved to Everett "Busy" Arnold's Quality Comics, where he assisted Will Eisner on *The Spirit* (when Eisner entered the army during World War II, Cole and Lou Fine filled in as his ghost artists) and created his own character, Plastic Man, to star in a backup feature in *Police Comics*. Plastic Man became an instant hit and was given his own title in 1943. The elastic Plastic Man was a satiric send-up of the muscle-bound superheroes of the Golden Age of comics, and the title was groundbreaking for its day, balancing Cole's wild humor and incredibly animated, taffy-pulling artwork with his experimentation with text and graphics, thus stretching the boundaries of comics and creating one of the most enduring comic book heroes ever. Cole also did freelance illustration for *True Crime Comics*, and one of his stories, "Murder, Morphine and Me," became a centerpiece of psychiatrist Dr. Fredric Wertham's crime/horror comics crusade in the fifties. After the superhero trend in comics began to fade, Cole turned his attention to creating "good girl" gag cartoons in wash for various men's humor magazines such as *Humorama*, using the pen name "Jake." When longtime *Plastic Man* fan Hugh Hefner launched *Playboy* in 1953, he instantly hired Cole as a regular contributor under his real name, and his beautiful lush watercolor cartoons became the centerpiece (as opposed to centerfold) of the new magazine. In 1958 Cole created his own more simplistic-looking syndicated comic strip *Betsy and Me*. Later that year, in one of the most baffling events in cartoon history, he sent two suicide notes, one to his wife and one to Hefner, before taking his own life with a shotgun.

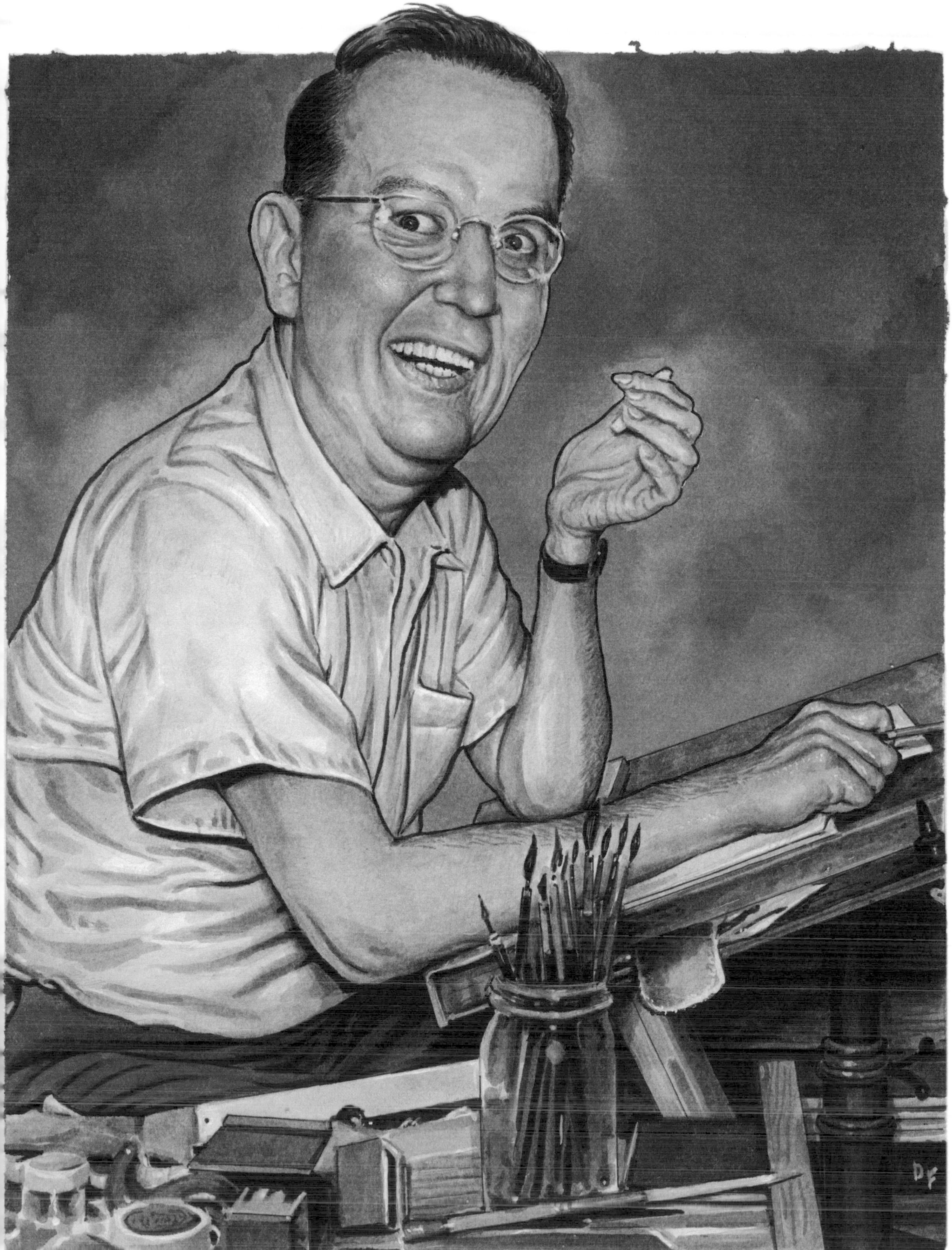
DF

DAN BARRY

1923–1997

plate
40

Daniel "Dan" Barry began his career drawing for comics in the early forties at age nineteen, assisting various artists and drawing for *Airboy*, *Blue Bolt*, and *Doc Savage*. Barry, like many other young artists of his generation, was particularly captivated and influenced by the more elegant Alex Raymond (the creator of Flash Gordon) school of art (as opposed to the Milton Caniff school of art) and paid special attention to his line work. After a brief stint in the air force, Barry returned to freelance for various comics publishers, drawing stories for *Crimebusters* and other titles, and then was hired to be Burne Hogarth's assistant on his *Tarzan* syndicated comic strip, which Barry took over in 1947 and drew for the next year. Barry also teamed with Charles Biro on memorable stories for the *Crime Does Not Pay* series for Lev Gleason Publications. In 1951 Barry was hired to revive the *Flash Gordon* newspaper comic strip for King Features. The strip was cowritten by none other than Harvey Kurtzman (who had greatly admired Barry's work for *Crime Does Not Pay*), and Jack Davis and Frank Frazetta occasionally assisted with the art. Barry and Kurtzman had a famously uneasy and brief partnership, but their version of *Flash Gordon* remains outstanding. Kurtzman lasted only two years as a writer on the strip, but Barry continued with *Flash Gordon* for almost three decades.

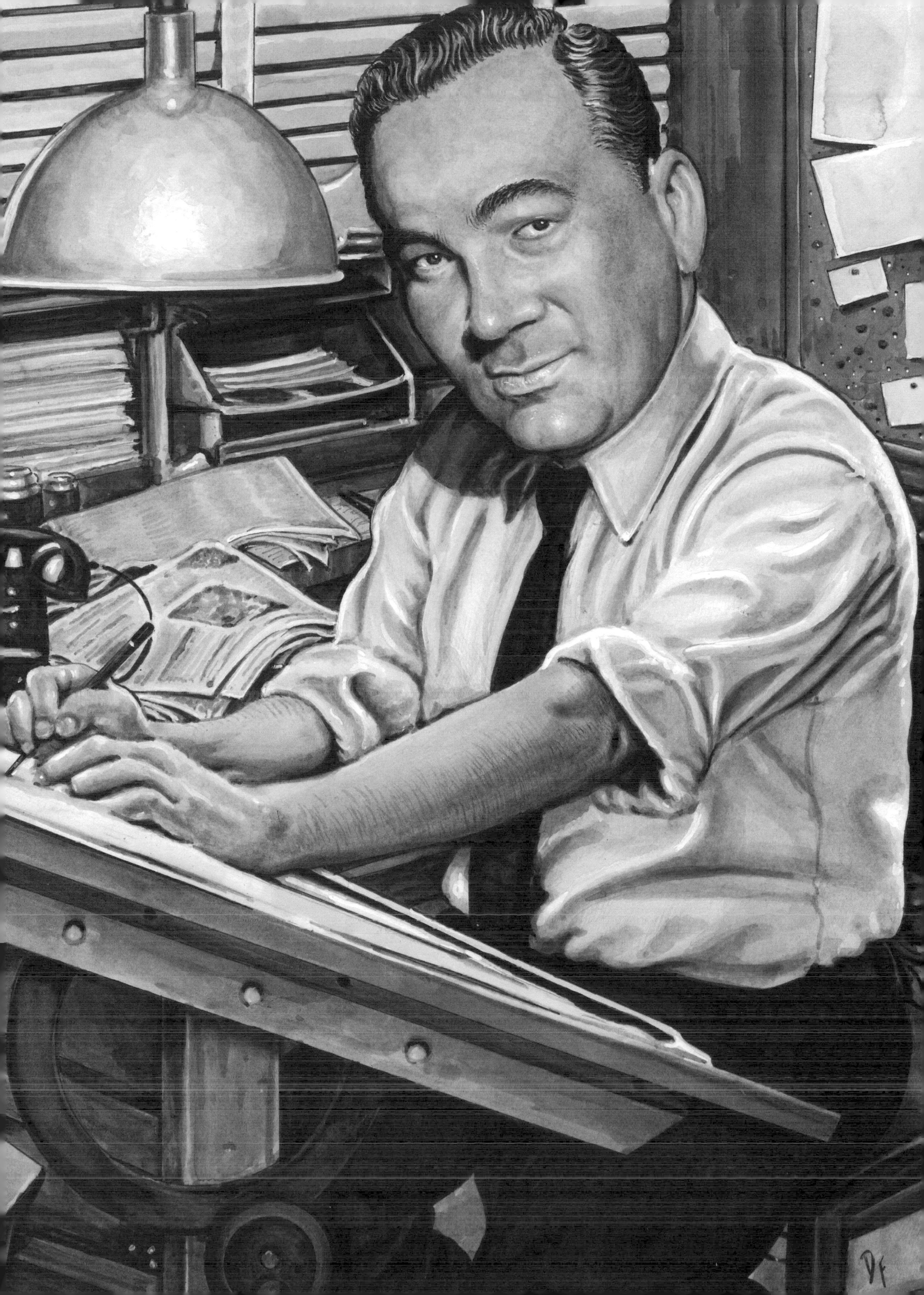
DF

ALFRED HARVEY

1913–1994

plate
41

Alfred Harvey (born Alfred Harvey Wernikoff), the publisher of iconic titles for young readers known as Harvey Comics, entered the business in 1939, working as a managing editor for Fox Comics alongside Joe Simon and Jack Kirby. After a brief stint in the military, Harvey returned in 1940 with something he'd hoped would stand out among traditional comics, publishing an experimental novelty title, *Pocket Comics*, a hundred-page half-size booklet. Its smaller size ultimately kept it hidden behind the larger comics on the magazine racks, and it sold poorly. Returning to the traditional comic book format, Harvey took over the successful title *Speed Comics*, relaunching it with his superwoman character Black Cat. He expanded his titles to include *Black Cat Comics*, which, following popular comic book trends, evolved into *Black Cat Western* in 1949 and *Black Cat Mystery* in 1951 to capitalize on the horror trend.

Harvey's most successful comic thus far was *Sad Sack*, created by ex-Disney animator George Baker. The Sack had appeared in the US Army magazine *Yank* sans dialogue, and Harvey recognized its potential as a comic book, launching it in 1949 with Baker drawing the covers and other artists handling the interior stories. The *Sad Sack* comic and its spin-offs lasted for decades. After horror comics disappeared from the landscape in the midfifties, Harvey, like his competition Dell Comics, focused on family-friendly titles. He acquired the rights to Famous Studios' *Noveltoons*, originally released through Paramount Pictures starting in the midforties. The *Noveltoons* characters included the already famous animated cartoon star Casper the Friendly Ghost as well as (Playful) Little Audrey. Harvey World Famous Comics soon added original Harvey characters including Baby Huey, Little Dot, Little Lotta, Spooky, Wendy, Richie Rich, and many other beloved childhood favorites.

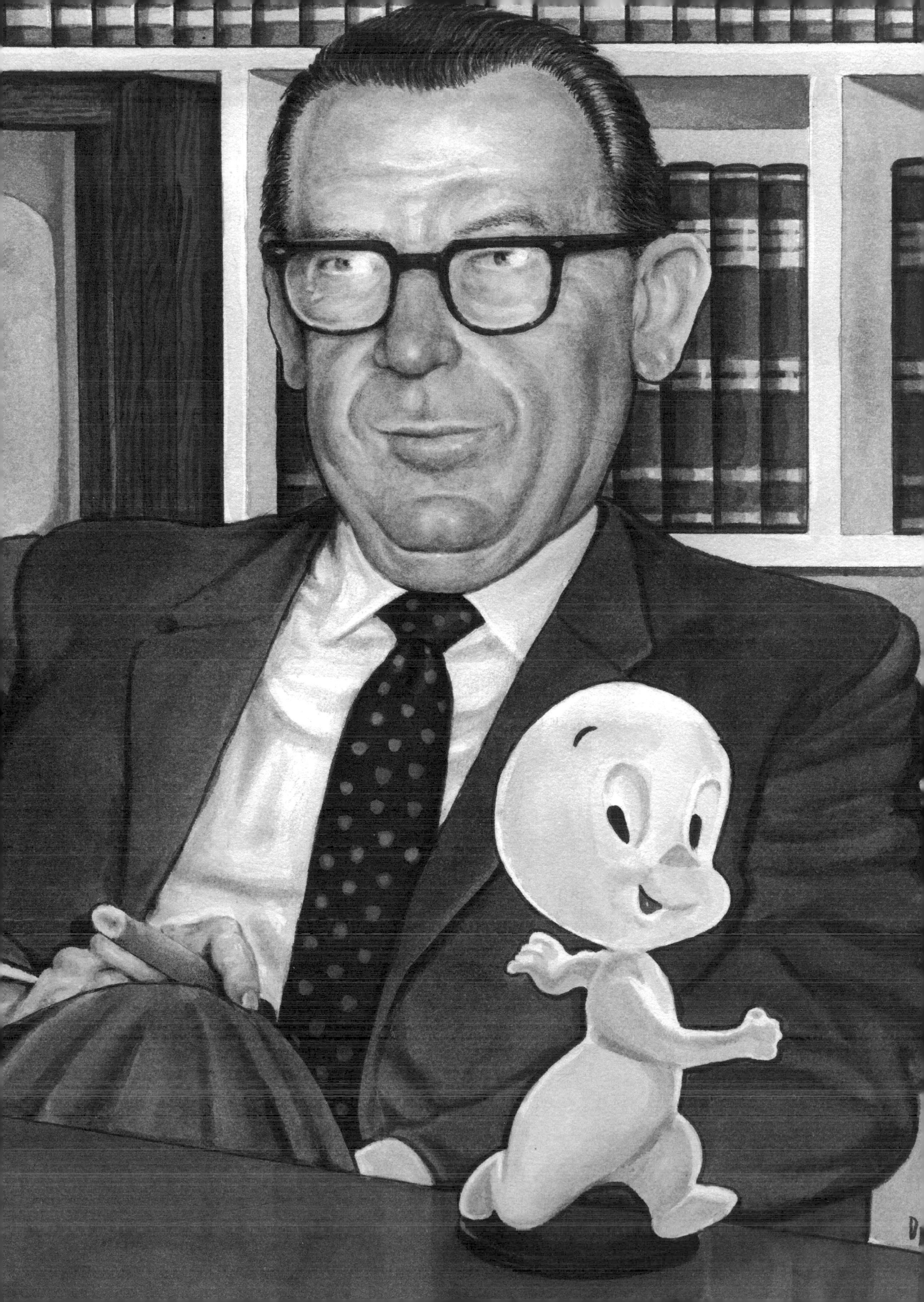

GEORGE CARLSON

1887–1962

plate
42

George Leonard Carlson enjoyed a long and prolific career as an art instructor, cartoonist, and commercial artist, illustrating classic children's books, magazine covers, political cartoons, gag cartoons, riddles, games, advertisements, several how-to books on cartooning, and perhaps most famously, the original book jacket for Margaret Mitchell's 1936 novel *Gone with the Wind*. Carlson was a one-man artistic factory and created so much varied work in his amazing career that sometimes it's hard to imagine it all stemmed from this one modest-looking man. Today Carlson is most celebrated for his visually staggering and unparalleled contemporary short fables "Jingle Jangle Tales," which were included in forty-two issues of Eastern Color's *Jingle Jangle Comics*, an anthology title of funny animal stories and fairy tales for small children, from 1942 to 1949. In his book *Art Out of Time*, Dan Nadel summed up George Carlson's joyous and absurd comic book work: "Carlson's stories blend slang, surrealism, theatricality, and narrative with a drawing style touched by more than a little bit of art deco."

Jingle Jangle Comics was not an outstanding success, and sadly Carlson's comic book work went for the most part unnoticed, buried between lesser artists' and former animators' uninspired funny animal stories, and he soon left comics for good to concentrate on his first love, children's books. His fun, unique, and distinctive artwork is only now being rediscovered and celebrated, and he's being compared to the likes of cartooning legends George Herriman, Milt Gross, Bill Holman, and Jack Cole.

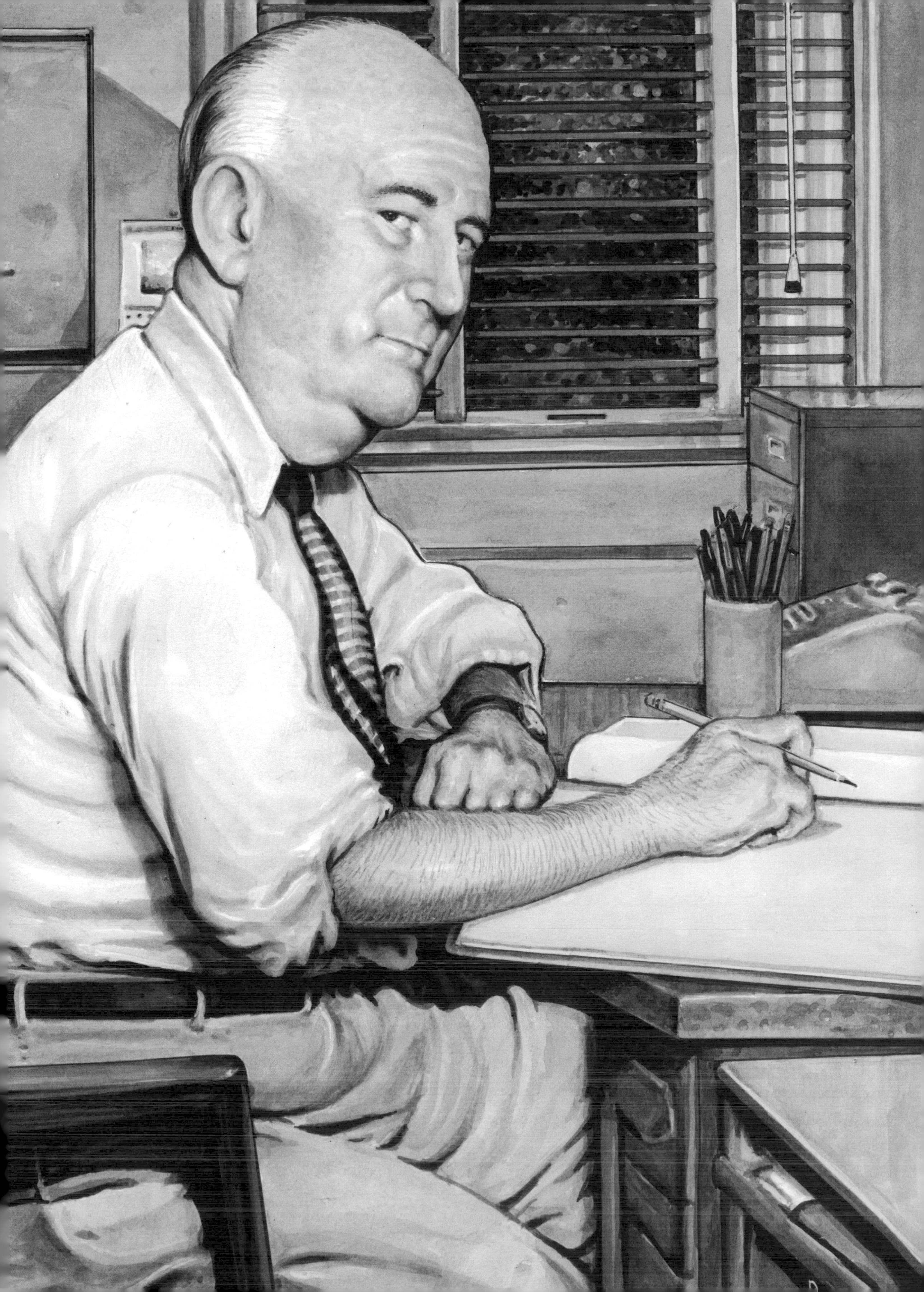

WALT KELLY

1913–1973

plate

43

Walter "Walt" Kelly Jr. worked as an animator, storyboard artist, and gagman at the Walt Disney studio until 1941, when he quit during the animators' strike. He adapted several Disney films, including *Pinocchio* and *The Three Caballeros*, into comic books for Dell Comics, leading to his new career as a comics artist. Kelly drew a series of charming comics based on Mother Goose fairy tales and nursery rhymes, before creating an early, crude, unrecognizable version of his most famous character, the possum Pogo, who first appeared in Dell's *Animal Comics* in 1942. Kelly was also asked to draw Dell's more realistic *Our Gang* comic book, based on the popular film shorts, and he subtly attempted to make changes to the characters not seen in the films, including shortening the black rascal Buckwheat's name to "Bucky" and playing down his stereotypical comic relief, giving him more maturity and dignity. Kelly continued working on the *Pogo* comic book as well as the *Our Gang* comic (even after the film series was canceled) throughout the forties, before dedicating his career to his hugely popular *Pogo* comic strip, a political satire that features anthropomorphic animal characters who inhabit the Okefenokee Swamp. *Pogo* was syndicated to newspapers for twenty-six years, and Kelly acquired the copyright and ownership of his strip, which was rare at the time, making him rich. Kelly became a celebrity, even appearing in magazine advertisements for fountain pens and concrete.

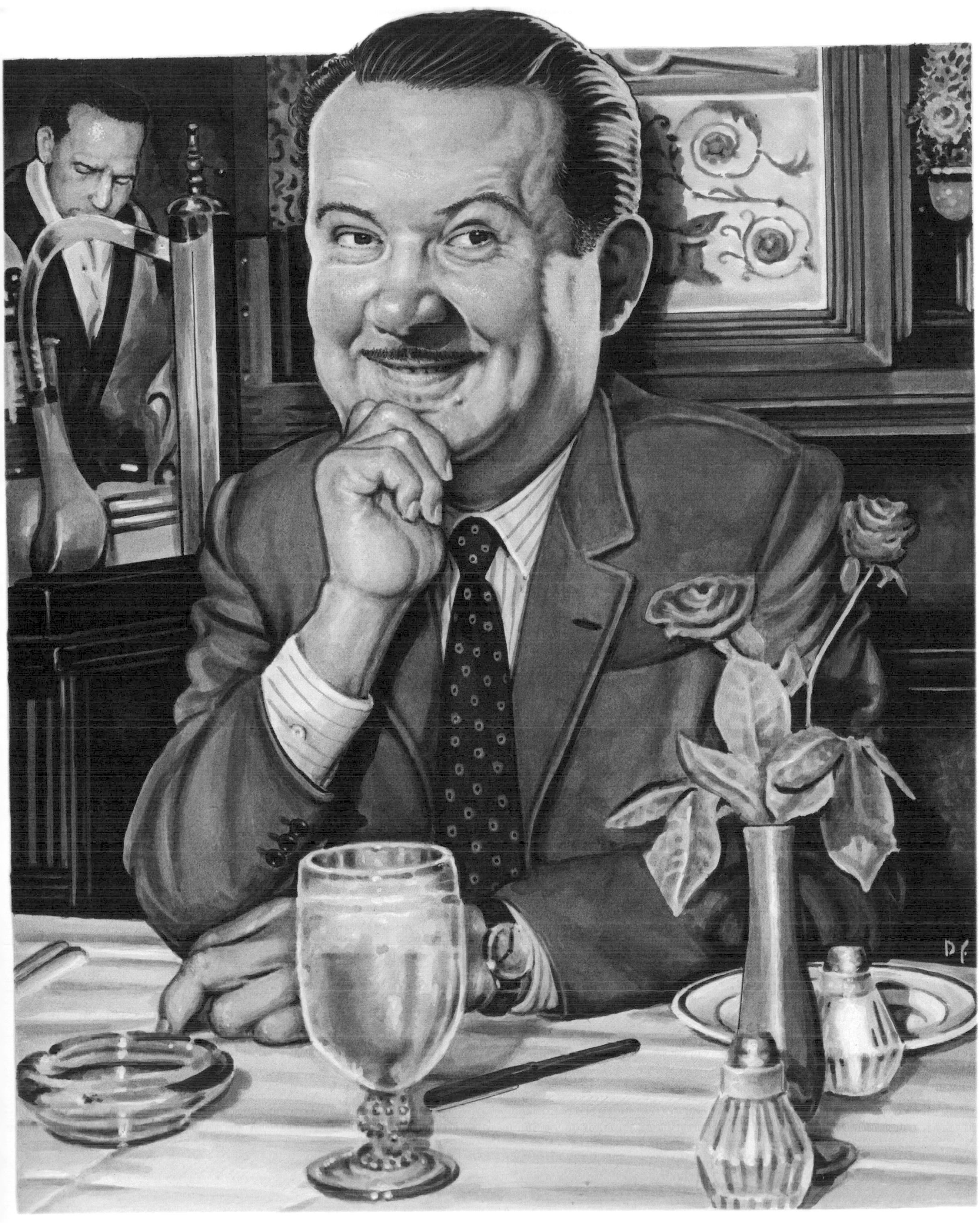
DF.

CARL BARKS

1901–2000

plate
44

Carl Barks, whose cartoon adventures of Donald Duck were published anonymously for decades, was known as "The Duck Man" and "The Good Duck Artist." Barks drew the Donald Duck stories for the front of *Walt Disney's Comics and Stories*, the most popular post–World War II comic book being published. Early on Barks worked odd jobs and drew cartoons for magazines, then became an editor of a spicy humor magazine. In 1935 Barks was hired as a full-time writer at the Disney film studios, but left in 1942 to become a full-time artist for Disney's comic book line, which included the bimonthly *Donald Duck*. Barks's duck stories stood out because of the deft flair he had for mixing the well-established Disney characters with unusually precise, realistic settings, whether high adventure or domestic comedies, not seen in other funny animal comics before. His stories also often exhibited a droll, dark, humanistic irony. Barks's Donald Duck stories featured a cast of eccentric, memorable, and colorful characters, including Donald's three nephews, the Beagle Boys, Gladstone Gander, and Donald's uncle Scrooge McDuck, the wealthiest duck in the world. Barks drew every issue of the quarterly adventures of the miserly duck. In his later years Carl Barks would re-create his beloved ducks in large oil paintings, some of which now fetch hundreds of thousands of dollars.

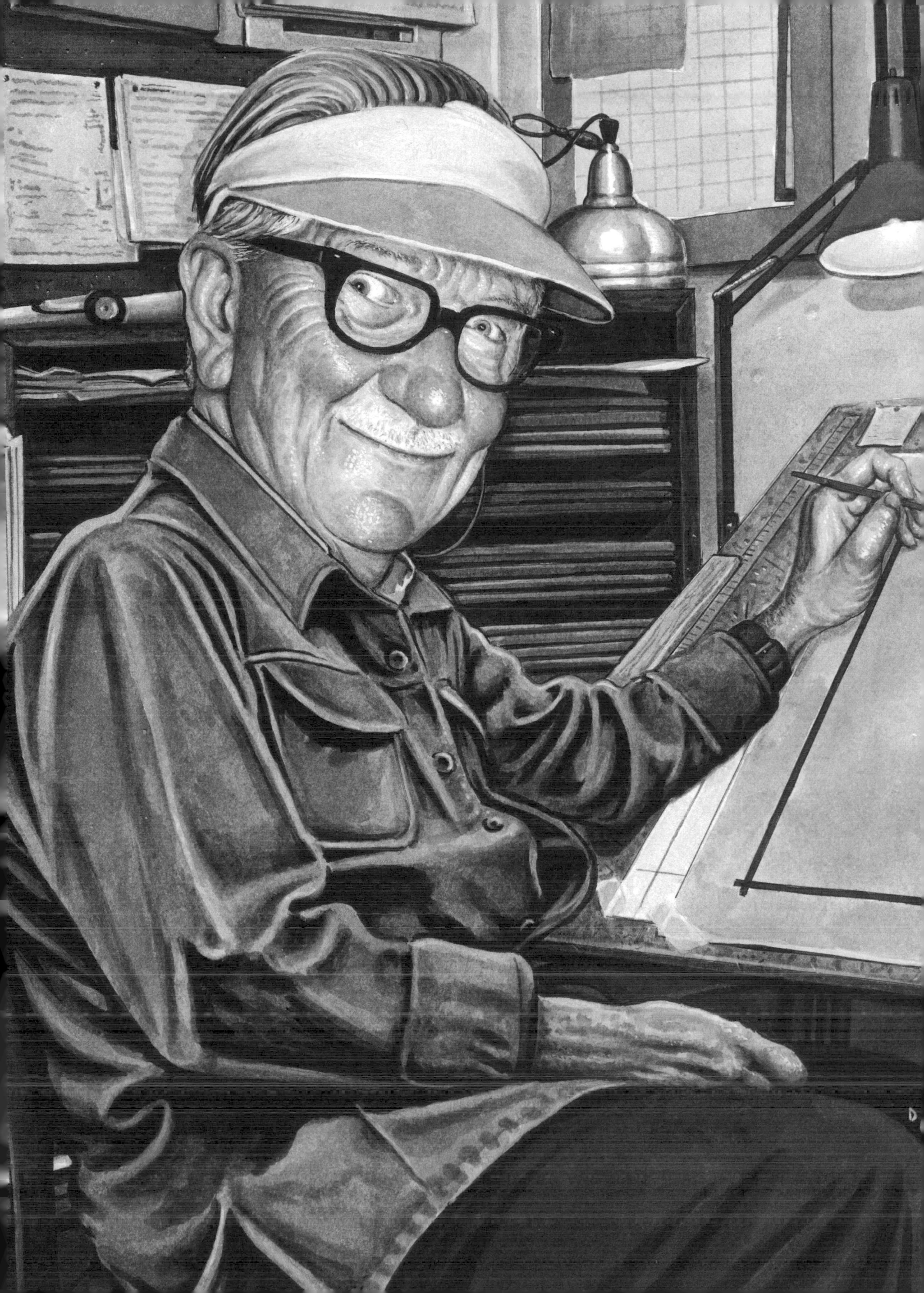

JOHN STANLEY

1914–1993

plate
45

John Stanley began his career in the early thirties working for the Max Fleisher animation studio as an opaquer and inbetweener, then drew for *Mickey Mouse Magazine* and also helped create merchandise for Disney. In the early 1940s Stanley began freelancing for Western Publishing (Dell), drawing their licensed characters Bugs Bunny, Raggedy Ann and Andy, Woody Woodpecker, and Andy Panda for editor Oskar LeBeck. In 1945 LeBeck asked Stanley to turn the single-panel-gag-cartoon character Little Lulu, who had been created by "Marge" for the *Saturday Evening Post* in the 1930s, into a comic book series. Stanley became the guiding spirit behind the *Little Lulu* comic book, initially drawing and writing several one-shots until 1948, when it became a regular series. Stanley expanded the cast of characters to include an entire neighborhood of children, including Tubby, Iggy, Alvin, and Lulu's friend Annie. Stanley, uninhibited by the condescension seen in other comics featuring children up until then, concentrated on the actual mannerisms, vocal patterns, and slang of children, showing a real appreciation for how they think and speak. By the fifties Stanley (usually uncredited) laid out the art, plotted the stories, and wrote the dialogue for *Little Lulu*, with the finished art (inking and coloring) handled by Irving Tripp and Charles Hedinger. The series ended in 1959, and Stanley began writing *Nancy and Sluggo* comics for Dell and continued working on other humorous titles into the sixties, most notably those featuring his own character, Melvin Monster.

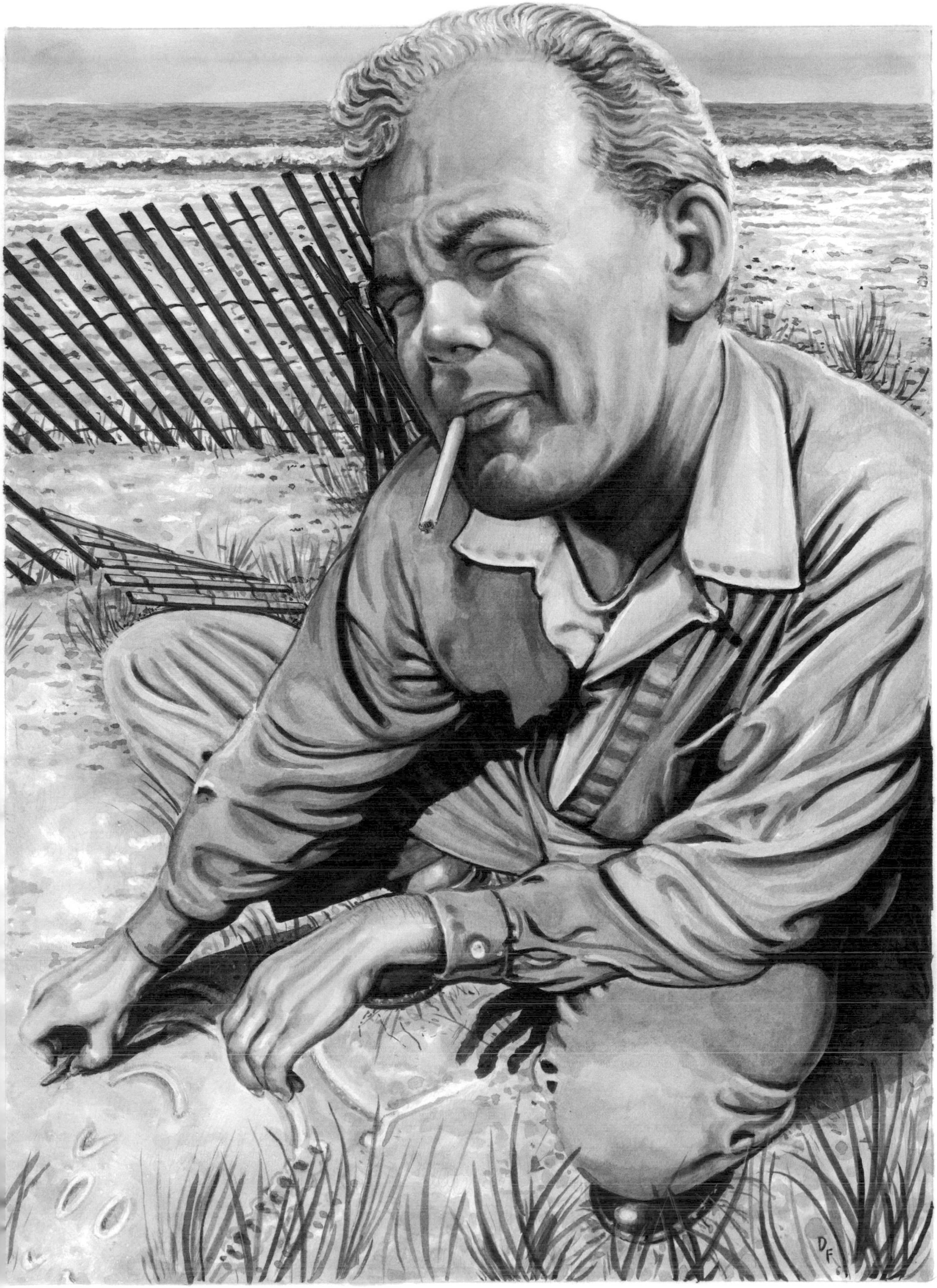

WOODY GELMAN

1915–1978

plate
46

Woodrow "Woody" Gelman began his career in the thirties as an animator, an opaquer, an inbetweener, and a scripter, moving from Brooklyn to Miami to work for Paramount Pictures. Later he worked for Paramount's animation division Famous Studios, where he worked on *Popeye the Sailor*, the feature film *Gulliver's Travels*, *Superman*, and *Little Lulu*. Gelman made an attempt to unionize the animators and was promptly fired. He returned to New York in 1944 and began writing and drawing funny animal comics for DC, including *The Dodo and the Frog* and *Nutsy Squirrel*, both of which were featured in *Funny Stuff* and *Comic Cavalcade*. Gelman, along with his friend and former coanimator Ben Solomon, created Popsicle Pete, who appeared in ads and packages for Popsicle ice pops for decades. Popsicle Pete caught the eye of the president of the Topps Company, Arthur Shorin, who hired Gelman and Solomon to work for him full-time in Brooklyn. Gelman worked as an editor and writer for Topps, and Solomon became its art director. Gelman soon became the head of the new product development department, where he developed the Bazooka Joe mini-comics (drawn by Wesley Morse) and had his hand in many successful innovations for trading cards and other products.

In 1953 Gelman helped design Topps' first baseball cards, and throughout his twenty-five years with the company, he helped develop several other trading-card series, including Mars Attacks (featuring the work of former pulp cover artist Norman Saunders), Funny Valentines (featuring art by a young Robert Crumb), the Civil War, beautifully painted Batman cards by Saunders, Ugly Stickers, and most notably Wacky Packs, which employed concepts and designs by future underground cartoonists Art Spiegelman, Jay Lynch, and Bill Griffith, and featured finished art by Saunders. Gelman was also a longtime fan and collector of vintage paper ephemera, including dime novels and early comic strips and comic books, and he helped Topps recruit several of the comics artists he had long admired, including former EC artists Wally Wood, Jack Davis, and Basil Wolverton. He also launched his own imprint in 1964, Nostalgia Press, with a Charlie Chaplin photo tribute book. Soon thereafter he pioneered the reprinting of vintage comic strips and comic books in large quality hardcovers, starting with Alex Raymond's *Flash Gordon* and an oversized collection of full-color EC horror comics, which would help revive a huge interest in EC in the seventies.

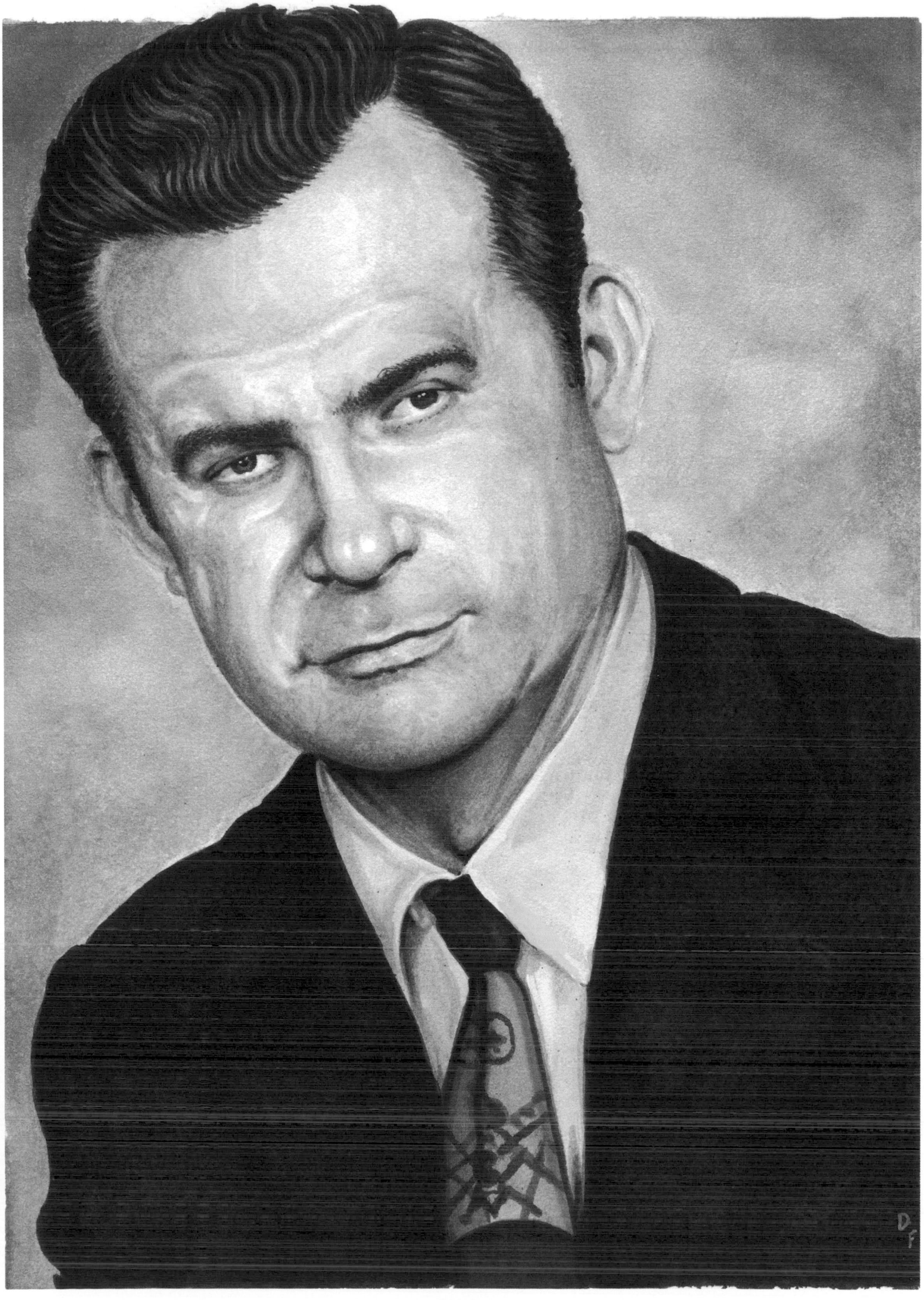
DF

OTTO MESSMER

1892–1983

plate **47**

Winsor McCay's early animated films inspired Otto James Messmer to create comic strips at a young age and to eventually work as an animator. In 1919 animator Pat Sullivan hired Messmer to work in his studio, where Messmer was asked to create a black cat character, the prototype of Felix the Cat. Felix was the first cartoon character (pre–Mickey Mouse) created exclusively for silent motion pictures, the first to become beloved and world famous, and the first to become licensed and mass merchandised, earning millions in royalties for studio head Sullivan, who took full credit for creating the character and received the only on-screen credit. The debate about who actually created the character continued for decades. Felix starred in over one hundred fifty cartoons until 1931, when sound films displaced silents and his star began to fade. Sullivan died in 1933, and Messmer never challenged Sullivan's claim that he invented Felix. Messmer also wrote and drew the *Felix the Cat* newspaper strip, which faded in popularity as the animated cartoons ended. Beginning in the 1940s he oversaw the art and writing for the popular, charming, and imaginative *Felix the Cat* comic books. He continued the comic book adventures of Felix into the fifties for various publishers, including Dell, Toby Press, and Harvey. In the early sixties Felix starred in his own popular television series, and Messmer was finally credited as the true creator of Felix the Cat.

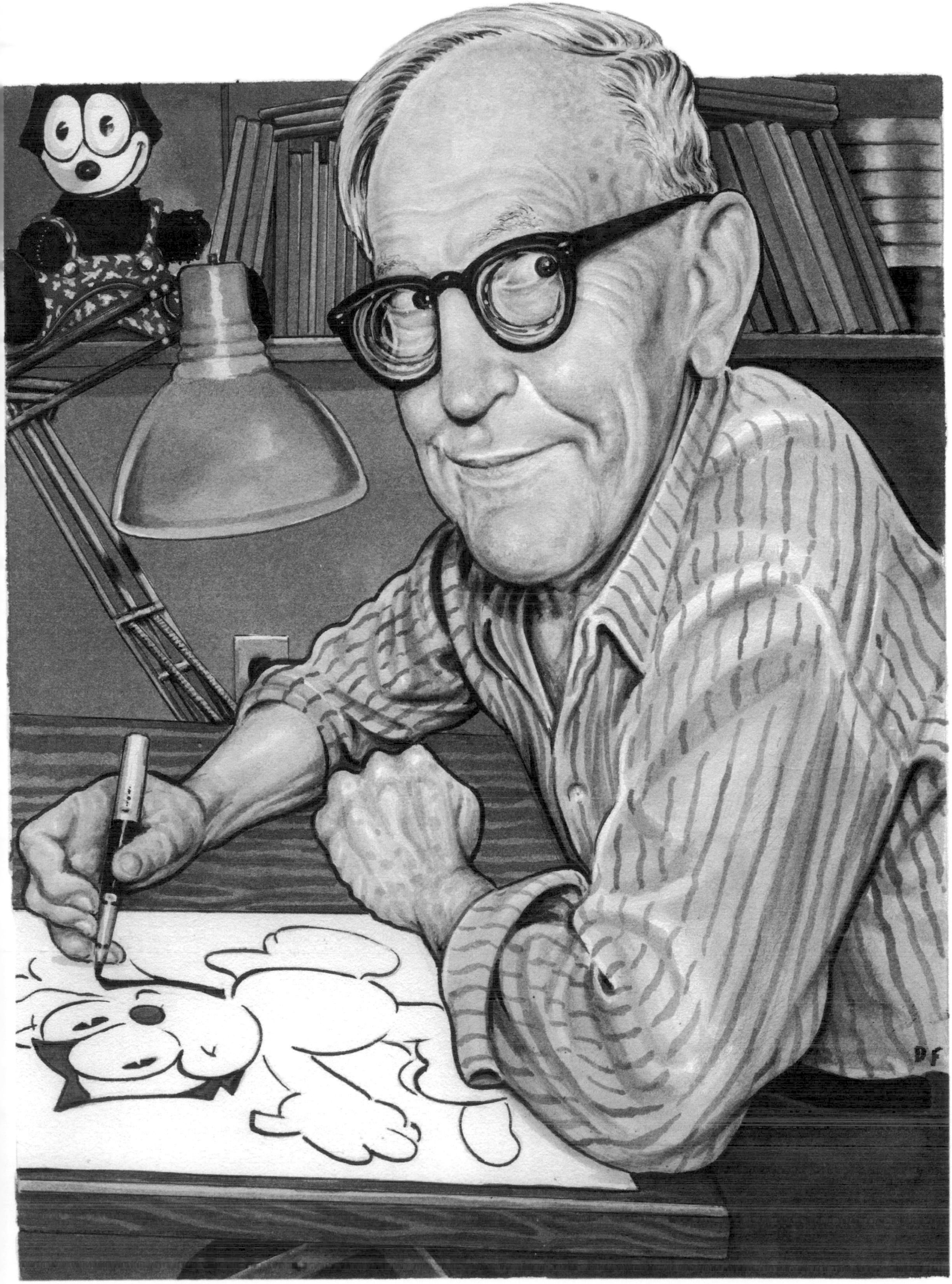

GIL KANE

1926–2000

plate
48

Gil Kane (born Eli Katz) was a venerable comic book artist whose career spanned six decades. He created artwork for just about every major comics company and updated the iconic superheroes Green Lantern and the Atom, infusing them with a new vibrancy. The self-taught Kane entered comics in the late thirties, working as a young teenager for MLJ, the future publisher of *Archie Comics*. He was soon creating artwork for Timely Comics, DC Comics, and many other comics publishers. Kane eventually created tens of thousands of pages of superhero comics, continuously elevating the form with his unique drawing abilities and his energetic page compositions.

During the Silver Age of comics in the 1960s, Kane created updated interpretations of the Hulk, Captain Marvel, and Spider-Man. He was instrumental in updating the archaic Comics Code by creating storylines for *The Amazing Spider-Man* at the directive of the US Department of Health, Education and Welfare that for the first time depicted drug abuse in mainstream comics. In 1968 Kane pioneered an early graphic novel prototype, *His Name Is . . . Savage!*, and he followed it up three years later with what is now generally considered to be the first graphic novel, the science fiction / sword and sorcery tale *Blackmark*. The tall, dapper, silver-haired Kane was a familiar figure at comic book conventions later on in his life, and was always an articulate, witty, and thoughtful spokesman for the field he chose and loved.

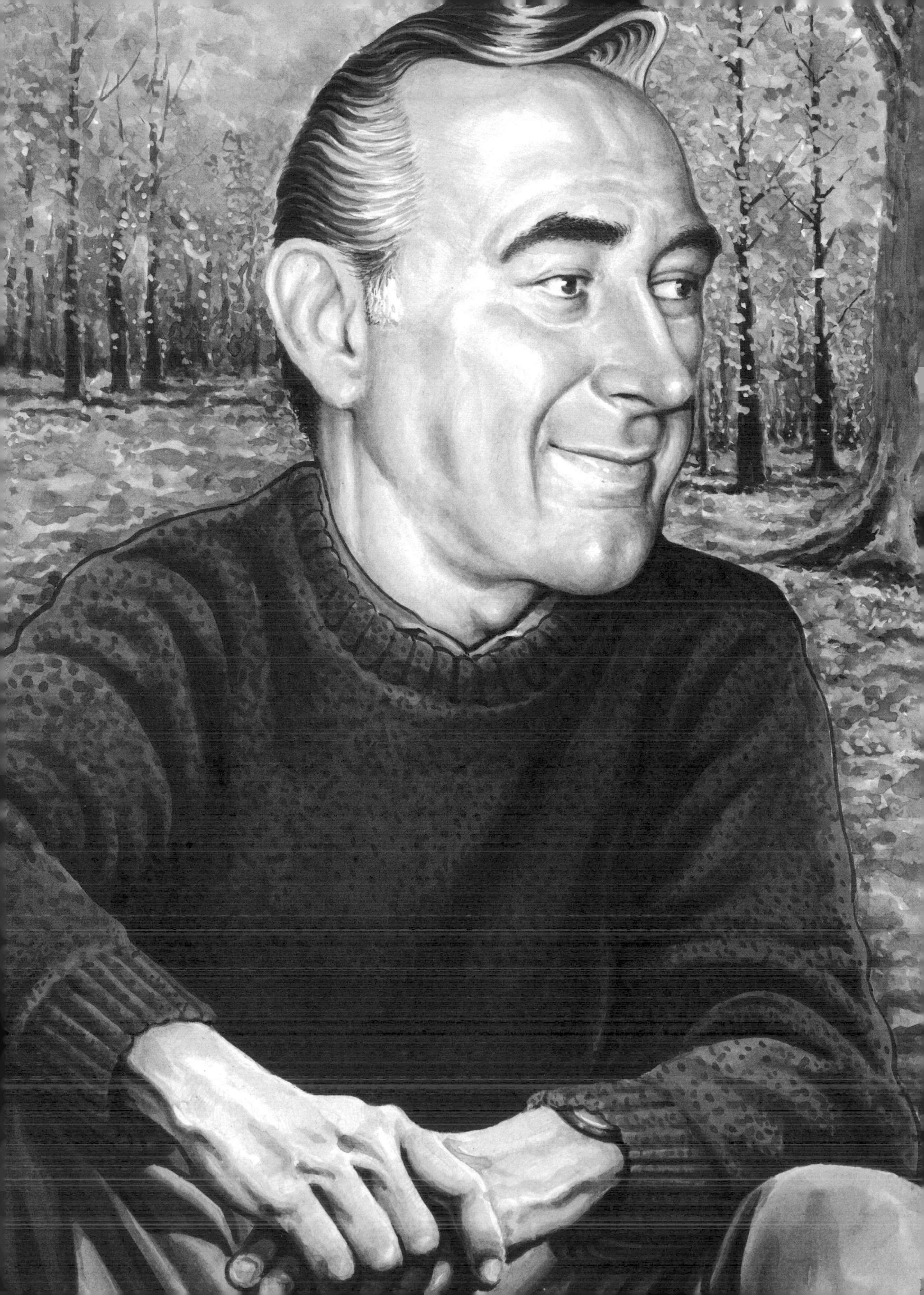

GARDNER FOX

1911–1986

plate
49

Gardner Francis Cooper Fox wrote more than four thousand comic book stories, making him probably the most prodigious *and* imaginative superhero comics writer in history. Fox began his comics career by writing stories for the early issues of National's *Detective Comics*, and by issue #33, he was helping to write and develop Bill Finger and Bob Kane's newly created character Batman, contributing to his evolution by creating Batman's utility belt and introducing Bruce Wayne's parents, Thomas and Martha Wayne. Fox helped create and wrote stories about dozens of iconic Golden Age comic characters, including The Flash, Sandman, Hawkman, and the Justice Society of America, which in the midfifties he'd turn into the *Justice League* of America for DC, while also revamping many of his earlier characters. Fox also freelanced for many other comics publishers, including Timely and EC, effortlessly writing for every genre, be it superheroes, westerns, science fiction, or horror. Fox was also a novelist and short story author, writing under many male and female pseudonyms.

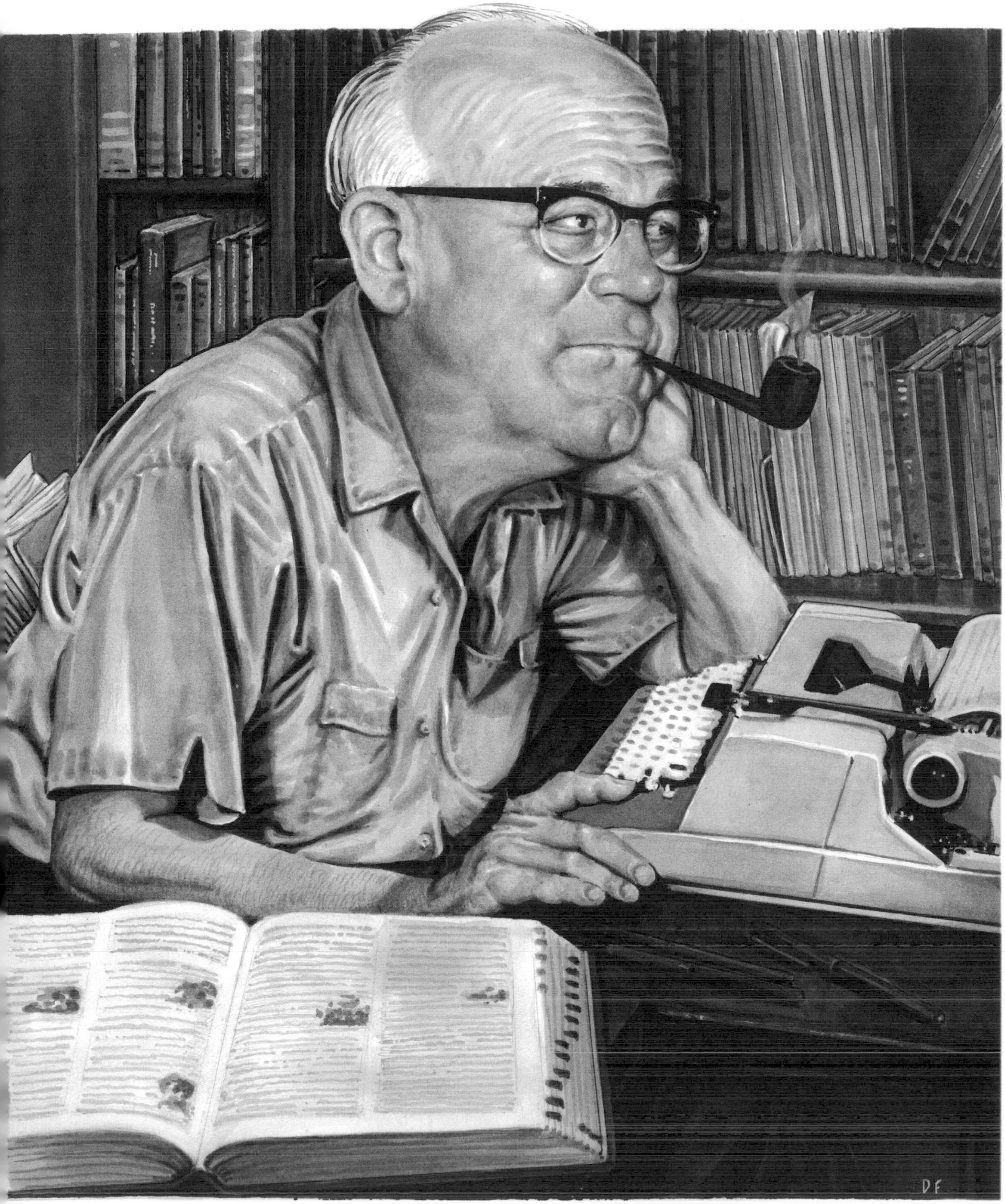
DF

BOODY ROGERS

1904–1996

plate

Gordon G. "Boody" Rogers of Oklahoma began drawing for syndicated newspaper comics in the 1920s. In the thirties he assisted Zack Mosely on his *Smilin' Jack* syndicated comic. Rogers's most famous character, Sparky Watts, debuted in 1940 in forty newspapers. Sparky Watts made his first comic book appearance in *Big Shot* #14 in 1941 and was featured in his own comic the following year. Rogers took time off to serve in World War II, later writing about his experiences in his autobiography *Homeless Bound*. He returned to work as a syndicated cartoonist and continued drawing for *Big Shot* and his screwball, sci-fi take on superheroes, the *Sparky Watts* comic, as well as for *Babe, Darling of the Hills*, which starred his bizarre, beautiful, buxom version of Li'l Abner. Rogers's work was vibrant and manic, and had a breathtaking screwball lunacy never before seen in mainstream comics. He drew and wrote some of the funniest, strangest, and most feverishly surreal comics ever inflicted on unsuspecting comics readers. In 1949 Rogers also attempted a short-lived *Archie*-like teenage comic, *Dudley*, which only lasted three issues. He soon retired from comics altogether, and in 1952 he moved to Phoenix, Arizona, to open an art supply store.

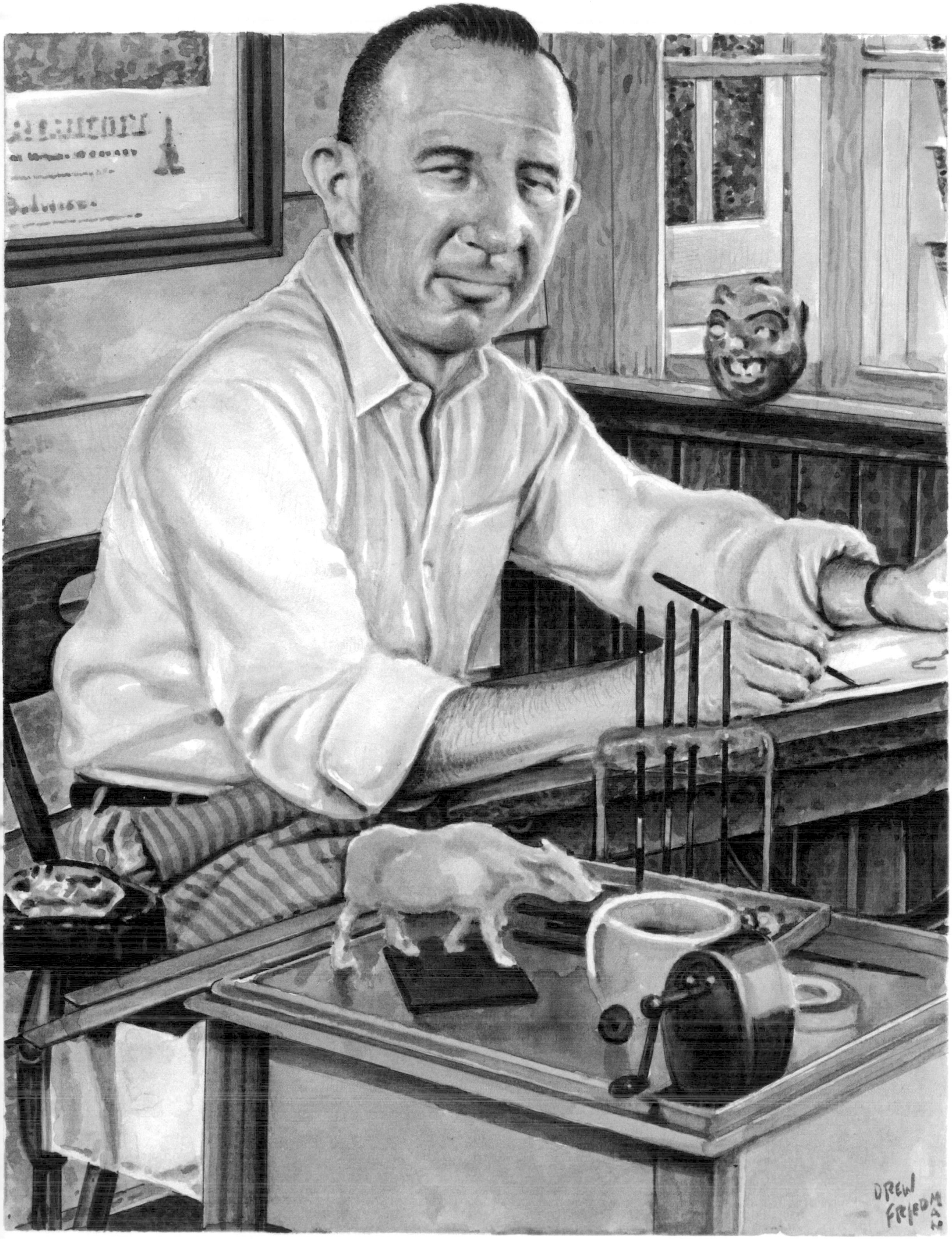
DREW FRIEDMAN

MATT BAKER

1921–1959

plate
51

Clarence Matthew "Matt" Baker is acknowledged as the first and most success-ful African American artist to work in mainstream comic books. Baker attend-ed Cooper Union, and by the early forties he was drawing comic book stories at the Jerry Iger (sweat) shop after Will Eisner had split off from Iger. The standard practice in those days was for artists working in the comics shops to use various pseudonyms to give the impression that the shop had more artists in its employ than it actually did. Baker's first confirmed work was penciling *Sheena, Queen of the Jungle* for *Jumbo Comics* #69 in 1944. The extremely handsome Baker soon established himself as the supreme "good girl" pinup artist, drawing gorgeous, buxom (white) women in skimpy, sexy costumes, as well as handsome, dash-ing, and elegant (white) men. In 1947 Baker was asked to redesign the popular *Phantom Lady*. He continued freelancing for various publishers in his adaptable, nimble style into the fifties, specializing in stylized romance comics for St. John Publications, until his tragic death by heart attack at age thirty-eight. Today Baker is hailed as the pioneering first African American comic book artist and a master of the art of glamour.

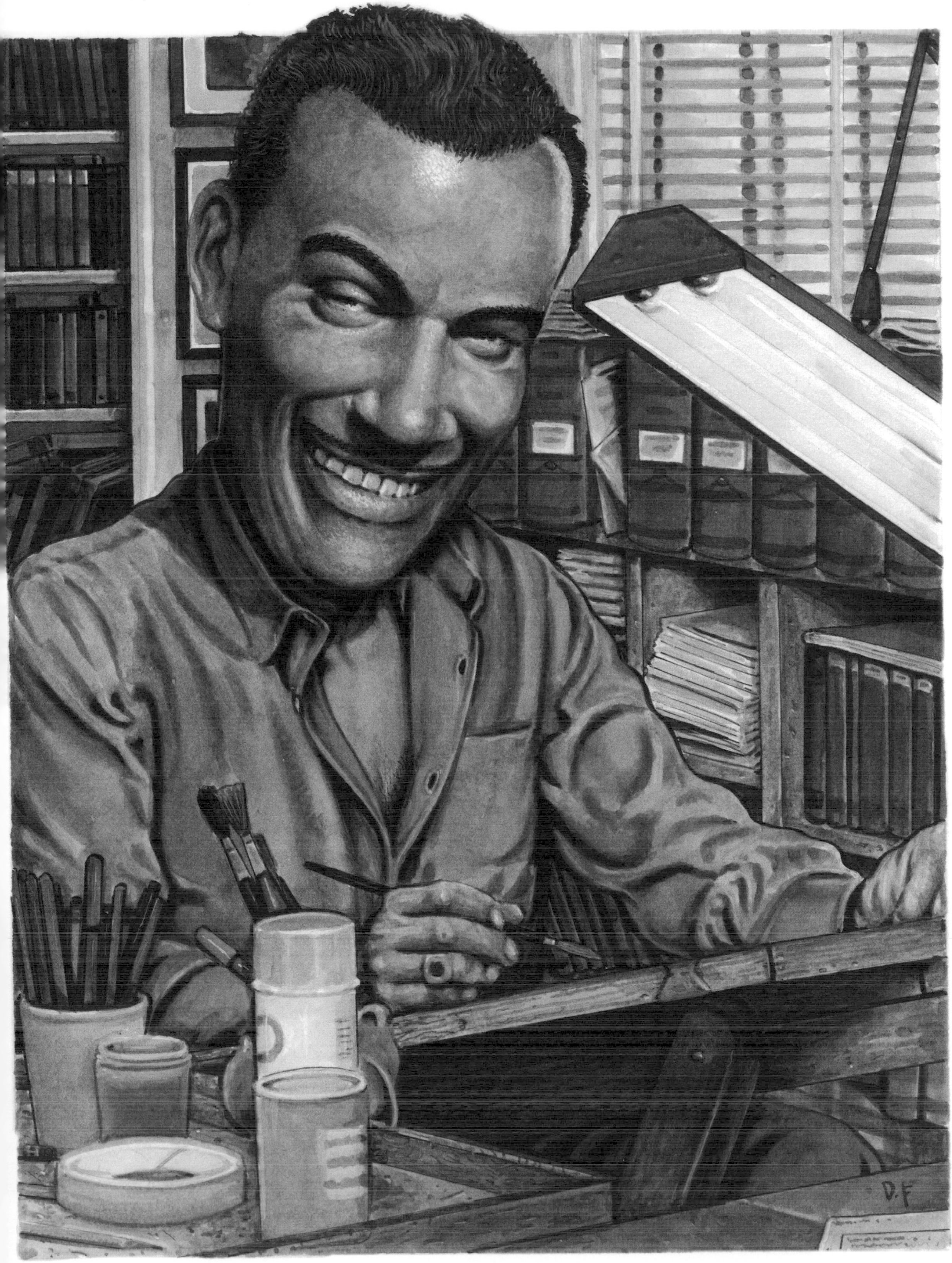
D.F

LILY RENÉE

b. 1925

plate
52

Lily Renée Wilheim was the first woman to work as a full-time comic book artist during the Golden Age of comics. Wilheim was born into a well-to-do Viennese Jewish family, but when the *Anschluss* happened in 1938 and the majority of Austrians welcomed the Nazis with open arms, her parents arranged to send their fourteen-year-old daughter to the safety of England. After a few false starts she would eventually reconnect with her parents in New York, although several of her relatives died in concentration camps. The artistically inclined Wilheim began taking classes at the Art Students League. Her mother showed her a newspaper ad placed by Fiction House, known for publishing *Sheena, Queen of the Jungle*, seeking new comic book artists, as many of its regular artists had left to serve in the war. Wilheim reluctantly answered the ad and got the job, at first erasing other artists' stray pencil lines and learning the ropes of drawing for comic books. Eventually she was penciling her own work. Soon (signing her work "L. Renee," keeping it unknown to readers that she was actually a woman) she was drawing the adventures of the female pilot Jane Martin and the beautiful Nazi-fighting spy Señorita Rio, for *Flight Comics*. She began freelancing for several other comics publishers, primarily St. John Publications, where she teamed up with her first husband, artist Eric Peters, a fellow Viennese refugee who was twenty-two years her senior. Together they worked on the *Abbott & Costello* comic book, with Peters drawing Bud and Lou, and Renée drawing the sexy ladies. She also worked on the company's various romance titles. After a few years she divorced Peters and remarried. She left the world of comics and didn't tell her two children that she had drawn comics until fifty years later, when comics historian Trina Robbins tracked her down and the two of them cocreated a graphic novel, *Lily Renée, Escape Artist*, which chronicled her incredible life. She attended her first comic book convention in 2007.

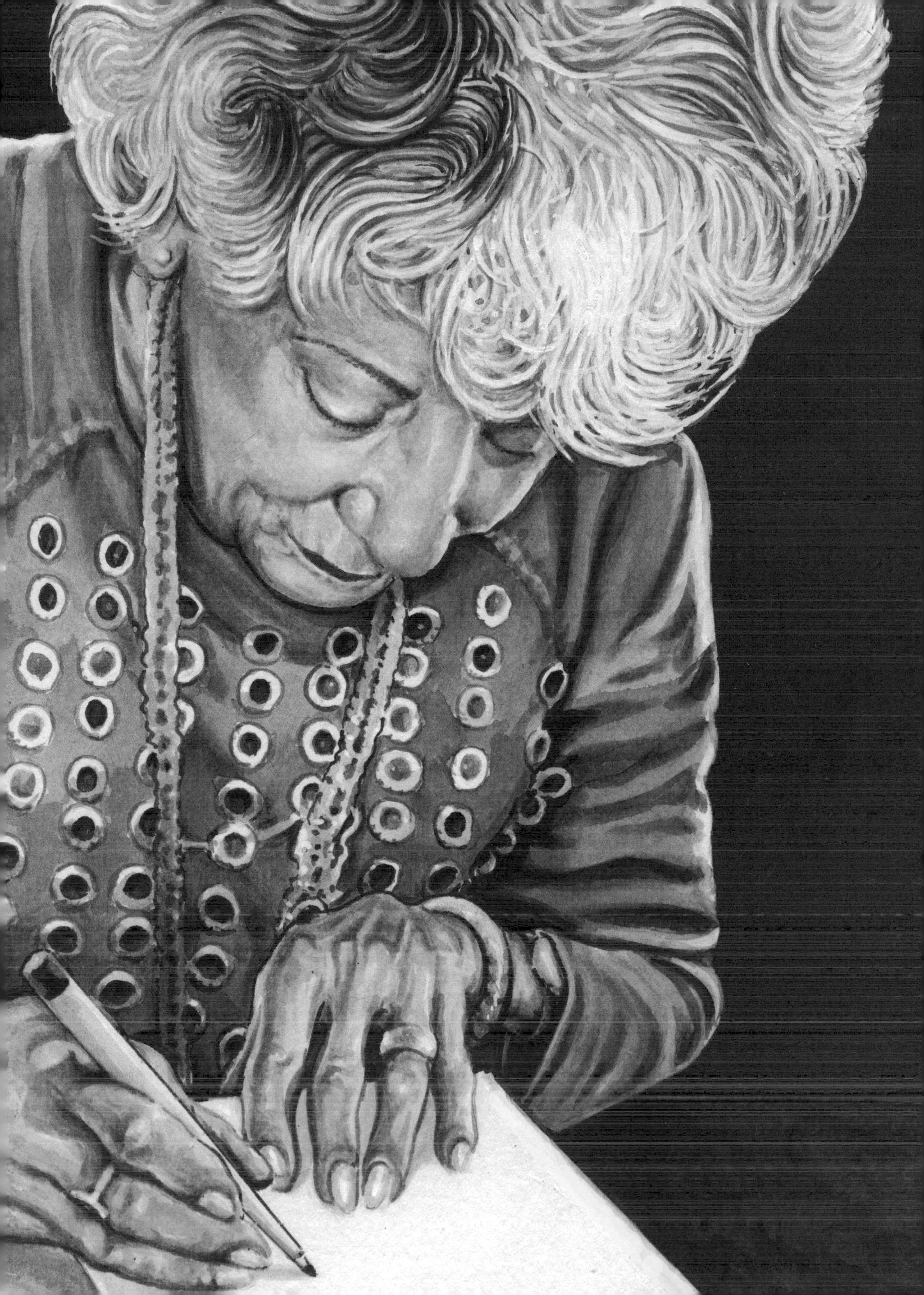

AL HOLLINGSWORTH

1928–2000

plate
53

Alvin Carl Hollingsworth, one of the first African American comic book artists, was born in Harlem and showed a talent for drawing and cartooning at a young age. When World War II broke out, many young comic book artists were called to duty, and an eager thirteen-year-old Hollingsworth (who had been a classmate of Joe Kubert at the High School of Music & Art) found work mainly drawing patriotic war and superhero comics for various publishers, including Fiction House, Fox, and Avon. His early work, drawn when he was a teenager, was crude, especially compared to other artists' output, but by the late forties it had matured, becoming more lively and dynamic, clearly influenced by several comics contemporaries, especially Jack Kirby and Joe Simon, whose studio he had worked in. Hollingsworth is credited by some as the artist on Fawcett's nonstereotypical *Negro Comics*, which certainly would have been apropos, but in those days artists were often uncredited or used pen names, so it can't be confirmed. He drew for many romance, jungle, crime, and horror titles until the midfifties, when comic book work all but dried up thanks to the senate hearings equating crime and horror comic books with delinquency. Hollingsworth switched gears and worked on newspaper comic strips, among them *Kandy* and *Scorchy Smith*. He also created sexy gag cartoons for various men's magazines at Martin Goodman's Magazine Management Company. Hollingsworth would eventually give up cartooning and comics to concentrate on fine art and on teaching at the High School of Art & Design and later at Hostos Community College.

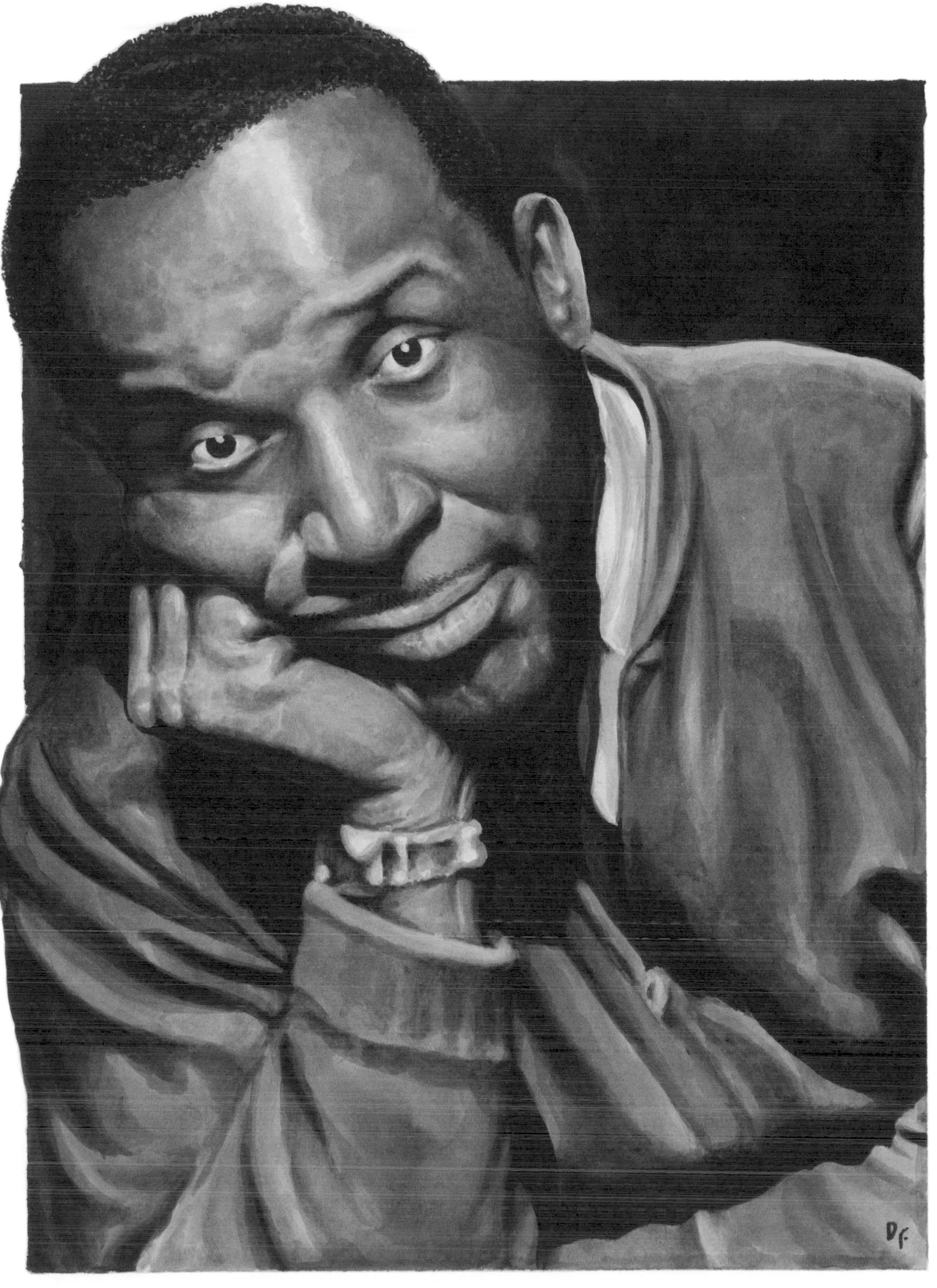

AL JAFFEE

b. 1921

plate
54

Abraham "Al" Jaffee is a legendary writer, artist, humorist, and cartoonist who, as of this writing, is still going strong. His *Mad* "Fold-In" created in 1964, has appeared in every new issue of *Mad* magazine except for one—some kind of record? His late-sixties series "Snappy Answers to Stupid Questions" hit a bull's-eye with *Mad* readers and helped to encourage generations of snarky kids and future stand-up comics and late-night hosts. Jaffee attended the High School of Music & Art, where he befriended fellow classmates and future collaborators Harvey Kurtzman, Will Elder, and Al Feldstein. He began his career as a comic book artist in 1941 at Martin Goodman's Timely Comics under editor Stan Lee and later edited humor and teen comics for Atlas Comics, including the popular *Patsy Walker.* Jaffee decided to go freelance in the midfifties, making his *Mad* debut then leaving with Harvey Kurtzman and Will Elder to create the short-lived *Trump.* Two thousand two hundred of his unique long and skinny *Tall Tales* ran in the Herald Tribune Syndicate from 1957 to 1963. He returned as a regular contributor to *Mad* in 1964, becoming one of the most essential and beloved of "the usual gang of idiots."

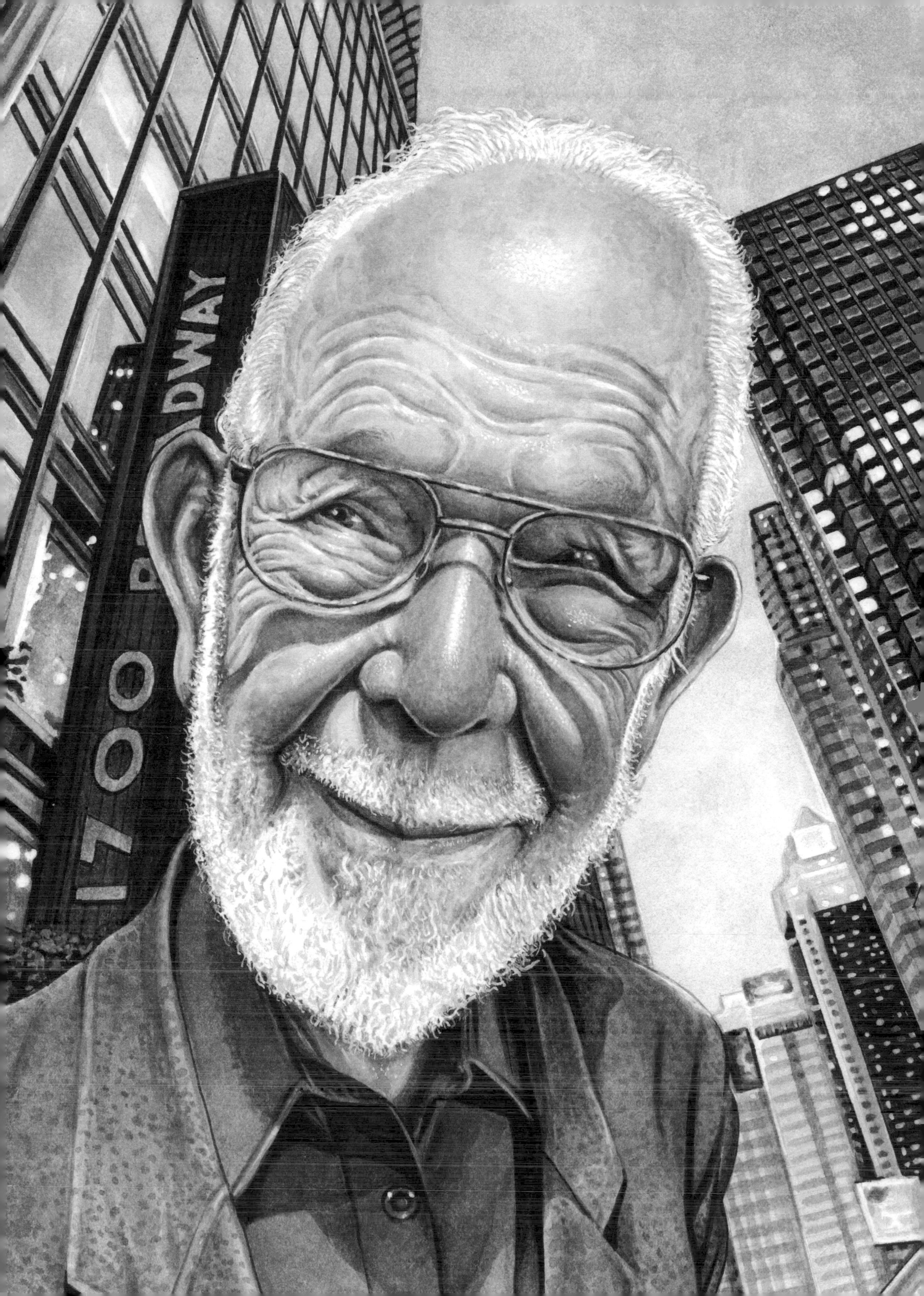
DWAY
1700

DAVE BERG

1920–2002

plate
55

Dave Berg was the artist and writer of the iconic *Mad* magazine feature "The Lighter Side of . . ." for four decades. Berg began his career in comics in 1940, assisting Will Eisner with *The Spirit*. Soon he was creating art for Quality, Dell, Fawcett, and finally Timely Comics under Stan Lee. After serving in the navy, Berg returned to freelancing for various comics publishers, now displaying more of a satiric edge in his work and drawing comics and covers for, among others, *Archie* and *Meet Merton*, as well as sexy "good girl" cartoons for novelty publications like *Humorama*. In 1952 EC's Harvey Kurtzman hired Berg to illustrate his story "Fire Mission" for *Two-Fisted Tales*. Kurtzman wasn't happy with the results though, feeling that Berg's humorous, lighthearted art, especially in the characters' faces, detracted from the drama and pathos of his story, and he didn't use him again at EC. He advised Berg to submit his work to *Mad* after it became a magazine, and under editor Al Feldstein, Berg began doing regular work for *Mad* in 1956. Five years later he created "The Lighter Side of . . ." which featured his whimsical barbs poking fun at benign omnibus topics, including men, women, young marrieds, grandparents, shopping, birthday parties, and summer camp. He later expanded his oeuvre to include subjects such as the generation gap, the "me" generation, God, and particularly himself, in the guise of his square-jawed pipe-smoking safari-jacketed moralizing everyman, Roger Kaputnik. "The Lighter Side of . . ." ran for forty years in *Mad*, humorously chronicling the ever-changing American scene.

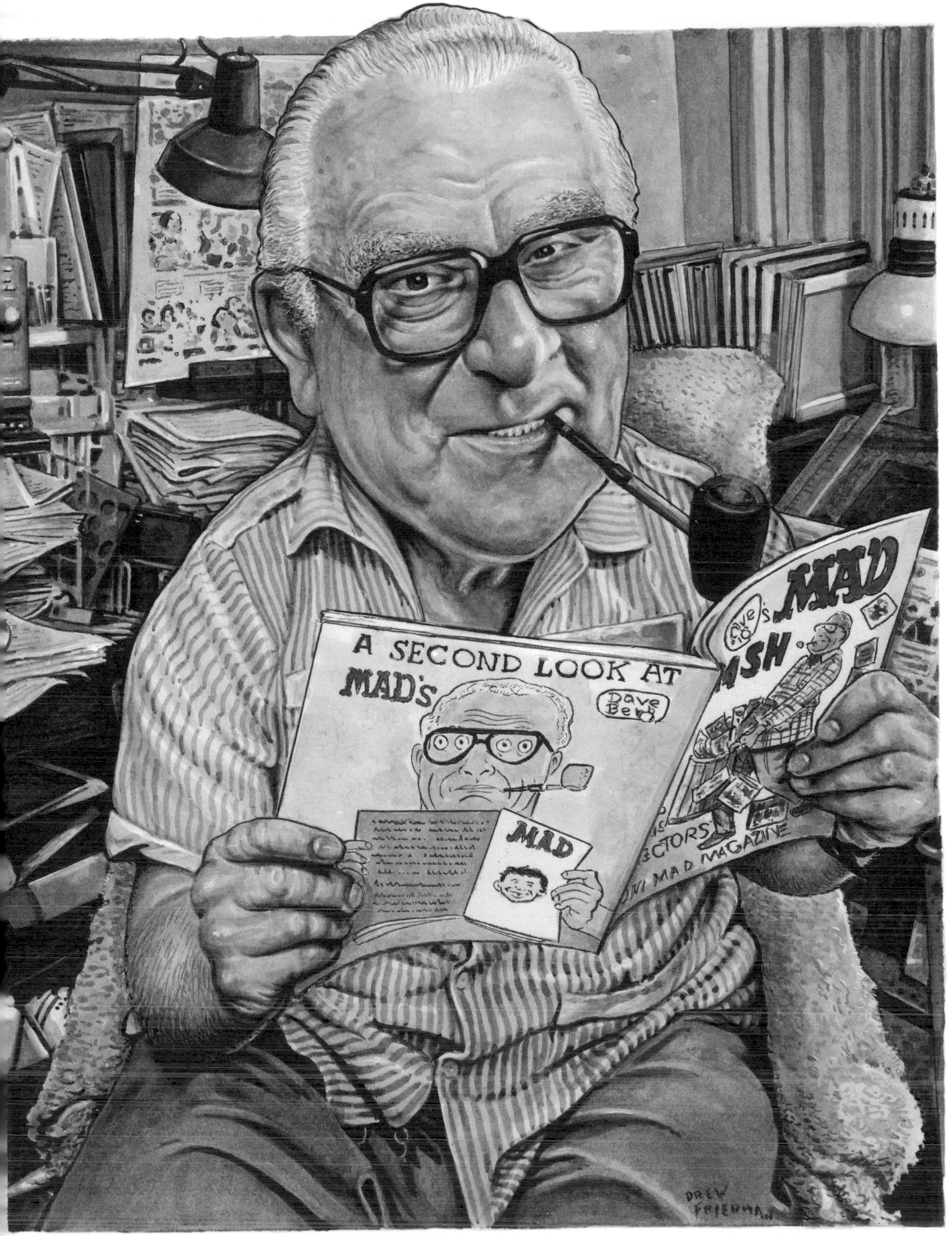
A SECOND LOOK AT
MAD's
Dave
MAD
MAD
MAD MAGAZINE
DREW FRIEDMAN

GRAHAM INGELS

1915–1991

plate
56

According to Bill Gaines, Graham Ingels was "Mr. Horror himself!" He signed his moody, visceral work for EC "Ghastly." His first published work appeared in pulps and science fiction comics in the 1940s, usually featuring sexy women in outer space who were somehow in the grips of space aliens. When he showed up at EC in 1948 looking for freelance work, he was first typecast in western titles, then romance, and finally crime. When EC introduced horror comics, it didn't take long for Bill Gaines and Al Feldstein to realize Ingels had a special appetite for their creepy stories and was the ideal choice to illustrate gothic tales featuring grotesque, cadaverous, shambling creatures. Soon they were tailoring their scripts specifically for Ingels's talents. Nobody before or since has depicted rotting, decaying, fetid corpses, let alone drooling hunchbacks and swamp-dwelling psychos, like the sensitive and shy Graham Ingels did. The saliva in his characters' horrified gaping mouths became Ingels's trademark. Ingels's work was featured in all three of EC's horror titles, and he became the lead artist on *The Haunt of Fear*, drawing all of its covers. Ingels also drew *The Haunt of Fear*'s hostess, the Old Witch—one of EC's three GhouLunatics. When EC went under in 1955, Ingels found little work in comics and eventually disappeared from sight, till it was revealed seventeen years later that he had moved to Lantana, Florida, to teach painting out of his home. He never acknowledged his horror comics work until shortly before his death, when he agreed to paint several commissioned oil paintings and several smaller studies of the Old Witch.

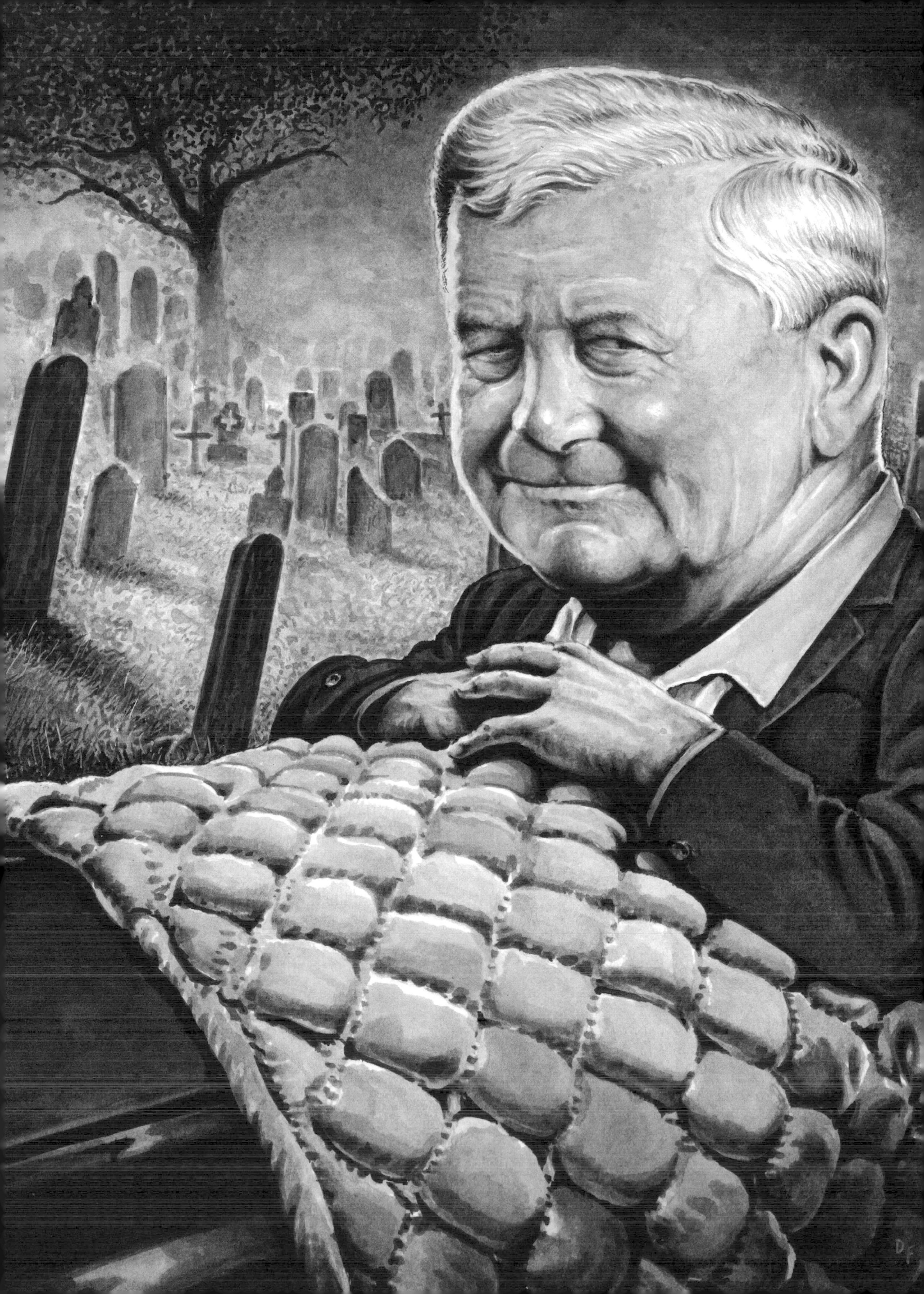

JOHNNY CRAIG

1926–2001

plate
57

"Johnny Craig drew the cleanest horror stories you ever saw." —Wally Wood

A slow, restrained, meticulous craftsman and perfectionist, artist and writer Johnny Craig first worked in comics in 1938 at age twelve, assisting with lettering and other odd jobs. He continued working for various comic lines till he joined the merchant marines and then the army. After the war, he returned to freelancing for several companies, including Lev Gleason Publications, Fox, and finally M. C. "Max" Gaines's Educational Comics, where he was hired to create covers and interior art for *Blackstone*, *Moon Girl*, and *The Prince*. After Gaines's tragic death in 1947, Craig continued on with EC, then called Entertaining Comics and run by Max's son Bill and his new editor Al Feldstein. Craig was present at the evolution of EC's new horror line of comics and soon became one of its main artists, drawing clean, crisp film noir–style horror stories usually involving voodoo, vampires, and zombies. But unlike his contemporaries Jack Davis and Graham Ingels, Craig rarely depicted anything gruesome, rather indicating that the horror lay just slightly out of frame. If Graham Ingels was known for his gaping mouths dripping saliva, then Craig was known for his neurotic characters' intense sweat. Craig also reimagined the *Vault of Horror*'s high-cheeked (a Craig specialty) mascot the Vault Keeper and edited, wrote, and drew the last six issues of that title.

When horror comics folded in 1955, Craig stayed on at EC to write and draw New Trend and Picto-Fiction titles, editing and writing *EXTRA!*, but when they also folded he left comics altogether to become an art director at a Pennsylvania ad agency. He missed comics, though, and started quietly freelancing. Using a pen name, Jay Taycee, to avoid giving himself away to his advertising clients, Craig drew (sweaty) horror stories for Warren's *Creepy* and *Eerie*, and eventually returned to work for both DC and Marvel. In his later years he re-created oil paintings of some of his early EC horror covers.

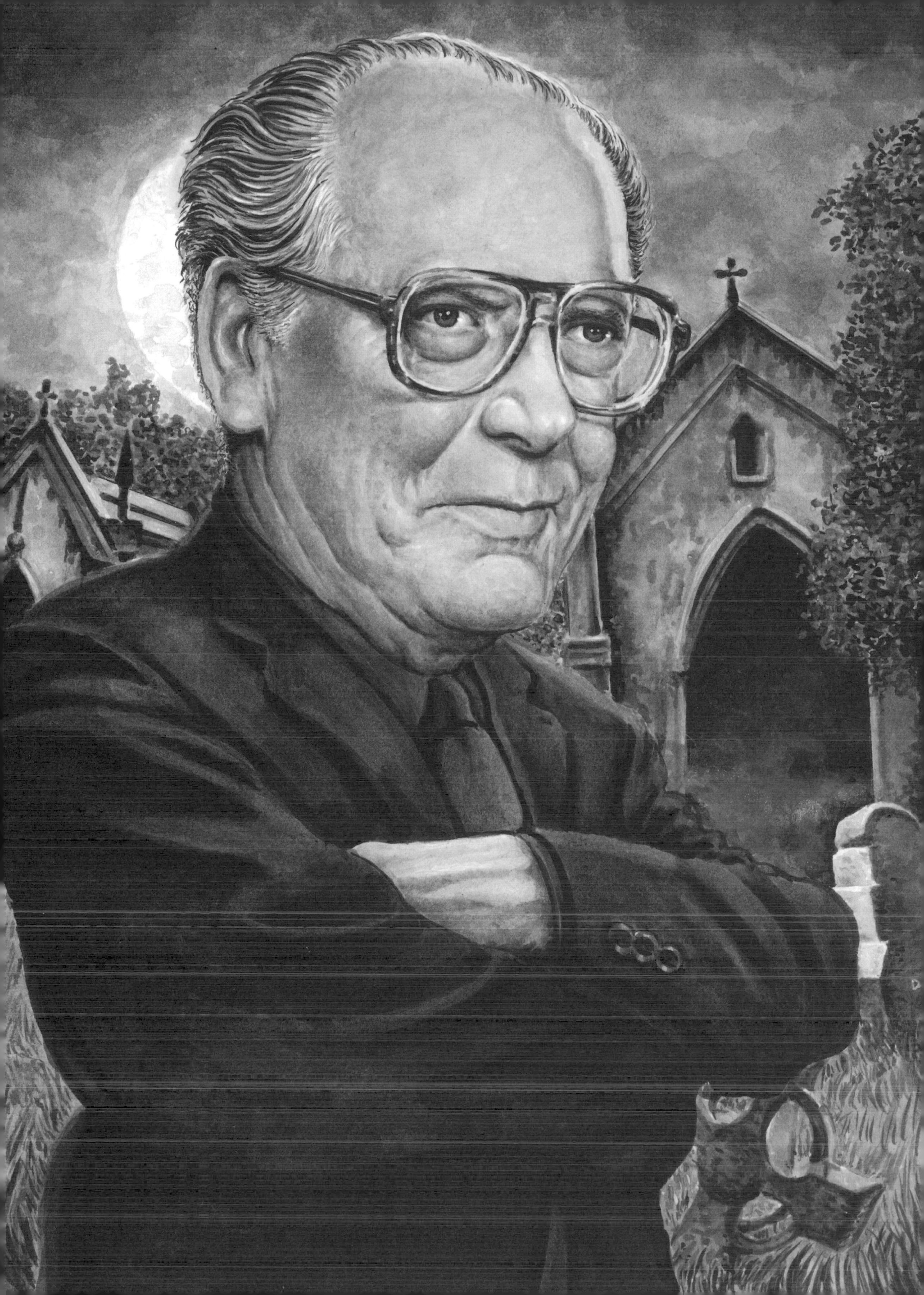

AL FELDSTEIN

1925–2014

plate
58

In 1948, shortly after Max Gaines was killed in a boating accident and his son William M. Gaines inherited the family business, EC (Educational Comics), a young artist named Albert B. "Al" Feldstein walked into Gaines's office, displaying examples of what was referred to as *headlight art* (simply put: ample young women with large erect nipples). It was serendipity. Gaines flipped for the art, and thus began a thirty-eight-year business association and friendship between the two men. Feldstein had worked in comics for several years after the war, specializing in drawing peppy-teenager books like *Junior* and *Sunny*. After arriving at EC, he combined his art with writing and soon became EC's main editor, while also continuing to draw in his appealing, yet stiff and static style. Feldstein and Gaines shared a love of old spooky radio shows like *Lights Out*, and both decided to create comic book versions of similar scary stories, at first slipping them into their crime comics. Soon Feldstein was editing and occasionally writing and drawing several science fiction titles for EC. He also had a great knack for recognizing new, untested talent, and he hired many of the finest young freelance comic artists, as well as several veteran artists, who walked through EC's doors. The EC comics formula became extremely successful, producing the most literate, well-crafted comics, which still remain unsurpassed in the field.

Unfortunately, it all ended in 1955 thanks to the hysterical outcry and eventual senate hearings that blamed horror and crime comics for juvenile delinquency. EC famously came crashing down, and when the dust settled, nothing was left in the rubble but *Mad*, now a black-and-white magazine. Gaines reluctantly let Feldstein go, and when *Mad*'s uneasy creator and editor, Harvey Kurtzman, had a deal firmly in place with *Playboy* publisher Hugh Hefner to create a new color humor magazine, *Trump*, Kurtzman left, taking *Mad*'s main artists along with him. Gaines instantly rehired Feldstein (who had edited the humor comic *Panic* for EC), who got right down to business, getting the word out that *Mad* was looking for contributors. Feldstein then watched as Don Martin, Dave Berg, Mort Drucker, Kelly Freas, Bob Clarke, and Norman Mingo, the entire usual gang of idiots, one by one walked through his door.

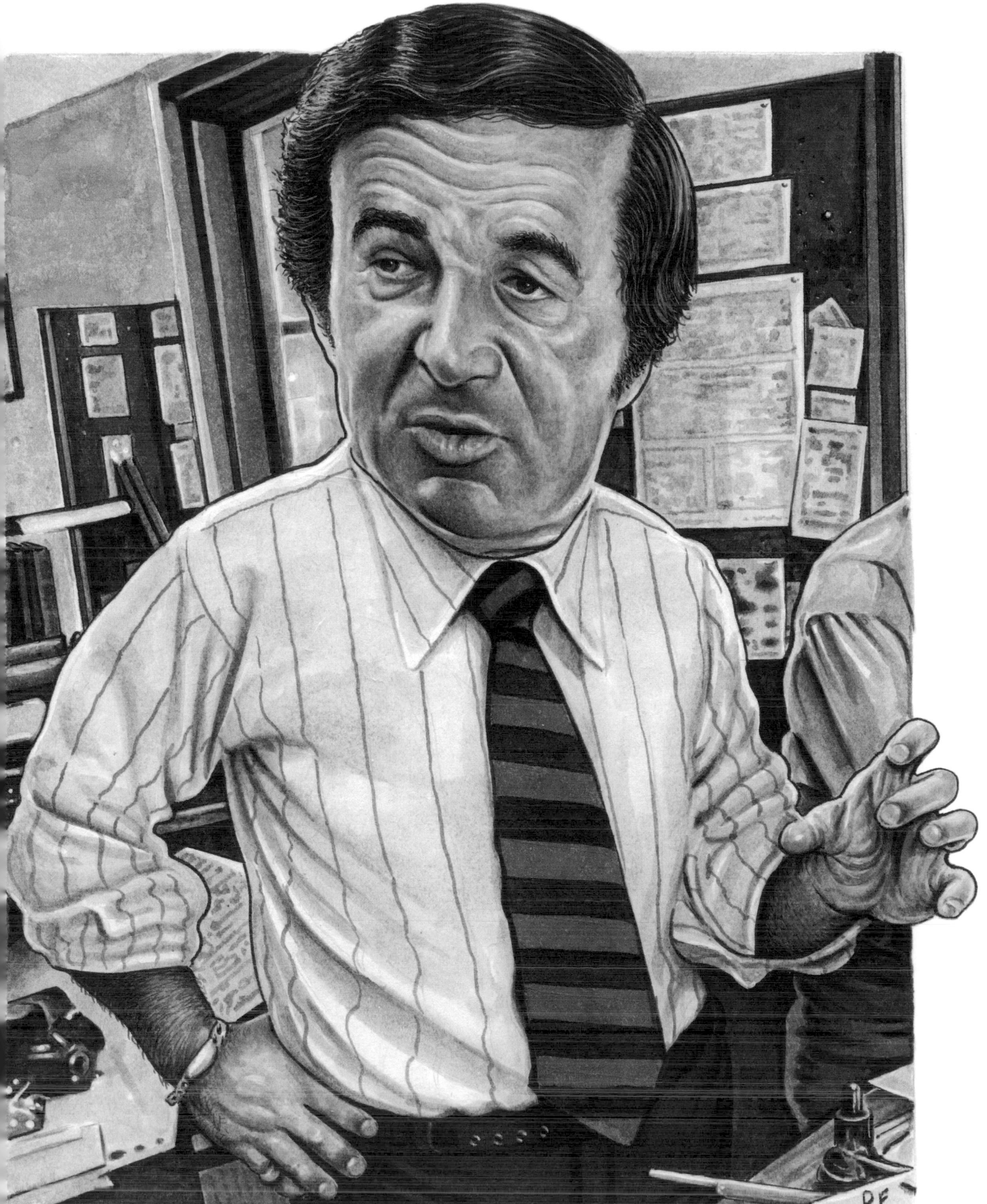

WILLIAM M. GAINES

1922–1992

plate
59

William Maxwell "Bill" Gaines was studying to become a high school chemistry teacher when his father, comic book pioneer M. C. Gaines, was suddenly killed in a boating accident in 1947, and his mother insisted that her reluctant twenty-five-year-old son head the family business, the floundering EC (Educational Comics). Bill Gaines had never shown any interest in the comic book business, let alone comic books, so at first he would show up at EC's offices only once a week just to sign payroll checks. But Gaines was an avid reader, and once he began to actually read his company's comics, as well as what other publishers were offering, he found himself enjoying them and became newly intrigued with his comics business. Gaines took control of EC and, little by little, phased out his father's humdrum titles and replaced them with new comics that followed the popular trends of the moment: romance, westerns, and crime. He also began assembling a younger staff, including artist Al Feldstein, who would become his editor and right-hand man, and artist/writer Johnny Craig, who had worked for M. C. Gaines. They began revising their line of comics by introducing experimental horror stories into their crime comics and officially renaming the company Entertaining Comics. The crime, horror, science fiction, and war titles (edited by Harvey Kurtzman) they introduced soon rose above the content of typical comics and eventually became the gold standard of the industry, featuring the finest writing and the most talented artists to ever work in comics.

EC's horror comics proved to be its best-selling titles, and Gaines and Feldstein went full tilt, perhaps occasionally pushing the envelope too far with their joyous depictions of depravity and horror. When ambitious psychologist Dr. Fredric Wertham published his book *Seduction of the Innocent* in 1954, declaring that horror and crime comics adversely affected children, he pointed a finger of blame directly at what EC was publishing. Bill Gaines felt compelled to testify before the Senate Subcommittee on Juvenile Delinquency, but his testimony wasn't well received, and he became the poster boy for greedy New York horror comics publishers. EC was essentially driven out of the newly emasculated comic book business with only *Mad*, now a magazine, still standing. Harvey Kurtzman left EC, taking all of *Mad*'s artists with him. Gaines had the last laugh though, and with loyal editor Al Feldstein, he guided *Mad* into becoming an American institution of humor. The eccentric Gaines evolved into essentially the world's oldest and fattest hippie. To quote Gaines himself: "My staff and contributors create the magazine. What I create is the atmosphere."

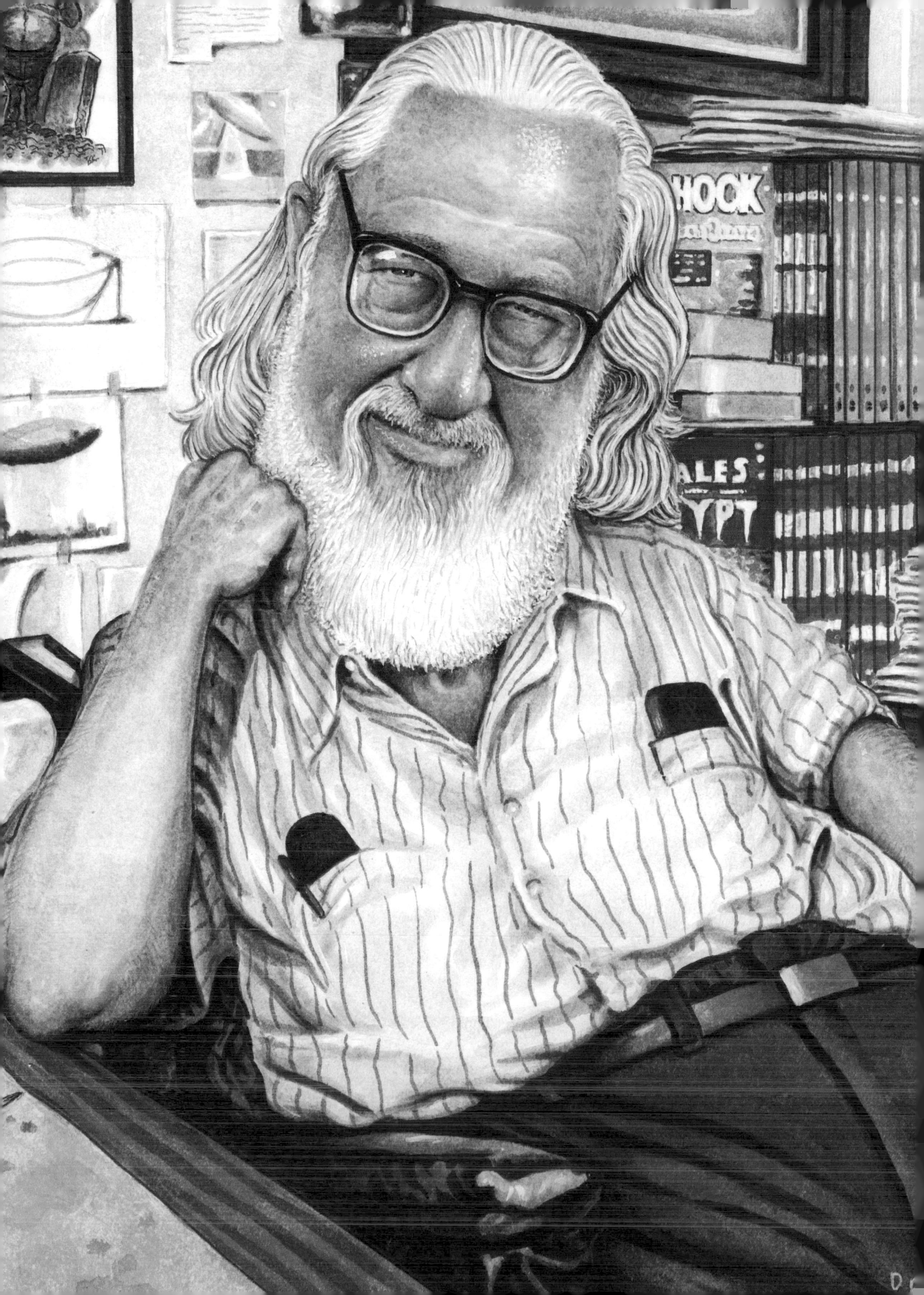
HOCK
ALES
YPT

HARVEY KURTZMAN

1924–1993

The legendary Harvey Kurtzman needs no introduction. So, here's one anyway: cartoonist, writer, editor, satirist, and teacher, he was the founder and creator of the iconoclastic *Mad*, *Trump*, *Humbug*, and *Help*. Along with his longtime partner, cartoonist Will Elder, he spent almost thirty years producing the lushly painted comic strip *Little Annie Fanny* for *Playboy*.

Kurtzman has had a huge, almost immeasurable influence on several generations of cartoonists and humorists, among them Robert Crumb and the (Monty) Pythons. His first appearance in a comic book was in 1939, when at age fourteen he won a cartooning contest, and his winning entry was printed in *Tip Top Comics* #39. He officially entered the comic book business in 1943 before being drafted. After the war he went freelance, creating his surreal one-page *Hey Look!* filler feature for editor Stan Lee at Timely, stretching and breaking the panels and boundaries of the comic book page, creating little masterpieces of humor, and preparing him for the eventual creation of the irreverent *Mad* comic book for EC, as well as his groundbreaking, truthful war comics *Frontline Combat* and *Two-Fisted Tales*.

Like many at EC, Kurtzman was a perfectionist, and as an editor, he expected his artists to faithfully follow his vision, providing them with vellum pencil overlays. Many happily complied, but several didn't, and heads were butted. Still, Kurtzman's EC war comics remain the most powerful and poignant comics reflecting the horrors of war ever created. Kurtzman (and EC) never dumbed down his comics to a perceived audience of children with low IQs; rather, he always aimed the comics he edited at a more intelligent reader. It was Harvey Kurtzman's vision and conception that would help guide *Mad* into the humor institution it would become. Harvey Kurtzman's legend continues to grow. Along with a recent gallery showing of his artwork at New York's Society of Illustrators, a huge biography and a film documentary are in the works. The *New York Times* got it right when they called Kurtzman "one of the most important figures in postwar America."

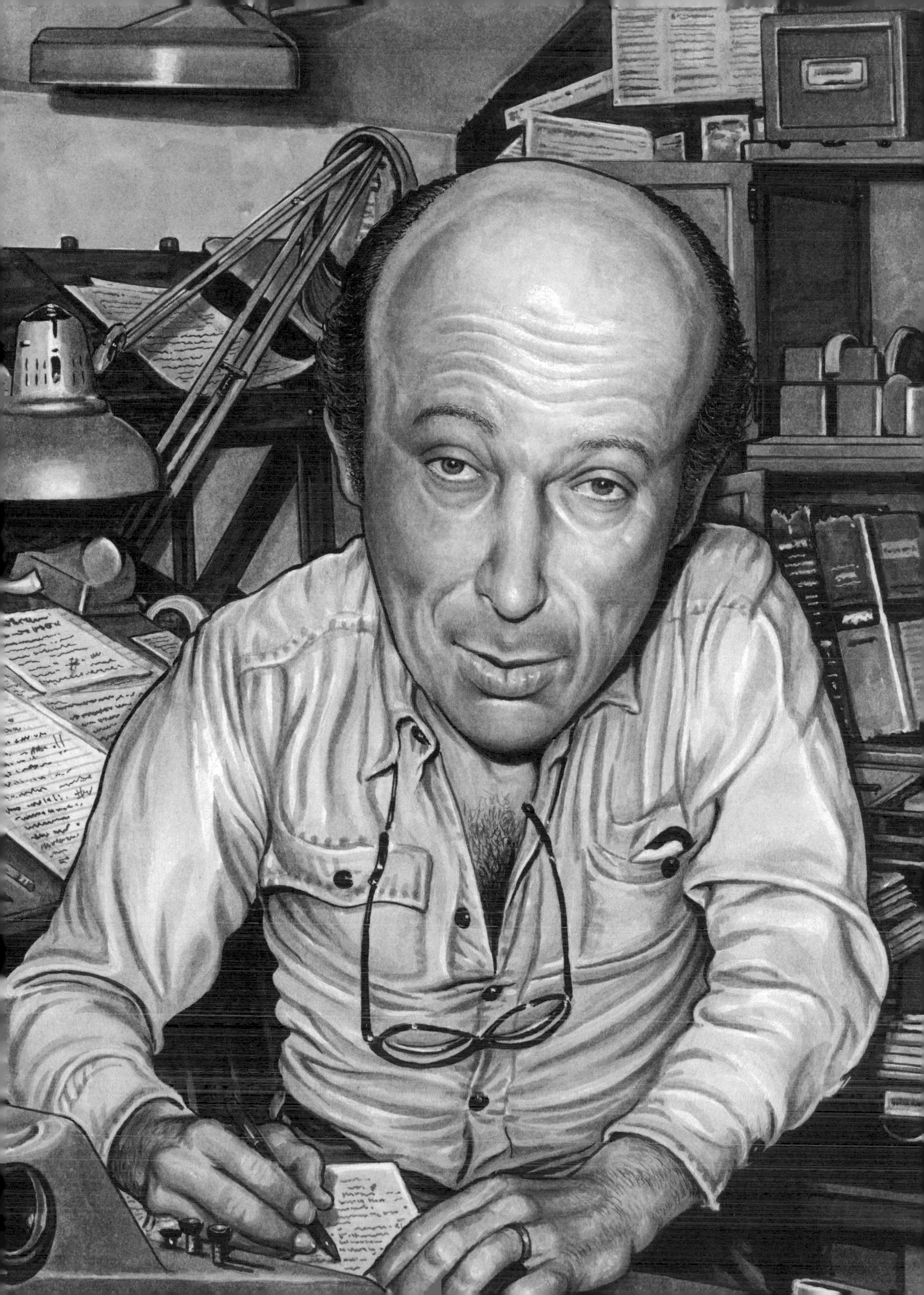

WILL ELDER

plate
61

"The Mad Playboy of Art," Will Elder (born Wolf William Eisenberg) was a force of nature, a dazzling artist that leaves you scratching your head asking "*How* did he do it?" Although personally shy, he was *Mad*'s original "maddest" artist, with a manic, insane eye for detail and (sometimes subversive) rampant background gags (referred to as "chicken fat"). Elder had an uncanny, deft ability to mimic or even improve on the styles of other artists, from Walt Disney to E. C. Segar to Norman Rockwell. He was truly a comedian on paper. Working with his long-time creative partner Harvey Kurtzman, whom he met at New York's High School of Music & Art, Elder created memorable comic book art for EC, mainly for the early *Mad* (and editor Al Feldstein's *Panic*, which ran his notorious take on "The Night Before Christmas"), then moved on with Kurtzman and others to create the short-lived publications *Trump*, *Humbug*, and *Help*, and finally *Playboy*'s bawdy *Little Annie Fanny*, which lasted for close to thirty years. A documentary on Will Elder's life, *Chicken Fat*, is in the works.

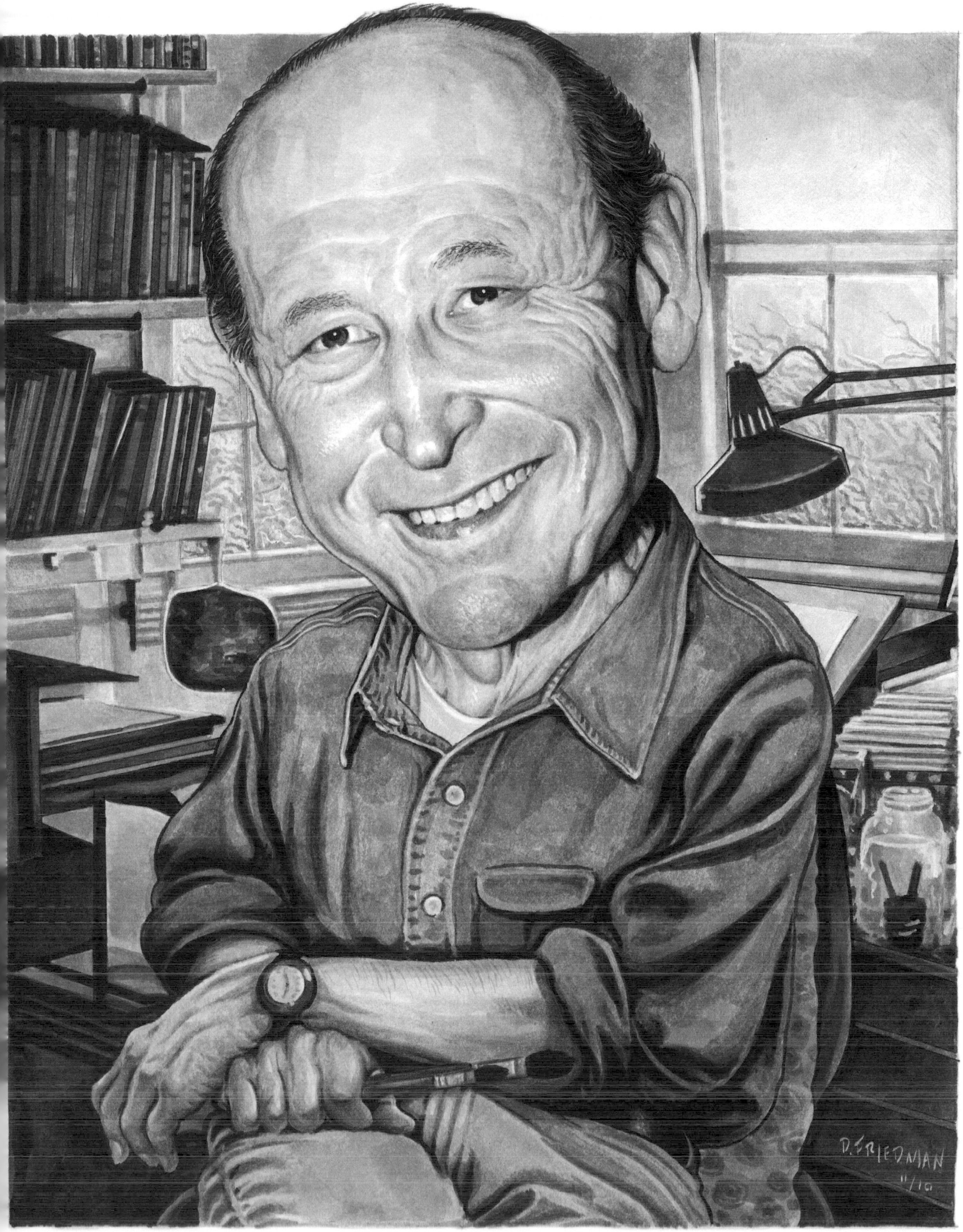
D. FRIEDMAN
11/10

JOHN SEVERIN

1922–2012

plate
62

John Severin was one of the most prolific and prodigious comics creators ever, producing thousands of pages and covers for 60 years, illustrating every imaginable genre, most notably for war and western comics and two particular humor publications, *Mad* and *Cracked*. Severin attended New York's High School of Music & Art, along with future collaborators Harvey Kurtzman and Will Elder, but amazingly had no further formal art training after that. After the war he formed a studio along with Kurtzman and Elder, and with Elder inking his pencils, began turning out work for comic books, already showing a flair for historical authenticity and a penchant for realism. He would arrive at EC in 1951 where Kurtzman put him to work on a seven-page story for *Two-Fisted Tales*. Kurtzman was unhappy with Severin's inking ability but loved his pencil work, so he teamed him up for the second time with Will Elder as his inker. When Kurtzman launched *Mad* in 1952, Severin appeared (sans Elder's inking) in nine of the first ten issues, clearly showing a flair for humor, and creating some memorable work ("Melvin of the Apes!"), but inevitably he and Kurtzman had a falling out. After EC imploded, Severin was invited by Al Feldstein to join as a regular contributor to *Mad* magazine, but Severin was then working for Stan Lee at Atlas, mainly drawing western comics, and didn't feel he could switch alliances. Severin freelanced for various publishers for the rest of his career, including Marvel and Warren, but is probably most remembered for his forty-five years beginning in 1958 working as the *Mad* imitation *Cracked's* featured artist, and created nearly all of their covers featuring their mascot Sylvester J. Smyth.

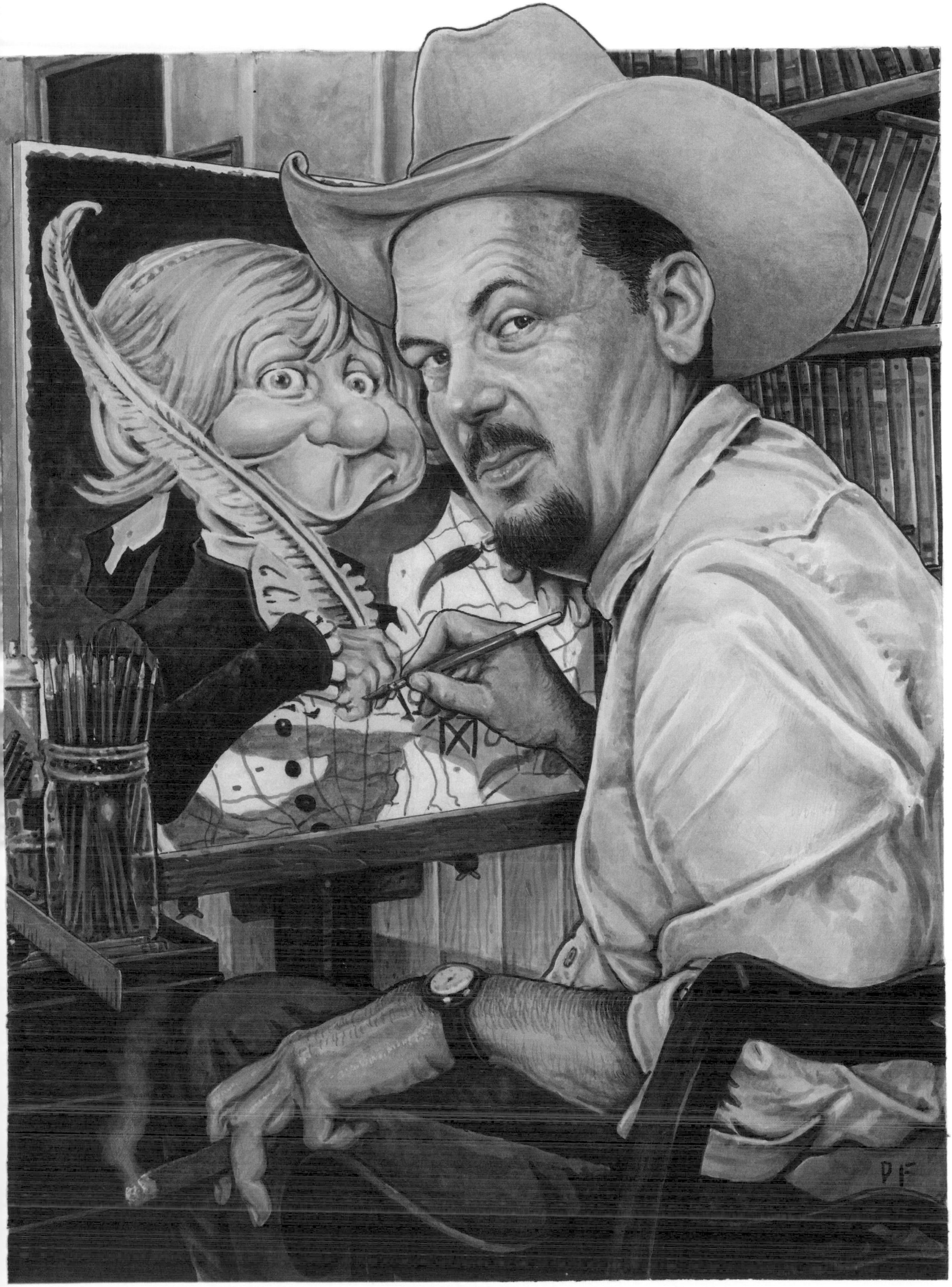
DF

WALLY WOOD

plate
63

"Wally may have been our most troubled artist, but he may have been our most brilliant." —William M. Gaines

Wallace Allan "Wally" Wood entered comics in 1948 as a letterer and background artist for romance comics but soon centered on his passion, science fiction art, sometimes in collaboration with the artist Joe Orlando, working for Avon comics and eventually for EC's *Weird Science* and *Weird Fantasy*. His work instantly stood out because of his intense attention to detail, particularly in his depictions of the inner machine workings of spaceships; sexy, voluptuous blonde women; and pulsating, oozing space monsters. Beginning in 1952, Wood's artwork literally exploded off of the pages of editor Harvey Kurtzman's new subversive humor comic book *Mad*, and along with Will Elder and Jack Davis, he became one of its main contributors, creating the art for the ultimate Superman send-up "Superduperman." Wood, along with Kurtzman, would eventually flee *Mad* to work for *Trump*, but he soon returned to *Mad* and worked as a regular till the midsixties, when he abruptly disappeared from its pages. Wood worked mainly as a freelance artist at this point, doing comic book work for Marvel (*Daredevil*) and creating the concept sketches for Marx Toys' Nutty Mad figures. He also worked for the Topps Company under its creative director Woody Gelman, producing sketches for its Mars Attacks series, Wacky Packs, and Ugly Stickers, and was more than happy to warp countless generations of children's minds in the process. According to Harvey Kurtzman, Wood internalized everything, was a slave to his work, and was filled with personal demons. He wound up drawing porno comics and sadly took his own life in 1981.

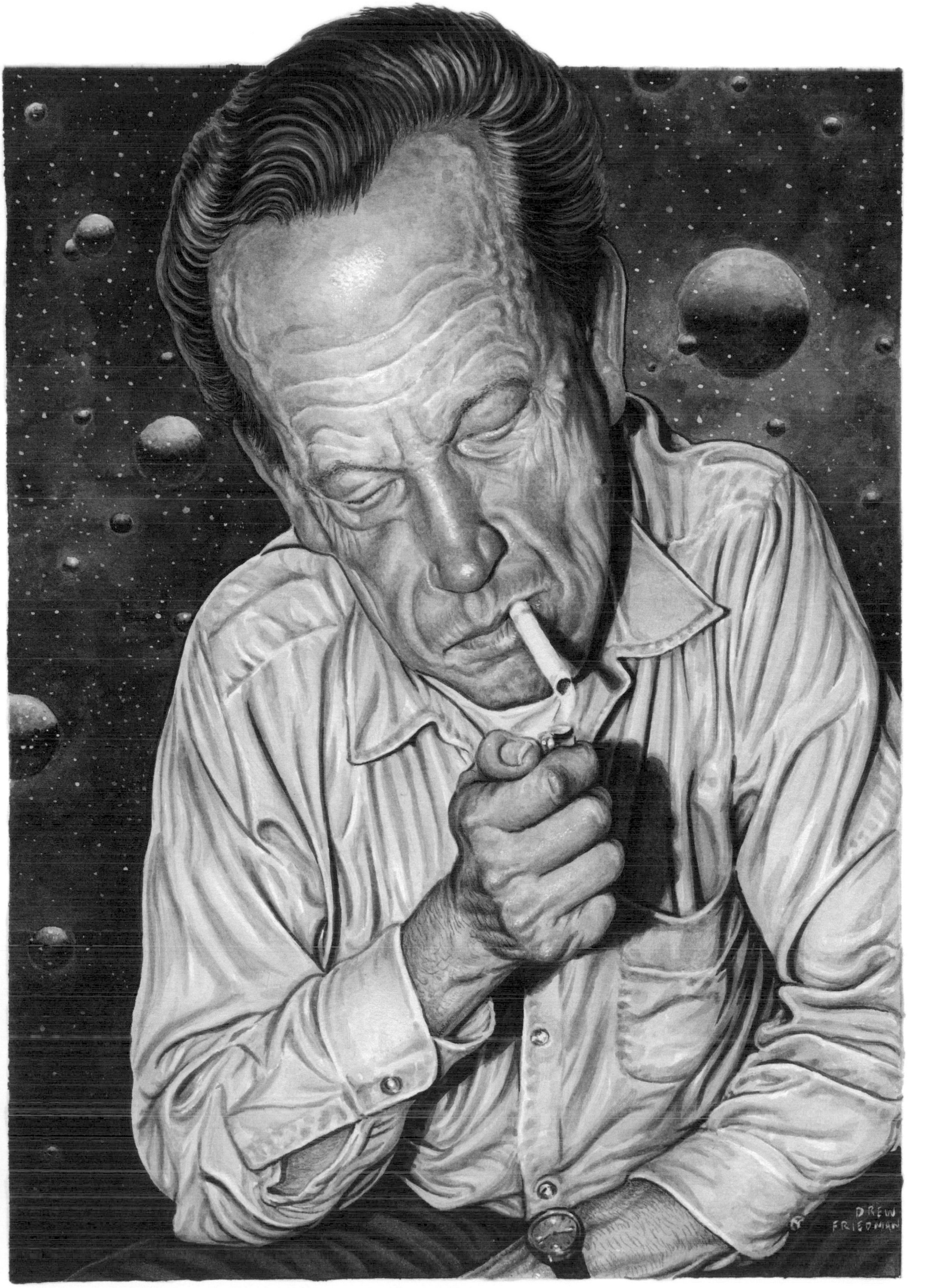
DREW
FRIEDMAN

JOE ORLANDO

1927–1988

plate
64

Born in Italy, Joe Orlando was often referred to as the "Godfather of Comics" due to his exaggerated Italian mannerisms and speech. After serving in the army during World War II, Orlando broke into comics as a penciler and inker, and soon met fellow artist Wally Wood. The two hit it off and began collaborating on comic book work, with Orlando inking Wood's pencils. Wood's talent and dedication to his craft had a strong influence on the young artist, and Orlando completely absorbed Wood's technique. Together with several other artists, they opened a studio to work mainly on their collaborations for Avon comics. Wood was freelancing regularly for EC comics by the early fifties and recommended his friend Orlando to editor Al Feldstein, who looked at his work and said, "Great, we have another Wally Wood!" Soon Orlando was an EC regular, creating excellent work for its science fiction, crime, and horror comics, as well as for *Panic*, EC's sister publication to *Mad*. When EC folded, the versatile Orlando freelanced for various comics companies, including Marvel. He also drew *Scenes We'd Like to See* and other features for *Mad*, illustrated horror stories for Warren's two horror titles *Creepy* and *Eerie*, and even took part in *National Lampoon*'s parody of *Mad*, poking fun at his old friend Al Feldstein. By the midseventies, Orlando was working almost exclusively for DC comics, mainly as an editor, and he eventually rose up the ranks, becoming vice president and editorial director, and overseeing *Mad*.

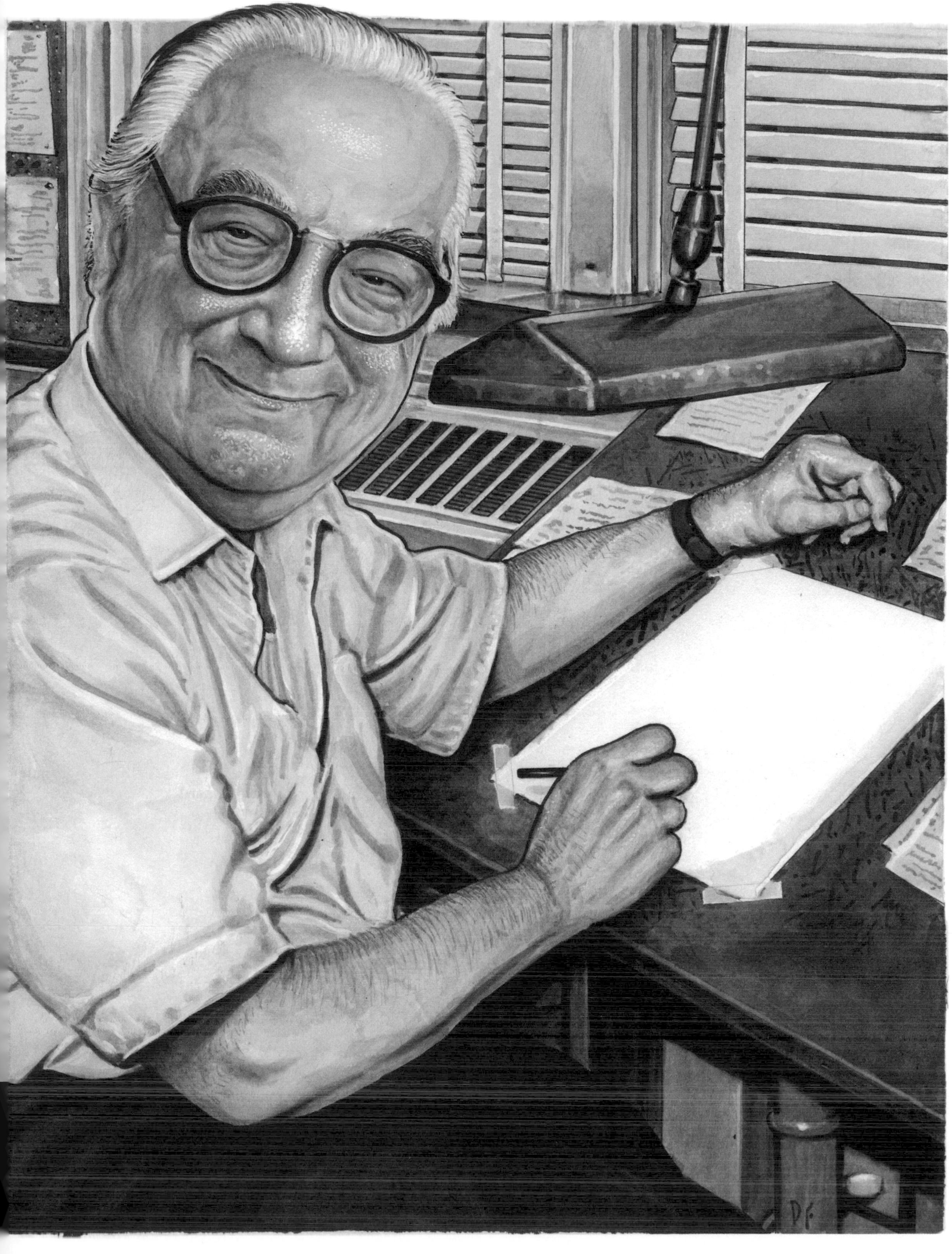

JACK DAVIS

b. 1924

plate
65

Jack Davis (born Jack Burton Davis Jr.) is quite possibly the most ubiquitous American humor illustrator of all time. Davis is a master cartoonist, caricaturist, and illustrator, and his funny, fast-paced, manic, beautifully rendered work has graced the covers of countless comic books, magazines, and record albums, and has also appeared on movie posters, bubble gum cards, and advertisements. A virtually mind-boggling one-man industry, Davis has been called "the fastest cartoonist alive" and "the master of crowd scene." It's astonishing to realize that this quiet Southern gentleman was usually finished with his assignments for the day and out on the golf course by 2:30 p.m. Davis did his first comic book work for EC in 1950, and, taking full advantage of his fast turnarounds and quality artwork, editors Al Feldstein and later Harvey Kurtzman kept him busy. Davis revamped the mascot of *Tales from the Crypt*, the iconic Crypt Keeper, and would appear in every EC horror comic over the next five years, becoming EC's most prominent horror artist while still somehow finding the time to contribute to all of its war, science fiction, and crime comics.

When *Mad* first appeared in 1952, Davis became one of its three primary contributors, and later he became one of main artists for *Panic*. He eventually left *Mad* with Harvey Kurtzman to work for the short-lived *Trump* and then *Humbug*. In 1961, Jack Davis edited and drew his own comic book for Dell, *Yak Yak*, and during several lean years, he drew gag cartoons for *Playboy* and created covers for *Mad*'s imitators *Cracked* and *Sick*. In 1963, he landed a job that would change everything for him, creating the running-crowd-scene poster art for *It's a Mad, Mad, Mad, Mad World*. He need never look back. He quickly became the most in-demand illustrator in the country and triumphantly returned as a *Mad* regular the following year.

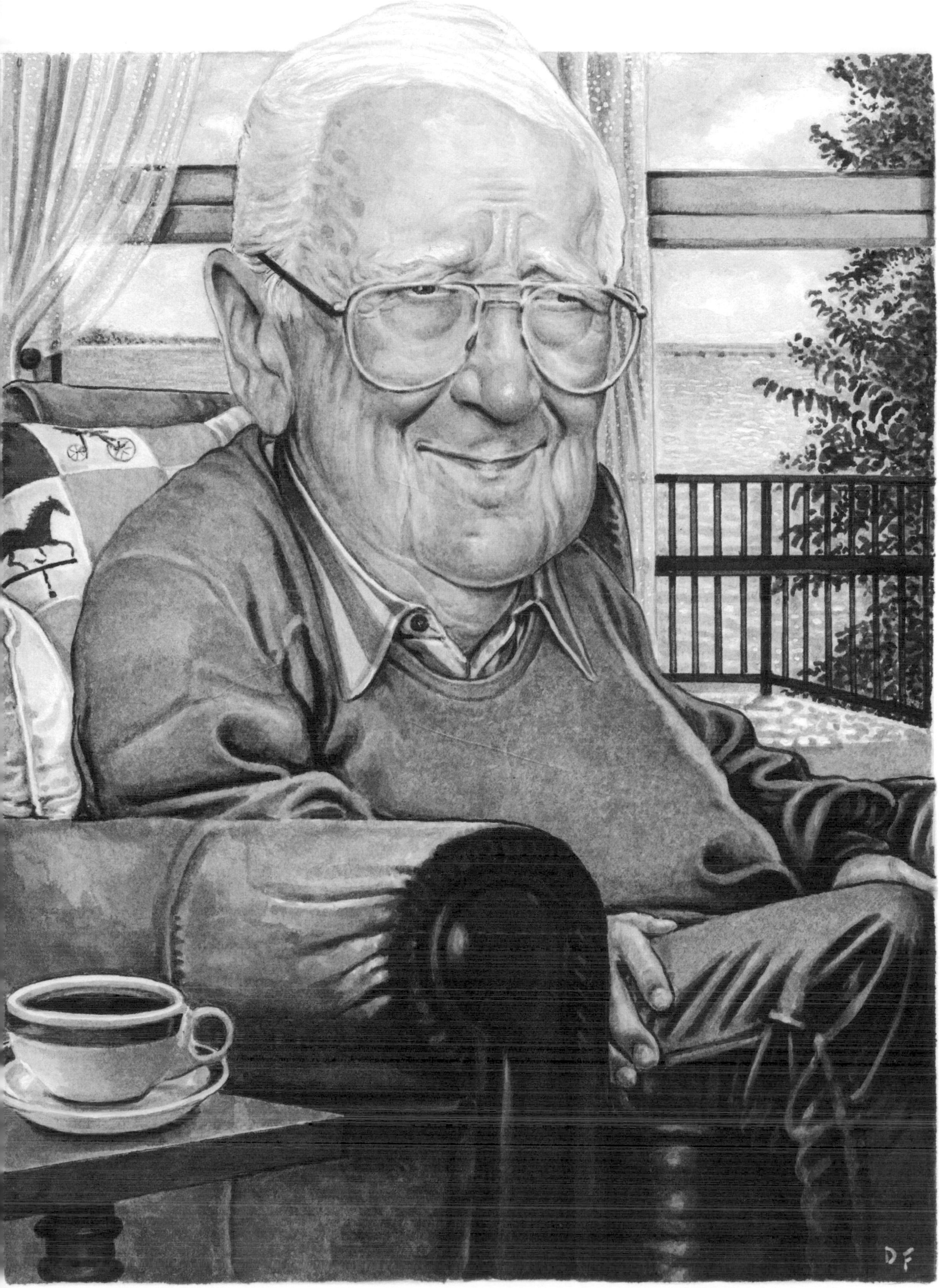
DF

GEORGE EVANS

1920–2001

plate

66

George Evans was described by Bill Gaines as looking like "a sweet, meek, and mild accountant." You would never dream that this man was capable of such brilliant depictions of brutality." Like many others, Evans first entered the world of comic books post–World War II, creating art and becoming a staff artist at Fiction House and Fawcett. Through the urging of several artist friends, including Al Williamson, Evans appeared at EC in the early fifties and soon became a semi-regular, creating his signature powerful, realistic art mainly for its crime and horror comics. He seemed to excel at drawing ordinary men who get mixed up in horrific situations and meek, henpecked husbands who eventually slaughter their shrewish wives. A cover Evans created for *Crime SuspenStories* of a man strangling his wife in a rowboat was held up as a shining example of comic book depravity at the senate hearings on juvenile delinquency in 1954. When EC ended its horror and crime comics, it ushered in its "new trend" titles, including *Aces High*, which was particularly geared toward George Evans, whose passion was World War I aviation. Evans created all the beautiful, cinematic covers and interior art for all five issues of *Aces High*. After EC closed shop altogether, Evans found work elsewhere in comics, including creating memorable art for Dell's *Twilight Zone* comic, for *Classics Illustrated*, and for stories in the EC tradition for James Warren's horror publications *Creepy* and *Eerie*.

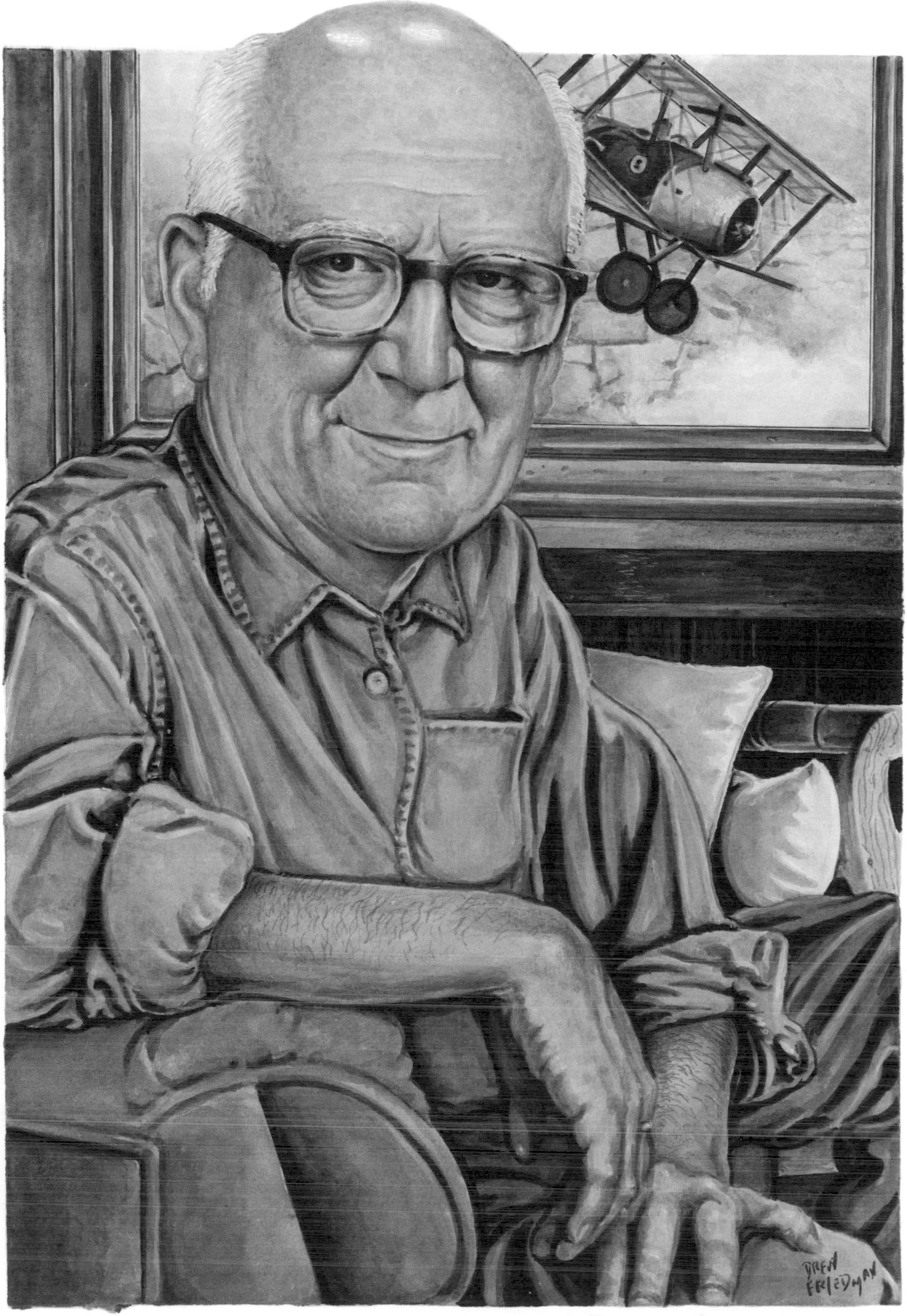
DREW FRIEDMAN

MARIE SEVERIN

b. 1929

plate
67

William Gaines has referred to Marie Severin as "the conscience of EC." Severin was EC's colorist and the only woman on the creative staff. She was also a very moral Catholic, known for coloring particularly gruesome panels dark blue to help tone down the gore. Marie Severin's older brother John first invited her to work as his colorist at EC in 1949, and soon she was coloring all of EC's comics, including the notorious horror titles. Comics lore has it that when she felt a particular artist (say Graham Ingels or Jack Davis) might have gone a bit overboard in the bad taste department, she would use her coloring as a kind of shield, helping to defuse the gore. After EC, Severin worked as a colorist for Stan Lee at Marvel's predecessor Atlas and later as a staff artist for Marvel, where she drew covers and interior pages for various Silver Age titles, including *The Incredible Hulk*, *Strange Tales*, and *X-Men*. She hit her stride while indulging her talents as a humorous cartoonist in *Not Brand Ecch*, which satirized Marvel's own characters, and in Marvel's later humor titles *Spoof*, *Crazy!*, and *Arrgh!*

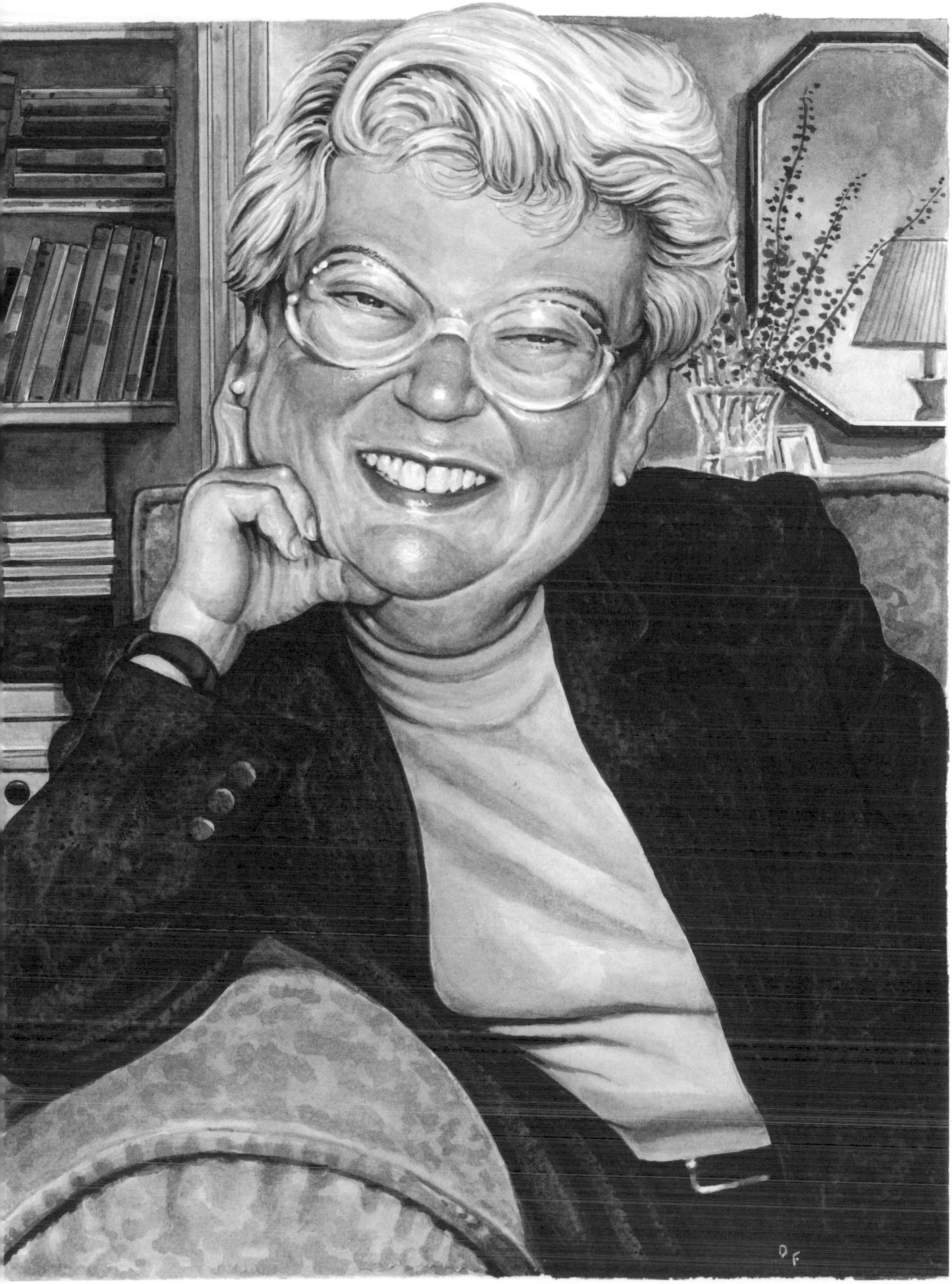
DF

JACK KAMEN

1920–2008

plate
68

Artist Jack Kamen was most famous for his "Kamen Girls," voluptuous yet cold and calculating babes who were rarely up to any good. Al Feldstein met Kamen when they both drew romance comics for Fox publications while working at the Jerry Iger (sweat) shop in the early forties, cranking out page after page for little money but for the chance to get published in comic books. After Feldstein became an editor at EC, he invited Kamen to stop by, and Gaines and Feldstein hired Kamen on the spot to create art for their romance and science fiction titles, and eventually for their crime and horror books. Kamen's pristine, sleek, controlled "cold" style never sat well with EC's horror fans, who vastly preferred Johnny Craig's deranged, sweaty femmes fatales and Graham Ingels's rotting corpses. But still, the well-liked pipe-smoking "jolly" Jack Kamen became one of EC's most prolific artists. Al Feldstein summed up his philosophy of using Jack Kamen to draw horror stories: "We gave Kamen those stories where the all-American girl and guy are married and then they chop each other to pieces." For *Tales from the Crypt*, Kamen drew a story by Feldstein, "Kamen's Kalamity," which depicted Kamen's uneasy transition from romance to horror and featured perhaps his finest art for EC. Kamen is probably best remembered for illustrating all the covers and stories for EC's oddball New Direction title *Psychoanalysis*, written by Al Feldstein, who was going through analysis himself at the time, as was Bill Gaines. After EC, Jack Kamen found (far more lucrative) work in advertising.

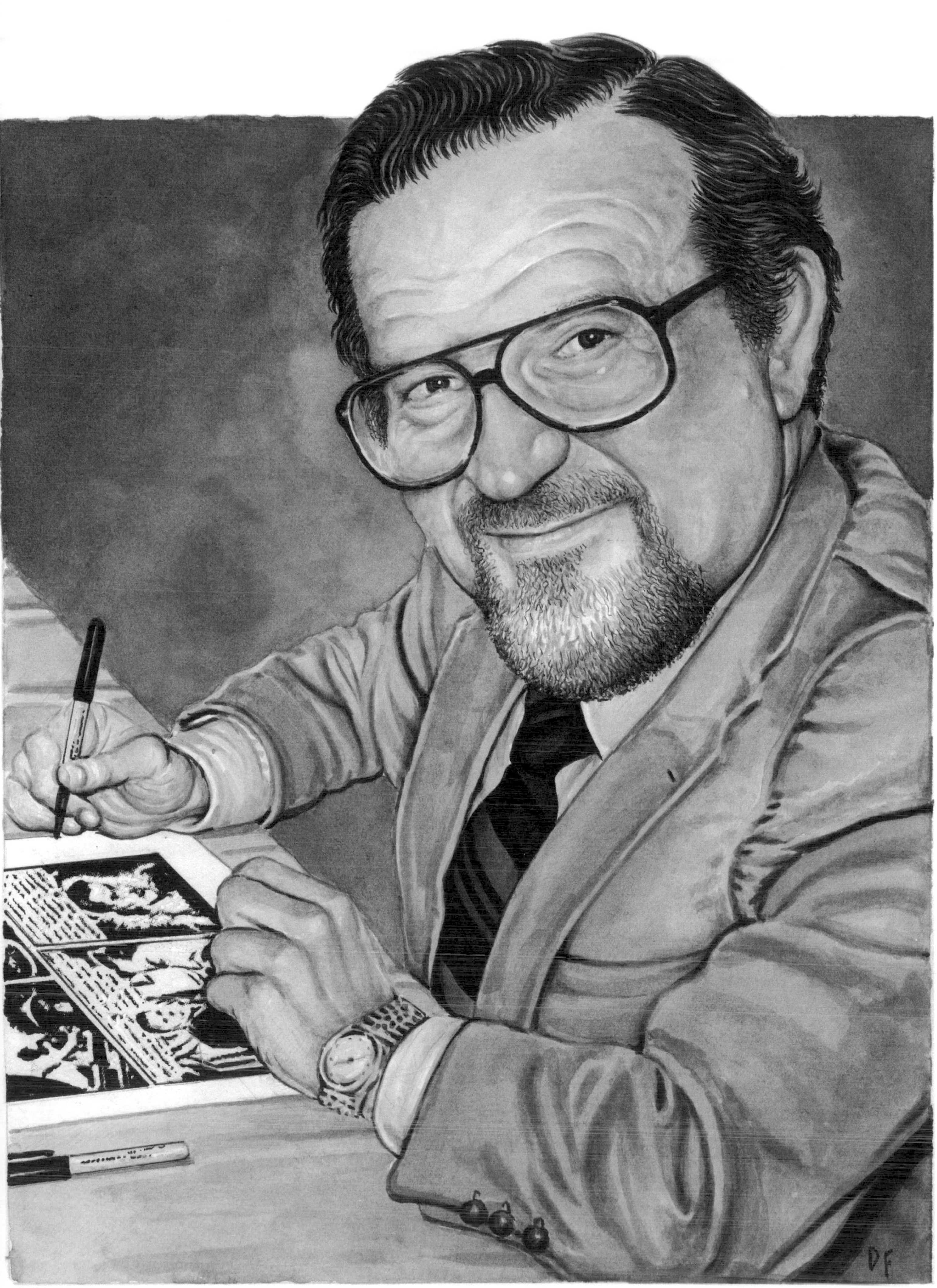
DF

FRANK FRAZETTA

1928–2010

plate **69**

Frank Frazetta is probably the most prolific horror and fantasy artist ever, producing mesmerizing, beautifully painted tableaux for magazine covers (most prominently for the midsixties Warren publications *Creepy* and *Eerie*), fantasy and horror paperback covers, and film posters (including many popular midsixties comedies). Frazetta didn't do a lot of work for comic books, but the little he did was memorable. In 1944, when he was fifteen and just breaking into comics, he was hired to do clean-ups for other comic book artists. Then little by little, he did some penciling and inking. He was soon creating artwork for various types of comics, among them westerns, fantasy, mystery, romance, celebrity biographies, and even funny animals. In the early fifties he did some work for EC, much of it in collaboration with his friends and fellow artists Al Williamson and Roy G. Krenkel. Frazetta's only published solo story created for EC was "Squeeze Play," a so-so morality tale that appeared in *Shock SuspenStories* and featured his passionate, spectacular (and sexy) art.

Frazetta memorably illustrated several covers in the midfifties for the long-running comic book series *Famous Funnies* featuring Buck Rogers. These are still considered some of the finest, must beautifully detailed and rendered covers ever created for comics. Based on those covers, Al Capp hired him to work as his assistant (ghost) on his wildly popular comic strip *Li'l Abner*, providing him with a steady income for nine years. Frazetta rarely did any more work for comic books aside from cover work for Warren publications, occasional work for *Mad* magazine, and superb and haunting covers for Ballentine Books' line of EC paperback reprints in the mid-1960s.

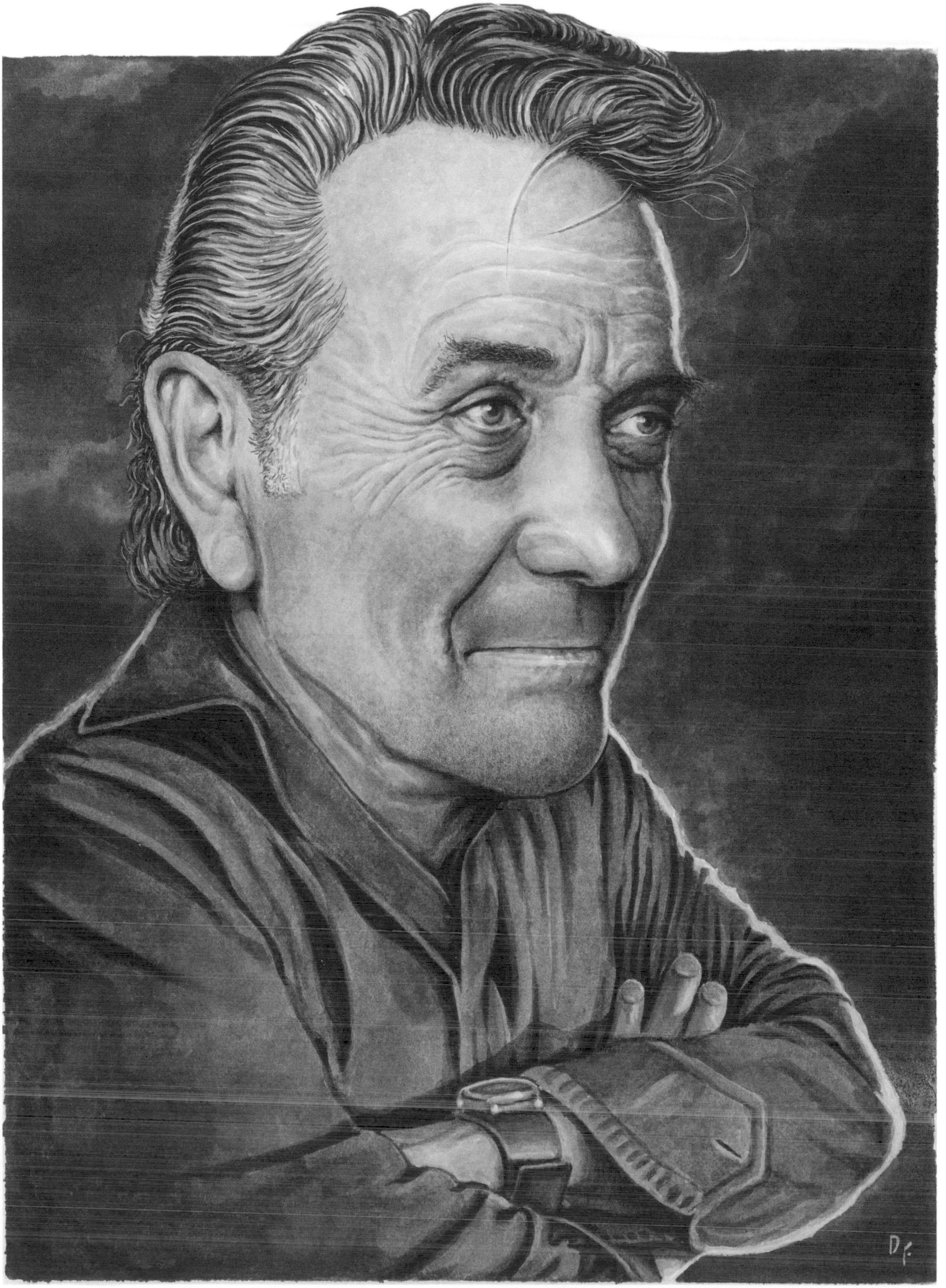

JACK OLECK

1914–1981

plate **70**

Jack Oleck was the brother-in-law of comics veteran Joe Simon and found work after the war scripting comics stories for the Simon and Kirby studio, turning out stories for Quality Comics and others. He became Quality's number-one writer, composing scripts for romance, crime, and war comics, as well as for horror comics, which were fast becoming the best-selling genre in the early fifties. EC was the standard-bearer in horror comics, and editor Al Feldstein, who had been writing most of the horror stories along with publisher Bill Gaines, except those written by Johnny Craig, was looking to lighten his writing workload a bit, so he contacted Oleck. Oleck soon found a welcoming home at EC, becoming one of the main scriptwriters for all of the horror, crime, and science fiction titles. When EC collapsed, Oleck left comics to publish and edit *Interior Decorator News*, but he returned in the late sixties to write for DC's EC-inspired horror titles including *The House of Mystery* and *The House of Secrets*. Oleck later wrote horror paperbacks, including the early seventies movie tie-ins for *Tales from the Crypt* and *The Vault of Horror*, and two *House of Mystery* paperbacks, both illustrated by Bernie Wrightson.

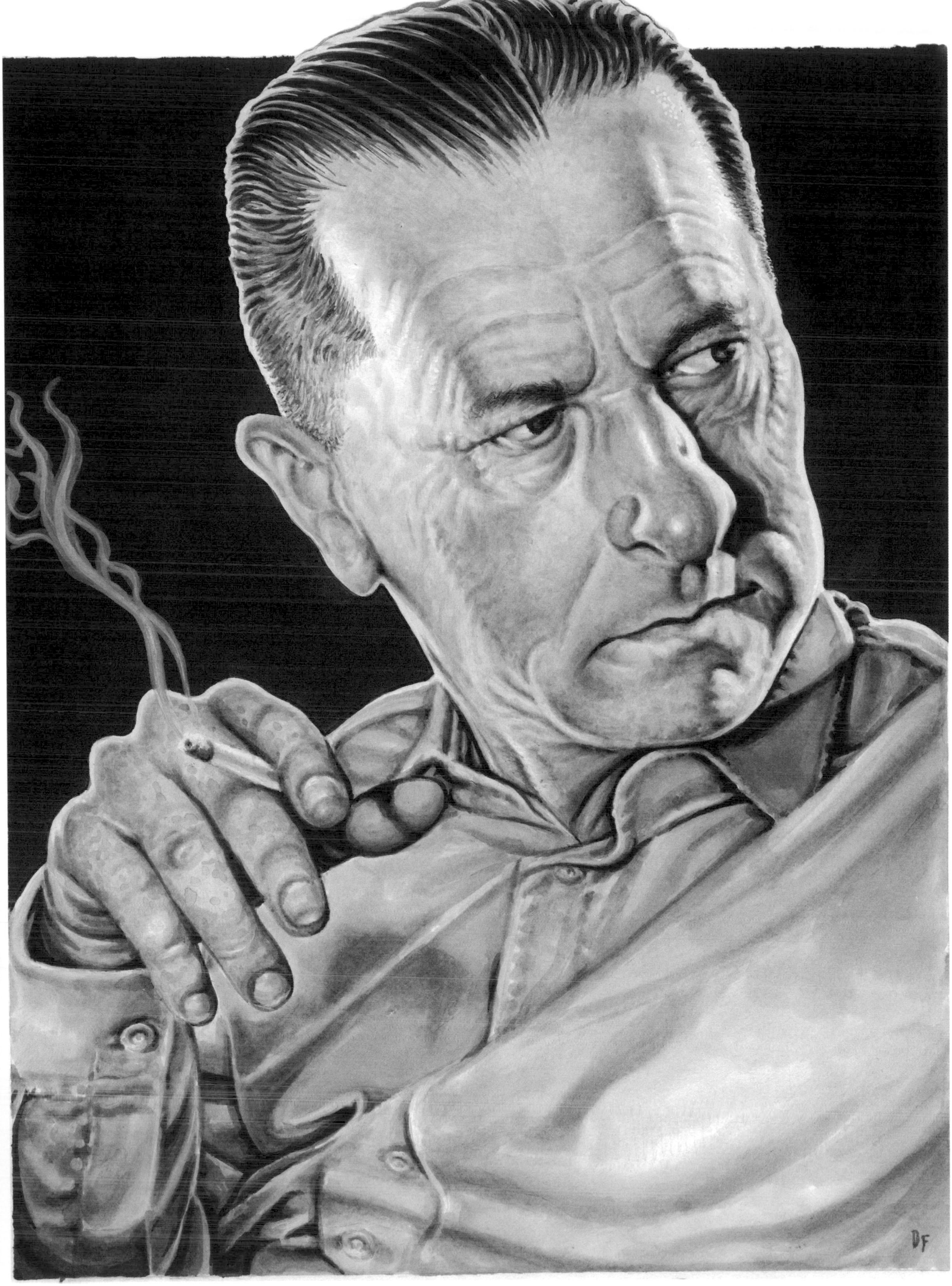
DF

RAMONA FRADON

b. 1926

plate
71

Ramona Fradon is a pioneering female comic book artist in the male-dominated field of comics. After Fradon graduated from Parsons, George Ward, a comic book letterer and friend of Ramona Fradon's husband, future *New Yorker* cartoonist Dana Fradon, urged the struggling artist to show some samples of her drawings to DC Comics. She had never considered drawing comics, let alone superhero comics, but she showed the samples to DC and was hired. Her first work for DC was 1951's *Shining Knight*. Soon thereafter, she revamped the Aquaman character for *Adventure Comics* and cocreated his Robin-like sidekick Aqualad before eventually handing over the characters to artist Nick Cardy. Fradon continued working off and on in comics, and in 1964 she cocreated and penciled the character Metamorpho (The Element Man), who debuted in *The Brave and the Bold* #57. Eventually she took some time off from comics work to raise a family. In the early seventies Fradon returned to work full-time for DC on various titles, including *Plastic Man*. In 1980 artist Dale Messick retired from drawing the popular syndicated comic *Brenda Starr*, and Fraden took it over for fifteen years before retiring to work on more personal projects.

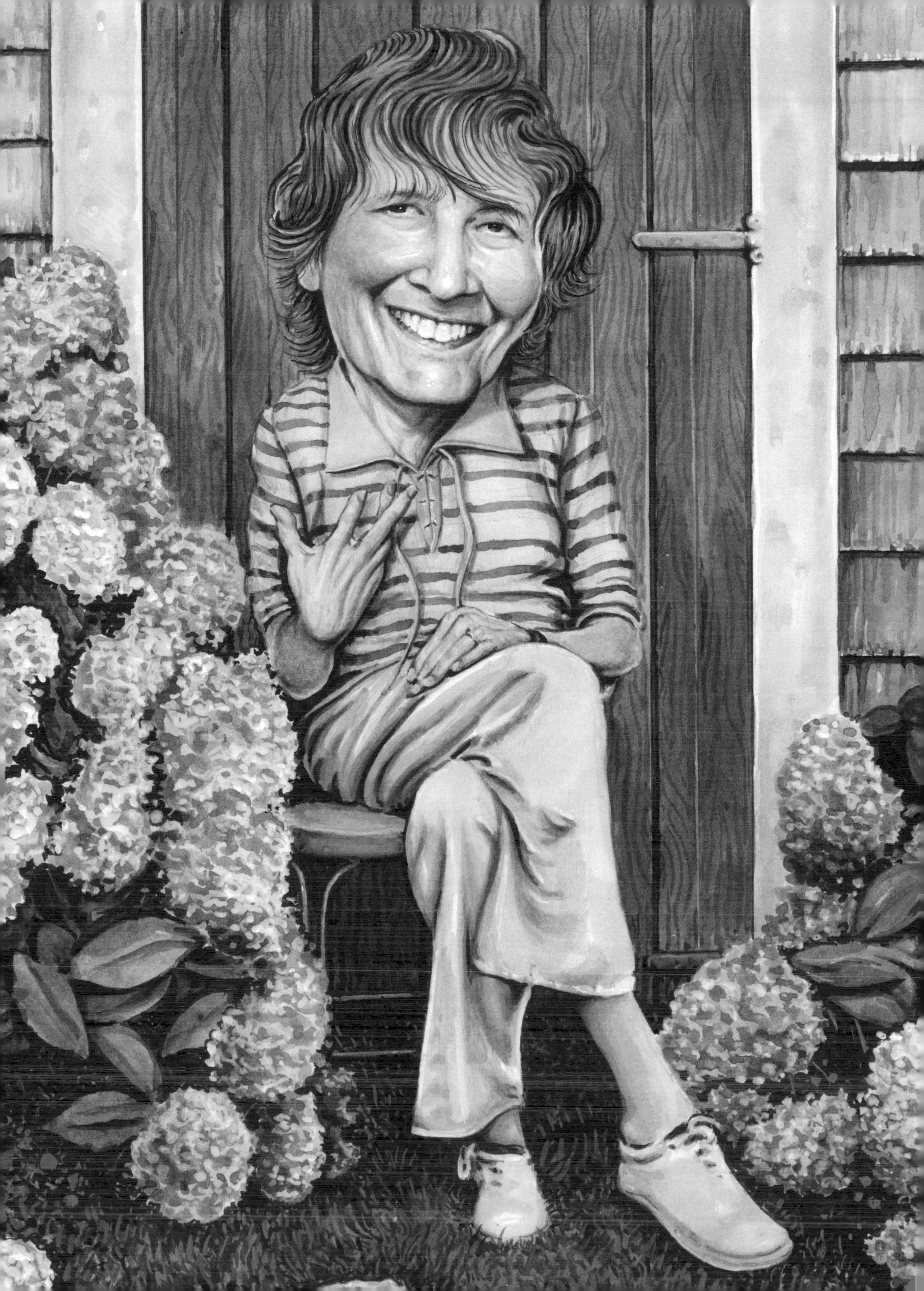

AL HARTLEY

1921–2003

plate
72

Henry Allan "Al" Hartley had been a prolific comic book artist for decades before he became a born-again Christian and began instilling his work with his new-found Christian beliefs. Hartley began his career in the late 1930s, selling spot cartoons and illustrations to various magazines before enlisting in the US Army Air Corps. He resumed his career after the war and drew for various comics publishers. In the late 1940s he began working for editor Stan Lee at Timely, writing and drawing their new teenage girl comic *Patsy Walker*, among many other titles. The versatile Hartley, who could draw satire, superhero, and adventure strips when needed, drew the red-headed Patsy with an alluring sexiness rarely seen in teenage comic titles. He had a teenage comics style all his own.

Hartley continued to work mainly for Timely, then Atlas, then Marvel until the late sixties, when feeling disillusioned with the "nudie cutie" secret agent feature *Pussycat*, which he was creating for several of Marvel publisher Martin Goodman's men's magazines, he had an epiphany, becoming a born-again Christian. He soon became a regular artist/writer for Archie Comics, aping the house style perfectly and attempting to imbue the characters with his Christian beliefs, until the powers that be asked him to cut back a bit, which he complied with. He found his outlet adapting Christian-themed novels such as *God's Smuggler* and *The Cross and the Switchblade* into comics form. He then helped launch the Spire Christian Comics line, where he could proselytize for his "Christian gospel message of salvation through Jesus Christ," adapting various bible stories and movies into comics (*Hansi: The Girl Who Loved the Swastika*). He also somehow convinced the president of Archie Comics, the Jewish John Goldwater, to license out the *Archie* comics characters to Spire, so he could "lead them to Jesus."

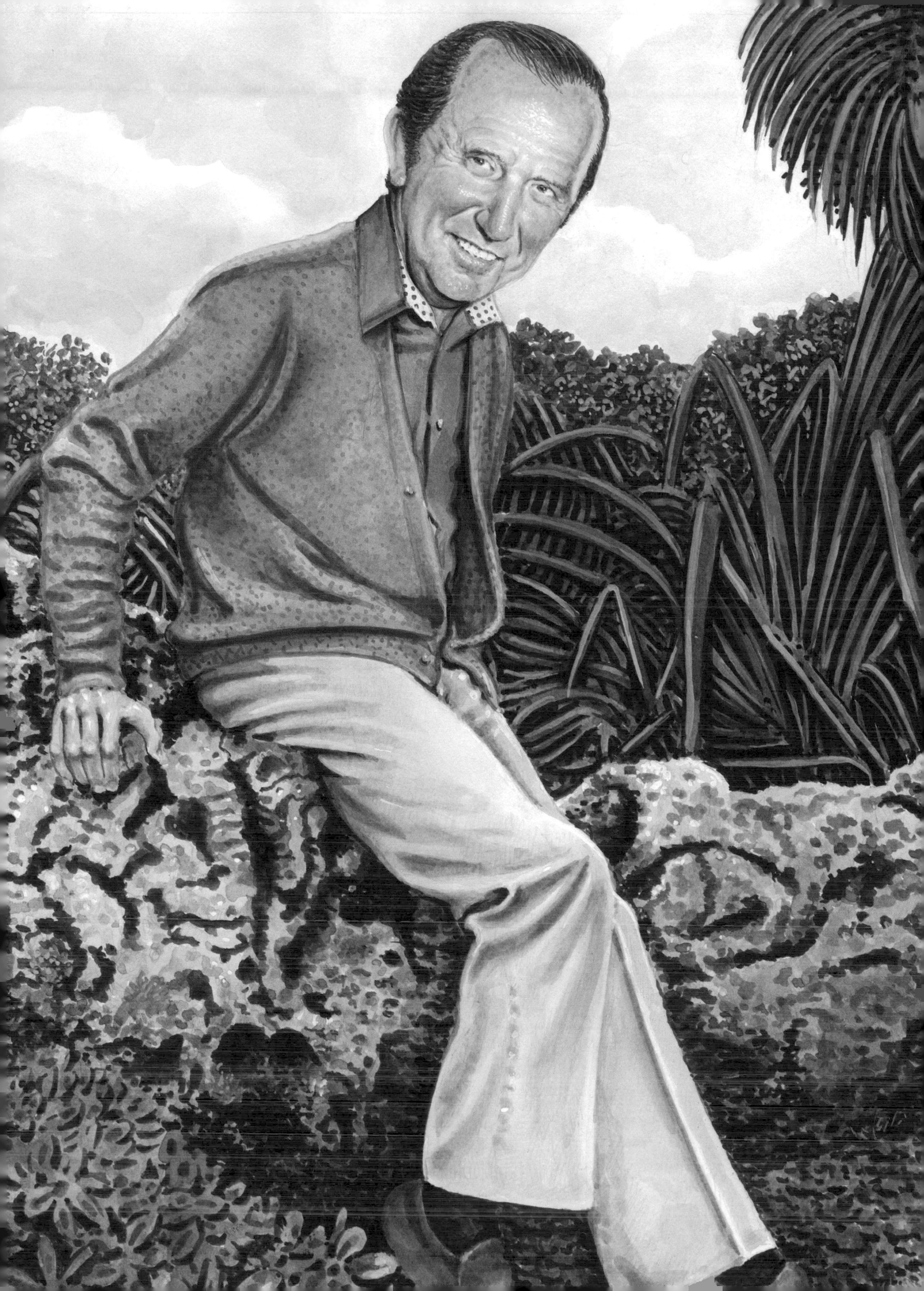

JESSE MARSH

1907–1966

plate **73**

Jesse Marsh worked as an animator and storywriter for Walt Disney in the early 1940s, working on various shorts and the features *Pinocchio* and *Fantasia*. In the midforties he worked full-time at the Southern California office of Western Publishing, the outfit that produced Dell Comics. Marsh began by drawing western titles for the company, among them the adventures of the popular singing cowboy Gene Autry. Soon Marsh was asked to draw the *Tarzan* comic book series, which up until that time had been composed of reprints of the *Tarzan* newspaper comic strip. Marsh collaborated with writer Gaylord DuBois on the comic, creating an innovative version of *Tarzan* that was spare, yet still contained an amazing amount of detail. He was an artist's artist, admired by peers such as Alex Toth and Russ Manning (who later took over the comic), but he remained one of the least recognized comics artists, since he worked for the low-key Dell. Marsh created more than one hundred fifty *Tarzan* comics over twenty years, first for Dell and then for Western Publishing's own label Gold Key, before turning over the title to his admirer Russ Manning in 1965, due to his failing health. Marsh's artwork has grown in popularity in recent years and has been particularly inspiring to many young comics creators, chiefly among them Gilbert and Jaime Hernandez.

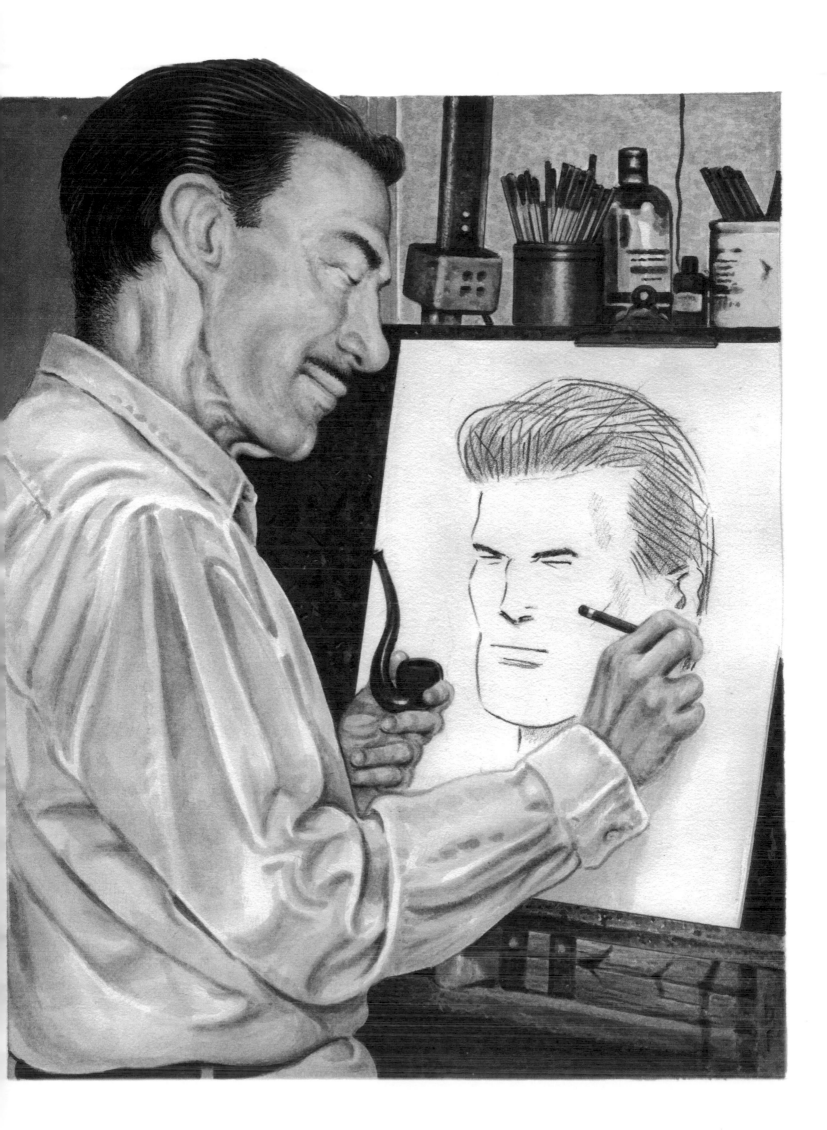

STEVE DITKO

b. 1927

plate
74

Steven J. "Steve" Ditko grew up as an admirer of Hal Foster's *Prince Valiant*, Will Eisner's *The Spirit*, Jerry Robinson's *Batman*, and the stylish comics of Mort Meskin. In 1950 Ditko studied with one of his idols, Jerry Robinson, for two years at the Cartoonist and Illustrators School (which would become The School of Visual Arts) in New York. In 1953 he was hired to work at the Simon and Kirby studio as an inker, and then he started working on horror and sci-fi comics for Charlton Comics.

Ditko began working for editor/writer Stan Lee at Atlas (later Marvel) in 1955. In 1962, with the overwhelming success of Marvel's new titles, particularly *The Fantastic Four*, superheroes were back in vogue, and Stan Lee asked his go-to artist, Jack Kirby, to develop a character Kirby had earlier conceived, a teenager who gains spider powers via a magic ring. Lee was unhappy with Kirby's new concept pages, finding the character "too heroic," and asked Steve Ditko to develop "Spider-Man." Unlike the popular mythological superheroes of the day, Ditko's teenage Spider-Man and his alter ego, Peter Parker, were grounded in reality, a first for superhero comics. Peter Parker was a neurotic college student with very human, everyday struggles who also had to deal with being a misunderstood superhero—a superhero young people could relate to. Spider-Man debuted in *Amazing Fantasy* #15 in 1962 and soon starred in his own title, which eventually became a huge hit. Steve Ditko's Spider-Man was revolutionary. Ditko created, designed (Marvel staffer Stan Goldberg helped develop Spidey's costume colors), and plotted (at first with Lee, then, as Lee's duties increased at Marvel, Ditko took full control of the plots) an identifiable, anxiety-ridden character who has grown even more popular over the last half century. Ditko also cocreated Marvel's Dr. Strange, a character who was also steeped in angst-ridden personal problems.

By the midsixties Ditko left Marvel for good over what he claimed were royalties issues. He returned to the lower-paying Charlton, where he revamped the character the Blue Beetle, and also did work for Warren and DC. Ditko, a devoted follower of the objectivist philosophy of Ayn Rand, has been referred to as the "J. D. Salinger of Comics." Unlike Stan Lee, he has never been interested in becoming a celebrity, leads a notoriously private life, has declined most interviews, and hasn't been photographed since 1959. He is one of the most revered and elusive comics artists in history, a genuine enigma and a legend.

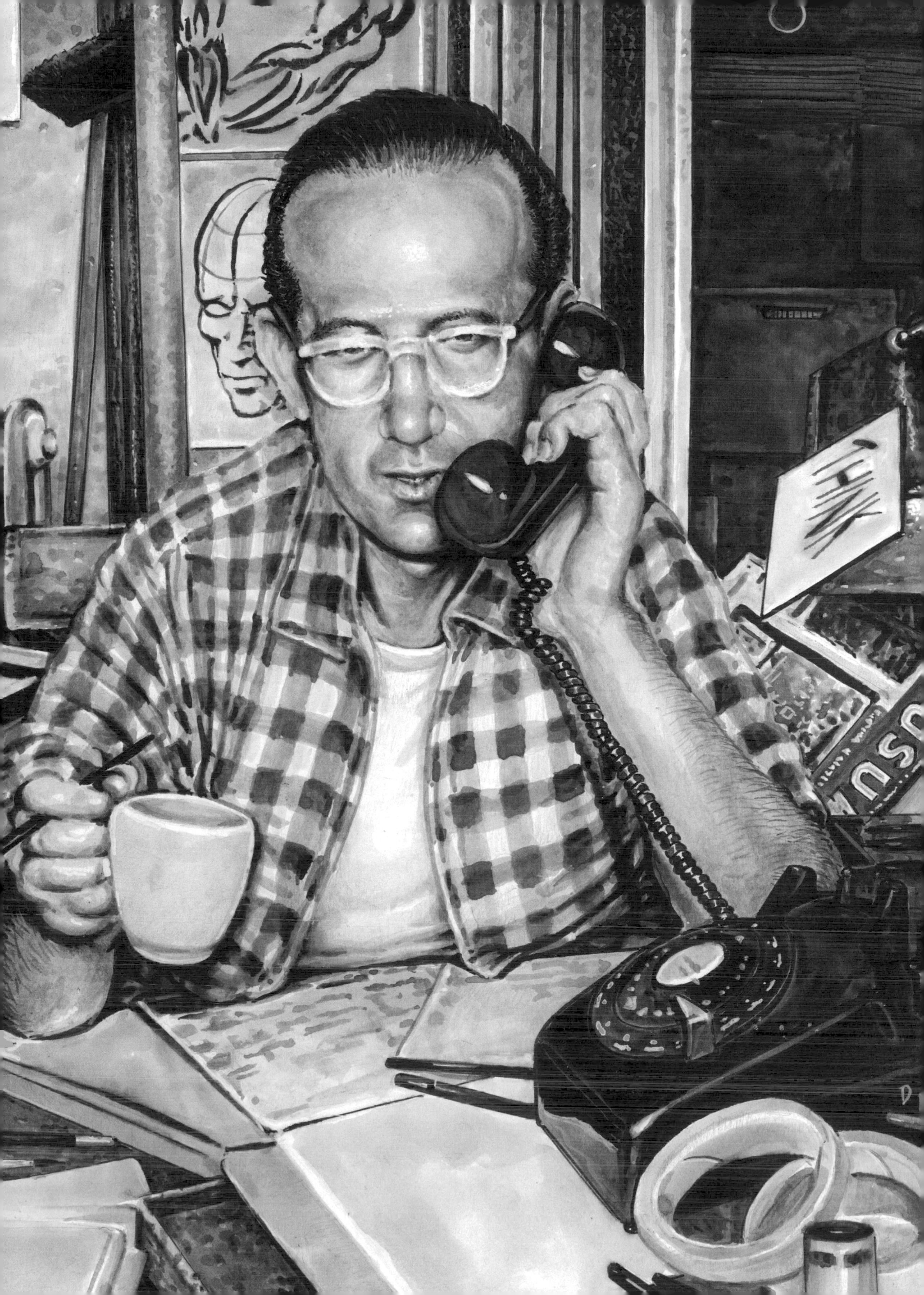

OGDEN WHITNEY

1918–197?

plate
75

Ogden Whitney started drawing comics in 1939 for National's *Adventure Comics* #39, before taking over duties from artist Creig Flessel on the popular character Sandman. A skilled and polished artist, Whitney created Skyman for *Big Shot Comics* and drew the character throughout the forties, taking time off to serve in the Philippines during the war. After Skyman's last appearance in *Big Shot Comics* in 1949, Whitney continued freelancing in comics for various publishers until he began mainly drawing fantasy and romance titles for the low-rent American Comics Group (ACG).

In 1958 Whitney and ACG editor Richard E. Hughes (under the pseudonym "Shane O'Shea") cocreated Whitney's best known character, Herbie Popnecker, a.k.a. "The Fat Fury." One of the oddest characters to ever appear regularly in mainstream comics, Herbie first appeared in *Forbidden Worlds* #73 and was given his own solo comic, *Herbie*, in 1964. *Herbie* stood out because Whitney's stiff, nondescript, understated artwork brought life to the oddball, outlandish slacker Herbie and the bland, white-bread mid-1960s world he inhabited. Whitney claimed that the deadpan, half-lidded Herbie with his bowl cut was based on his own appearance as a child. Herbie was a short, fat, emotionless boy, aimlessly wandering through life, always sucking on a lollipop. Herbie also became a flying (actually, walking on air) superhero, "The Fat Fury," with a plunger stuck to his head. His lollipop became magical, and he turned invisible, talked to animals, and traveled through time and across the world to encounter Fidel Castro, Winston Churchill, the Loch Ness Monster, or to fight Sonny Liston. Herbie was naturally irresistible to women, and his parents were completely unaware of his powers or his worldwide fame. *Herbie* was a masterpiece of deadpan absurdity and remains a cult favorite, continuing to grow in popularity over the years and influencing a generation of cartoonists, chiefly among them Daniel Clowes. *Herbie* lasted for twenty-three issues, until ACG ceased publication in 1967. Soon thereafter Whitney descended into alcoholism, and he died at some time in the early seventies.

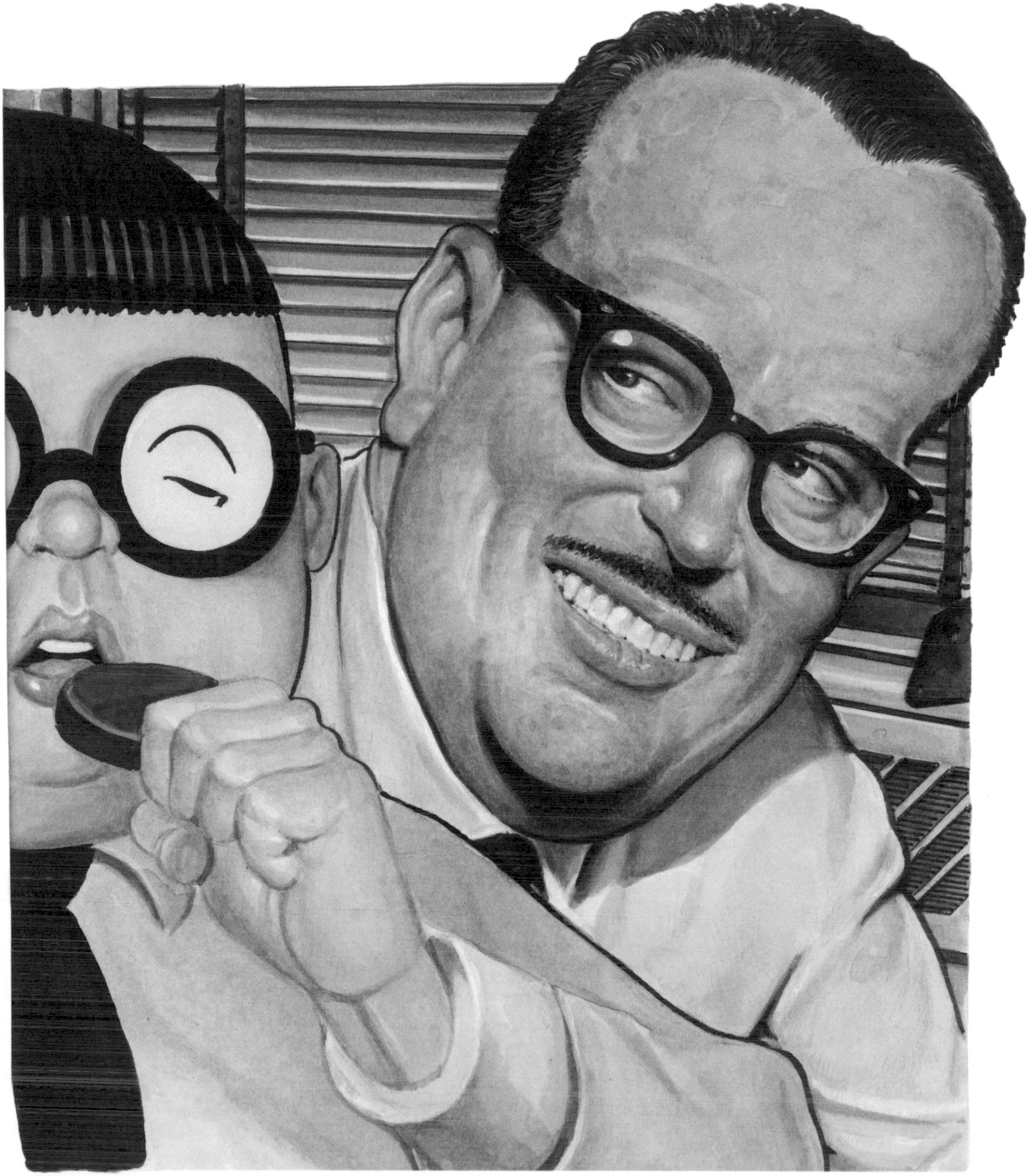

JOE KUBERT

plate
76

Joseph "Joe" Kubert was a comics legend whose prolific comics career lasted close to eight decades. By the time he was a teenager in the late 1930s, he had already worked for Will Eisner and for the Harry "A" Chesler comics packaging shop in New York, where his tasks included erasing, inking, and sweeping up. Kubert attended the High School of Music & Art, where he would meet his future collaborator Norman Maurer, future son-in-law of stooge Moe Howard. Kubert freelanced for various publishers, including DC, while still in and out of high school. After serving stateside in the army, he became a full-time comics artist, at first working on the popular Golden Age superheroes of the forties, including a long association with the Hawkman.

In the 1950s Kubert teamed up with his old friend Norman Maurer and Maurer's brother Leonard to produce the first 3-D comic books for St. John Publications, including *The Three Stooges*, which did very well—for a short period. Around this time Kubert also freelanced, creating artwork for several Harvey Kurtzman–scripted stories for *Frontline Combat* and *Two-Fisted Tales* at EC. In 1953 he created his most long-lasting character, the prehistoric human Tor, for St. John. In the midfifties Kubert worked exclusively for DC Comics, beginning with work on *Our Army at War* #32, and swiftly and effortlessly bounced back and forth between superhero, war, and jungle titles for the next fifty years. He earned acclaim for his work on *Sgt. Rock*, giving the ragged characters unusual depth and focusing on details in his patented stylized crosshatching technique, rarely seen in mainstream comics, where most artists were encouraged to crank out pages. He became DC's director of publications in 1967, continuing to draw for the company, including the new *Tarzan* and *Korak* comics. In 1976 he opened the Joe Kubert School of Cartoon and Graphic Art in Dover, New Jersey.

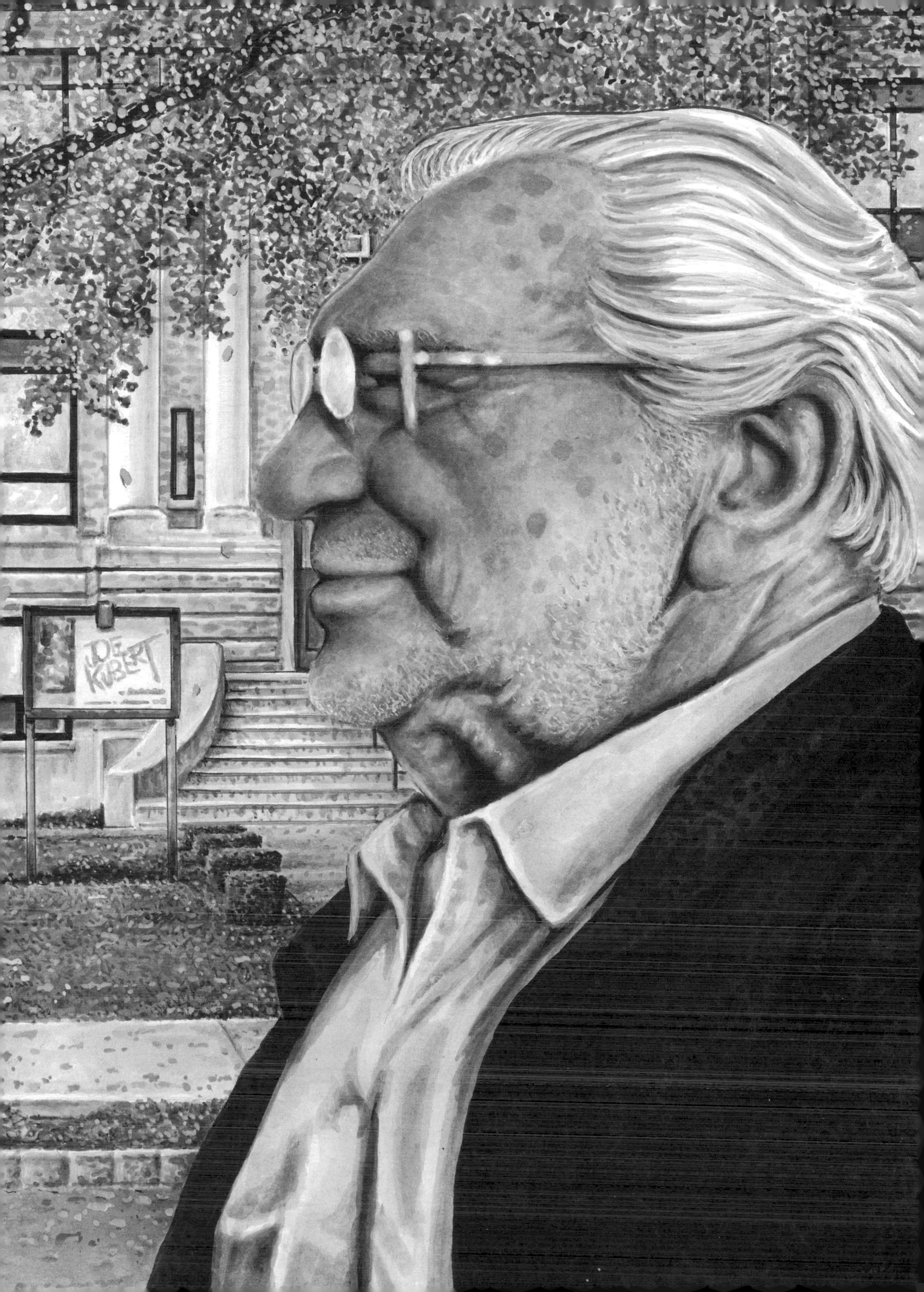
JOE KUBERT

HOWARD NOSTRAND

1929–1984

plate
77

Howard Nostrand, known as the "Jack Davis–type artist," enjoyed perhaps one of the briefest and oddest comic book careers. He entered comics in 1948, assisting comics artist Bob Powell on various comic book work created for Fawcett and Harvey Comics. When EC's horror comics took off in the early fifties, the pre-family-friendly Harvey joined in on the trend, and Powell and Nostrand collaborated mainly on horror stories. Nostrand, by that point a talented artist, broke off from Powell in 1952 and continued to create work for Harvey titles, including *Black Cat Mystery*, *Chamber of Chills*, *Tomb of Terror*, and *Witches Tales*. He soon earned a reputation for being able to duplicate other popular comics artists' styles, including an almost flawless imitation of EC horror artists Jack Davis and Wally Wood. Nostrand went so far as to appropriate a Wally Wood sequence from *Two-Fisted Tales*, merely adjusting the positioning and layouts of every panel. Nostrand also channeled Bob Powell's old boss Will Eisner's distinctive style and was clearly influenced by Harvey Kurtzman's EC page layouts, especially for *Mad*. But since this probably didn't sit well with EC's editors Kurtzman and Al Feldstein, he was never actually hired to create any work for them. When the horror trend in comics came to a crashing end in the midfifties, an overall slump in the industry took hold, and Nostrand left comics to concentrate on advertising work, occasionally continuing to ape Jack Davis's style, including for the cover of the early sixties Transogram game Screwball: The Mad Mad Mad Game (which was accused of appropriating *Mad* magazine and its mascot, Alfred E. Neuman), for the *Mad* clone *Cracked* magazine, and later for *National Lampoon*.

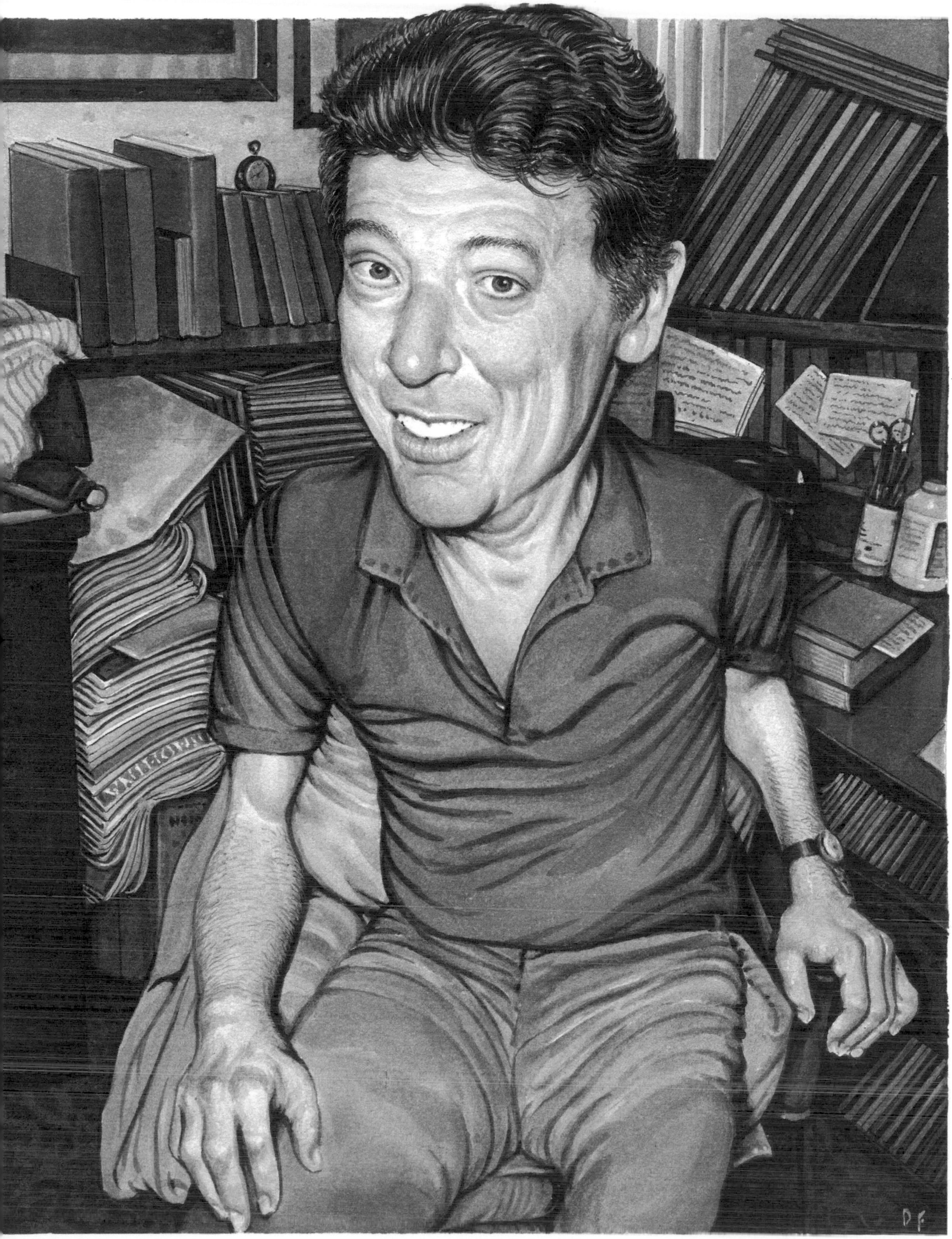

MORT DRUCKER

b. 1929

plate
78

The incredibly gifted *Mad* magazine caricaturist Mort Drucker entered comics in 1947 at age eighteen, assisting comics artist Bert Whitman on his popular newspaper strip *Debby Dean*. Whitman had worked for DC Comics and suggested Drucker seek employment there, and he was soon hired to retouch art and assist staff artists. Soon he drew comics himself and began honing his caricature skills, creating covers and interiors for several humorous DC titles like *Jackie Gleason and the Honeymooners*, *The Adventures of Bob Hope*, and *The Adventures of Jerry Lewis*, as well as the western title *Hopalong Cassidy*. Drucker also freelanced for other publishers, creating work for various war, romance, and science fiction titles. With comic book sales plunging in the late fifties and comics work becoming harder to come by, Drucker answered an ad placed in the *New York Times* by *Mad* magazine seeking new contributors. Drucker found his calling when he showed his work to *Mad* associate editor Nick Meglin, who liked what he saw but was most impressed with his *Hopalong Cassidy* work. Despite more than three hundred artists answering the *Times* ad and *Mad* already having a full lineup of artists (the usual gang of idiots), he was hired.

Drucker's unparalleled attention to facial expressions, including their flaws and quirks, as well as his amazing background details, made his monthly movie and TV parodies for *Mad* the magazine's defining centerpiece and the gold standard of great caricature for decades. Drucker also continued working for DC into the sixties, on the *Bob Hope* series (as well as his hip one pagers *Beat Nick* and *Lola*, which appeared buried in the Bob Hope and Jerry Lewis comics) and *The Fox and the Crow*. Aside from drawing close to two thousand pages of art for *Mad*, Drucker also created art for countless magazine and book covers, record albums, film posters, and advertisements, and continues to have a profound influence on generations of young artists.

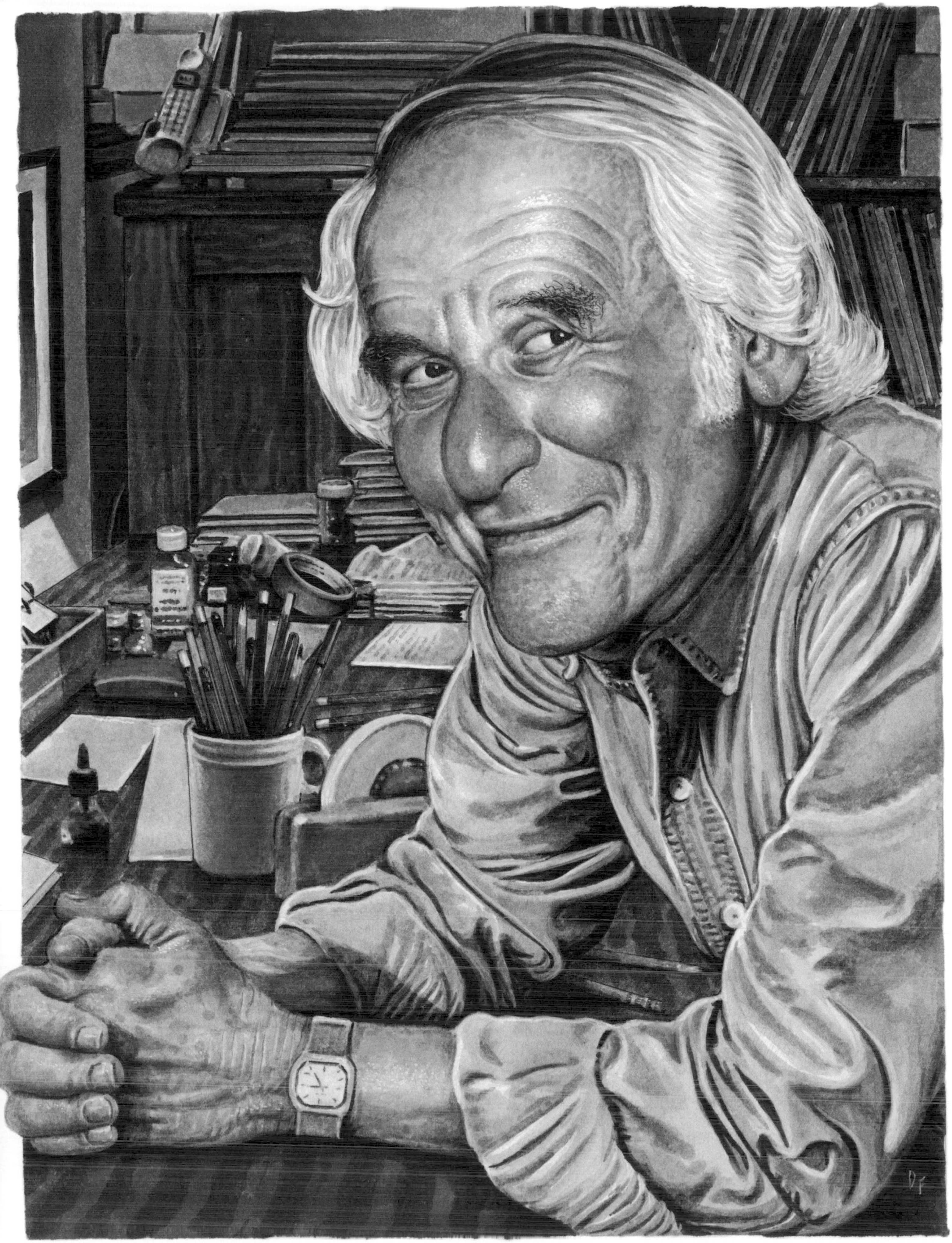

RUSS HEATH

b. 1926

plate
79

Russell "Russ" Heath Jr. began drawing for comics in 1944 and was later hired for a staff position at Timely Comics. He initially drew for many of Timely's then popular western and combat titles, and rendered his first superhero work for *Captain America* in 1949. Heath also freelanced for EC Comics, creating artwork for Harvey Kurtzman's scripts for EC's two war titles, *Frontline Combat* and *Two-Fisted Tales*. Kurtzman also hired the versatile Heath to draw his satire of Jack Cole's *Plastic Man*, "Plastic Sam!," for *Mad* #14, and Heath followed Kurtzman's tight breakdowns to a tee, essentially coloring Kurtzman's acetate sketches. Kurtzman was not happy with the results and never used Heath for *Mad* again (Kurtzman would later admit that *Plastic Man*, a parody in itself, was hard to parody). Despite that setback, Heath had at that point developed a reputation for his stunningly authentic war comics and his amazing attention to detail, down to the specific types of weapons and uniforms. He would continue to freelance, mainly for DC, St. John, and Atlas on their horror, combat, and superhero titles.

In the early sixties Heath was surprised to see that some of his random panels of fighter jets that had appeared in DC's *All American Men of War* comic book had been appropriated and enlarged without his permission by pop artist Roy Lichtenstein, most notably for his painting *Blam!*. Lichtenstein made millions off of Russ Heath's artwork, while Heath received nothing. In the midsixties Heath created some beautifully realistic black-and-white artwork for Warren Publishing's EC-like war title *Blazing Combat*, with scripts by the talented writer Archie Goodwin. He also continued to draw comics for DC (mostly war titles) and assisted with the art from time to time on Kurtzman and Elder's *Little Annie Fanny* comic strip for *Playboy*.

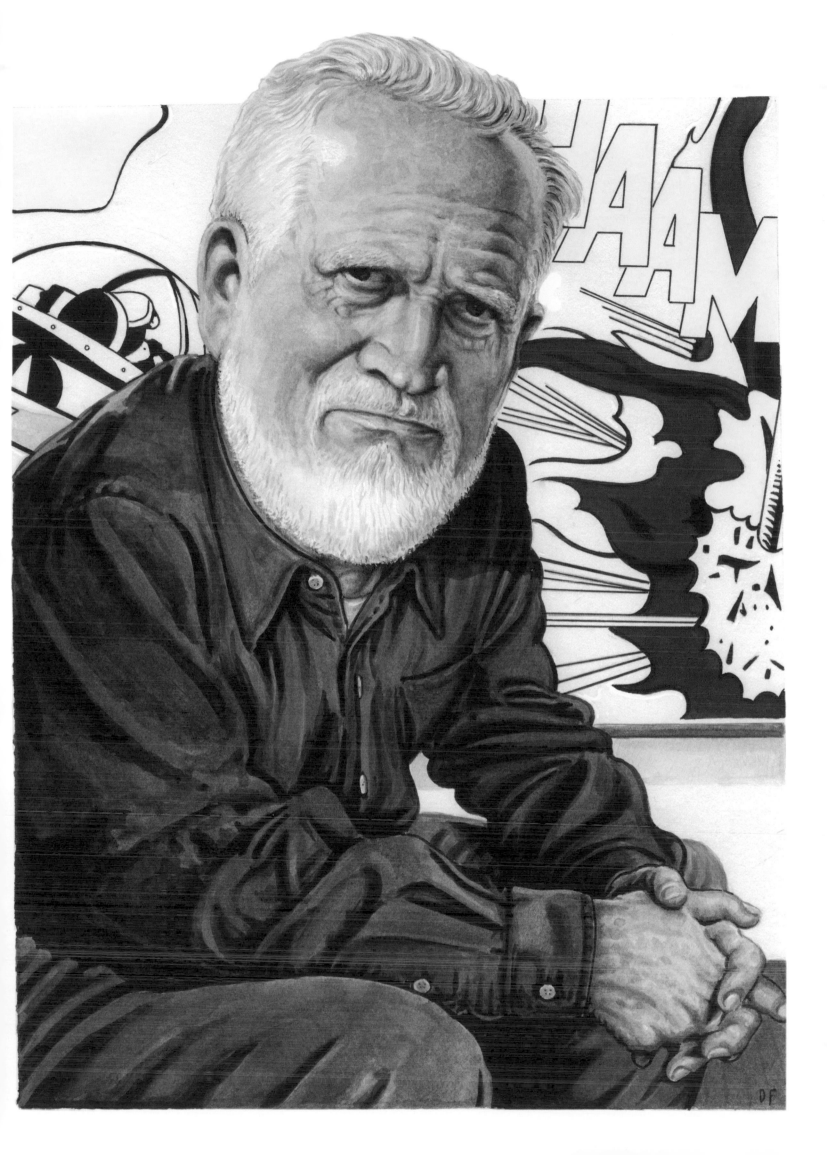

ALEX TOTH

1928–2006

From an early age Alexander "Alex" Toth was an admirer of artist Milton Caniff and dreamed of creating his own newspaper comic strip. He did his first work for comic books at age sixteen in 1944, and in 1947 editor Sheldon Mayer of All-American Comics hired him to work on superhero characters, including the Flash, the Green Lantern, the Atom, and Doctor Mid-Nite. Toth honed his artistic skills and began to introduce techniques of modern magazine illustration into his work, focusing on intricate composition, patterns, tonal values, and depth of field and shape. His bold, clean style made him stand out from other artists working in comics, and his peers soon considered him to be an "artist's artist."

Harvey Kurtzman, who was editing war comics at EC, was also impressed with Toth's abilities and hired him to illustrate his two war titles, but Toth found Kurtzman's "considerable control" over his layouts not to his liking, and they parted ways after working on just three stories together. Toth also worked on various crime, romance, and war comics for Standard Comics. In the midfifties he was inducted into the army, and he returned to find little work in comics aside from at Dell, which had not been affected by the new strictly enforced comics code. In 1960, having moved to Los Angeles, Toth began his career in TV animation, art directing the science fiction series *Space Angel*, which led to his being hired by Hanna-Barbera as a storyboard and design artist. His most famous cartoon designs were for *Space Ghost*, *Super Friends*, and *The Herculoids*. He also found time in the sixties to contribute work to Warren's two horror magazines, *Creepy* and *Eerie*, and to draw *Hot Wheels* and *The Witching Hour* for DC. Toth's economical black-and-white compositions made him a legendary creator of comic art, who lifted the craftsmanship level of the medium to new heights.

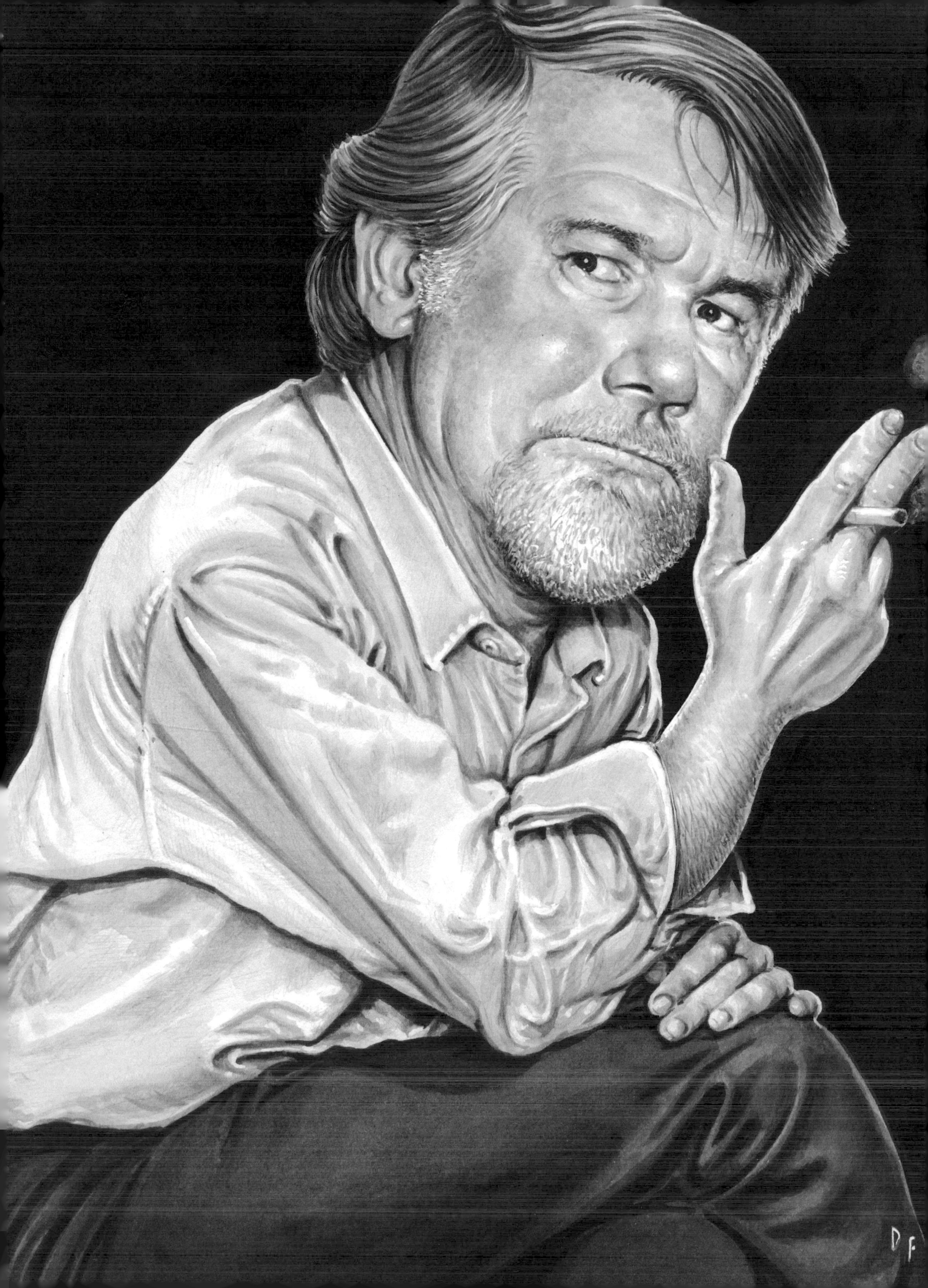

BERNARD KRIGSTEIN

1919–1990

plate
81

Bernard Krigstein approached comics as a serious art form, and his inventive, beautifully composed, almost cinematic use of panels (like quick jump cuts in a film) has never been equaled in comics. Krigstein began creating work for various comic book publishers in the early forties, turning out art in artist Bernard Bailey's assembly-line shop. After the war he returned to comics and his work began to stand apart, so much so that Harvey Kurtzman contacted him and invited him to illustrate one of his EC war stories. Soon, Krigstein became a regular (if reluctant) contributor to EC, illustrating a total of forty-seven stories over the next four years, including several pieces for *Mad*, which highlighted his brilliant gift for caricature. Krigstein's masterpiece "Master Race," a groundbreaking triumph of sequential storytelling, appeared in the debut issue of EC's New Direction comic book *Impact* in 1955. Al Feldstein wrote the psychologically suspenseful narrative as a six-page story, but Krigstein expanded it to eight pages. It took place in a New York subway station with flashbacks to Nazi death camps and was the first mainstream comic story to deal directly with the still fresh and painful memory of the then decade-prior Holocaust. After parting ways with EC, Krigstein left comics forever to work as an illustrator, a fine artist, and a teacher at New York's High School of Art & Design for twenty years. His work for EC was both startling and unusually thoughtful, especially in the world of 1950s comic books.